T0318294

The American Workplace
Skills, Compensation, and Employee Involvement

Many managers are frustrated by a bewildering array of advice about what works in the workplace. This volume contributes to a growing consensus about effective workplace practices. The volume combines detailed studies of single industries (automobile assembly, apparel, and machine tools) with cross-industry studies of financial performance. Compared with most past investigations, the research described here has better measures of both workplace practices and organizational performance. The contributors find that systems of innovative human resource management practices can have large effects on business performance. Success comes not from any single innovation, but from a coherent system encompassing pay, training, and employee involvement. Although a majority of contemporary U.S. businesses have adopted some innovative work practices, only a small percentage have adopted a coherent new system. A concluding chapter outlines barriers to diffusion and discusses public policies to remove barriers and enhance dissemination of effective management.

Casey Ichniowski is a professor at the Graduate School of Business, Columbia University, where he has taught since 1984, and a research associate in the Labor Studies Program of the National Bureau of Economic Research. He is coauthor of *The Competitive Edge: Managing Human Resources in Union and Nonunion Firms*.

David I. Levine is an associate professor at the Haas School of Business, University of California, Berkeley, where he has taught since 1987. Professor Levine is the editor of the journal *Industrial Relations*, associate director of the Institute of Industrial Relations, and director of research at the Center for Organization and Human Resource Effectiveness.

Craig Olson is a professor of business and industrial relations at the University of Wisconsin, Madison, where he is also Wolfe Professor of Business Research. His recent research focuses on human resource practice in firms and organization performance. Professor Olson has also held faculty positions at Purdue University and the State University of New York, Buffalo.

George Strauss is Professor Emeritus of Organizational Behavior and Industrial Relations at the Haas School of Business, University of California, Berkeley. He is the editor or coauthor of nine books, including *Organizational Participation: Myth or Reality, Researching the World of Work: Strategy and Methods in Studying Industrial Relations*, and several texts.

The American Workplace
Skills, Compensation, and Employee Involvement

Edited by

CASEY ICHNIOWSKI
Columbia University

DAVID I. LEVINE
University of California, Berkeley

CRAIG OLSON
University of Wisconsin, Madison

GEORGE STRAUSS
University of California, Berkeley

 CAMBRIDGE
UNIVERSITY PRESS

CAMBRIDGE UNIVERSITY PRESS
Cambridge, New York, Melbourne, Madrid, Cape Town, Singapore, São Paulo, Delhi

Cambridge University Press
The Edinburgh Building, Cambridge CB2 8RU, UK

Published in the United States of America by Cambridge University Press, New York

www.cambridge.org
Information on this title: www.cambridge.org/9780521650281

© Casey Ichniowski, David I. Levine, Craig Olson, George Strauss 2000

This publication is in copyright. Subject to statutory exception
and to the provisions of relevant collective licensing agreements,
no reproduction of any part may take place without the written
permission of Cambridge University Press.

First published 2000
This digitally printed version 2008

A catalogue record for this publication is available from the British Library

Library of Congress Cataloguing in Publication data
The American workplace : skills, compensation, and employee involvement / edited by
Casey Ichniowski . . . [et al.].
p.   cm.
Includes also five articles which were first presented at a January 1995 conference.
Includes index.
ISBN 0-521-65028-3
1. Industrial management – United States.   2. Organizational effectiveness – United
States.   3. Management – Employee participation – United States.   4. Creative ability
in business – United States.   I. Ichniowski, Casey.
HD70.U5A56   1999
658'.00973–dc21   98-45617
                                                                                      CIP

ISBN 978-0-521-65028-1 hardback
ISBN 978-0-521-08997-5 paperback

Contents

Preface

Many managers are frustrated by a bewildering array of advice about what works in the workplace. In 1995 the National Center for the Workplace and the Alfred P. Sloan Foundation sponsored a conference on the links between workplace practices and organizational performance. This volume presents revised versions of five papers from that conference, coupled with two invited chapters, an introductory chapter, and a concluding one that outlines obstacles to diffusion and draws out lessons for public policy.

The introductory chapter (by the editors and Thomas A. Kochan) reviews the problems researchers face in identifying the effects of workplace practices. With these cautions in mind, it then summarizes the literature on such practices. Results show that systems of innovative human resource management can have large effects on business performance. Success comes not from any single innovation, but from a coherent system encompassing pay, training, and employee involvement. Finally, although a majority of contemporary U.S. businesses have adopted some innovative work practices, only a small percentage have adopted a coherent new system.

This volume contributes to a growing consensus about effective workplace practices. It combines detailed studies of single industries (automobile assembly, apparel, and machine tools) with cross-industry studies of financial performance. The chapters are among the very best on the adoption and effects of innovative workplace practices. The research described here has better measures of both workplace practices and organizational performance than does most past research. In addition, most of the chapters analyze data spanning many years.

Several of these chapters appeared in the Summer 1996 issue of *Industrial Relations*, and we are grateful to Blackwell Publishers for permission to reprint them, as well as to the Sloan Foundation (especially Hirsch Cohen) and the U.S. Department of Labor for sponsoring much of the research presented here.

Contributors

Eileen Appelbaum
Economic Policy Institute
Washington, DC

Thomas Bailey
Institute on Education and the
    Economy
Teachers College, Columbia
    University
New York, NY

Brian E. Becker
School of Management
State University of New York at
    Buffalo
Buffalo, NY

Peter Berg
School of Labor and Industrial
    Relations
Michigan State University
East Lansing, MI

John T. Dunlop
Department of Economics
Harvard University
Cambridge, MA

George S. Easton
Goizueta Business School
Emory University
Atlanta, GA

Kevin B. Hendricks
School of Business
College of William and Mary
Williamsburg, VA

Mark A. Huselid
School of Management and Labor
    Relations
Rutgers University
Piscataway, NJ

Casey Ichniowski
Graduate School of Business
Columbia University
New York, NY

Sherry L. Jarrell
Georgia State University
College of Business Administration
Atlanta, GA

Arne L. Kalleberg
Department of Sociology
University of North Carolina
Chapel Hill, NC

Maryellen R. Kelley
H. John Heinz III School of Public
    Policy
Carnegie Mellon University
Pittsburgh, PA

Thomas A. Kochan
Sloan School of Management
Massachusetts Institute of
    Technology
Cambridge, MA

David I. Levine
Haas School of Business
University of California, Berkeley
Berkeley, CA

John Paul MacDuffie
Wharton School
University of Pennsylvania
Philadelphia, PA

Craig Olson
School of Business
University of Wisconsin
Madison, WI

Frits K. Pil
Katz Graduate School of Business
University of Pennsylvania
Pittsburgh, PA

Vinod R. Singhal
Dupree School of Management
Georgia Institute of Technology
Atlanta, GA

George Strauss
Haas School of Business
University of California, Berkeley
Berkeley, CA

David Weil
School of Management
Boston University
Boston, MA

CHAPTER 1

What Works at Work:
Overview and Assessment

Casey Ichniowski, Thomas A. Kochan, David I. Levine,
Craig Olson, and George Strauss

The past two decades have witnessed considerable experimentation and research on new work practices and human resource policies. Why have businesses adopted them? What has been their effect on performance?

This study has two primary goals. The first is to review features of the research methods employed in studies on workplace innovations. This review of methodological issues serves as a framework for evaluating existing studies and to encourage new research on workplace innovations to incorporate the most persuasive research designs possible. The second goal is to review the findings from a broad set of studies that employ different research designs. Because different research designs have their own particular strengths and limitations, we highlight those results that emerge consistently from different studies. Much more than a typical volume introduction, this chapter presents a critical review of the strengths, weaknesses, and results of research on what works at work.

The Nature of Workplace Innovations

The term "innovative work practices" has no settled meaning. For many scholars and practitioners it refers to employee involvement efforts such as work teams (e.g., Katz, Kochan, and Gobeille, 1983). For others, it means employee participation in the financial well-being of a company such as profit-sharing, employee stock ownership, or pay-for-performance. Still others have in mind flexible and broadly defined job

This chapter is a revised version of an article that originally appeared in *Industrial Relations* 35:3 (July 1996); reprinted by permission of Blackwell Publishers.

We thank the National Center for the Workplace and the Alfred P. Sloan Foundation for their support of all our work in the Human Resource Network, as well as the Department of Labor for its support to Ichniowski and Kochan under contract 41USC252C3.

1

assignments, employment security policies, or improved communication and dispute resolution mechanisms. Often, managers and workers refer to a special workplace "culture" that is not easily captured by the measurement of a single work practice.

What these diverse work practices have in common is that they depart from the traditional work systems and labor–management relationships that evolved in the United States out of the "New Deal system of industrial relations" (Kochan, Katz, and McKersie, 1986). The traditional system is characterized by tightly defined jobs with associated rates of pay, clear lines of demarcation separating the duties and rights of workers and supervisors, decision-making powers retained by management, and the channeling of communications and conflicts through formal chains of command and grievance procedures. Current workplace innovations seek greater flexibility in work organization, cooperation between labor and management, and worker participation in the decisions and financial well-being of a company. In this chapter, we use the term "workplace innovations" or "new work practices" to refer generally to all these kinds of non-traditional work practices that have become increasingly common among U.S. businesses in recent years (Ichniowski, Delaney, and Lewin, 1989; Osterman, 1994; Lawler, Mohrman, and Ledford, 1995).

Theoretical Explanations

Elaborate theories have been developed to explain why new high-skill, high-involvement workplaces may be more effective (for a review see Levine, 1995). These can be divided into theories that focus on the effort and motivation of workers and work groups and suggest that individuals work harder, and theories that focus on changes in the structure of organizations that improve efficiency.

High-involvement workplaces may lead workers to work harder if the work is less onerous. Workers may enjoy work more when the characteristics of the job make work interesting and ensure that the work provides feedback and rewards. They are also less likely to resent a job if they help design it.

Innovative work practices may also lead workers to work more efficiently. Workers often have information that higher management lacks, especially as to how to make their jobs more efficient. Further, greater participation permits a variety of views to be aired, and many such views lead workers to redesign their jobs so that they can better coordinate their efforts. Indeed, Berg, Appelbaum, Bailey, and Kalleberg (Chapter 3, this volume) conclude that in the apparel plants they studied "working smarter" is more important than any changes that make work more interesting or enjoyable. Work groups may encourage both working harder and working smarter if their norms change from discouraging high performance – for example, by punishing "rate busters" – to reward-ing high performance. These changes, in turn, are more likely if the group is rewarded for its collective success, perhaps with bonuses or gainsharing.

Innovative work practices can also produce structural changes that improve performance independent of their effects on motivation. Cross-training and flexible job assignment can reduce the costs of absenteeism; decentralizing decision-making to self-directed teams can reduce the number of supervisors and middle managers required while improving communication; training in problem-solving, statistical process control, and computer skills can increase the benefits of new information tech-nologies; worker and union involvement in decision-making can reduce grievances and other sources of conflict and thereby improve operating efficiencies. These kinds of organizational changes that are often associ-ated with employee involvement processes make it difficult to isolate any single causal mechanism that produces their effects on economic performance.

Thus, theories of new work practices imply that these new arrange-ments can cause workers to work harder and share more ideas. Further, they can make organizational structures more efficient regardless of any effects they may have on worker motivation. In either case, companies that adopt these practices should enjoy higher productivity and quality (as in Berg et al., Chapter 3, and Kelley, Chapter 4, this volume), leading to lower costs and higher product demand, all else equal. But any savings may be offset by the expenses of employee involvement programs, such as the costs of extra meetings and of related human resource policies. Cost reductions and stronger demand, holding other things constant, should lead to higher sales and earnings (Dunlop and Weil, Chapter 2, this volume) and ultimately better performance on financial measures such as cash flow and return on investment. Ultimately, these financial improvements should be reflected in the value of the enterprise's stock (Huselid and Becker, Chapter 5, this volume).

Performance measures vary widely, from those close to the workplace such as worker stress (Berg et al.), to intermediate outcomes such as machine time per piece in the machining industry (Kelley), to outcomes quite distant from the workplace such as stock market value (Huselid and Becker). For public policy, knowing the effects of innovative work practices on workers and productivity may suffice. For private-sector decision-makers, such as investors and managers, financial and stock market returns are the arbiters of success. Because these latter groups have far greater influence on management practices than do union leaders or policy-makers, we need to know how work practices affect the bottom line. Unfortunately, as discussed later in this chapter, a number of factors imply that even fairly successful workplace innovations may have effects on financial performance that are difficult to detect.

Recent research further suggests that high-involvement work practices are more effective when "bundled" with supporting management practices (Milgrom and Roberts, 1990, 1993; Holmstrom and Milgrom, 1994). Workers cannot make good decisions without sufficient information and training, and they are unlikely to make suggestions if they feel this will cost them their jobs or reduce their pay (Levine, 1995, ch. 3). Dunlop and Weil, and Pill and MacDuffie (Chapter 6, this volume), shed light on theories of "internal fit," that is, how bundles of work practices support, or fail to support, each other.

The external context also matters. For example, bundles of work practices that support a highly flexible work process may be effective in a product market with rapidly changing demands, but have fewer advantages in a stable market. Dunlop and Weil find evidence that the organization's environment in the apparel industry has affected who adopts innovative work practices and how effective they are. More generally, they argue that new work practices must be analyzed within the context of the organization's overall strategy and market environment, not as an isolated human resource policy initiative.

Types of Workplace Research

It may be useful to place the research reported here in broader perspective. Empirical research began with laboratory experiments. These identified the theoretical principles that might underlie effective work practices such as participation and goal setting. Unfortunately, what works in a short-term laboratory experiment (often with college students) may not work in the real world. Early field experiments in workplaces were more realistic, but usually were confined to single departments, lacked controls, and lasted for short periods of time (e.g., French and Coch, 1948; Whyte et al., 1955).

The late 1960s and 1970s saw experiments in which various forms of employee involvement were introduced into entire plants. The effects of these workplace changes on various outcomes such as attitudes, production, accidents, and turnover were carefully monitored, both qualitatively and quantitatively and over considerable periods of time (e.g., Marrow, Bowers, and Seashore, 1967; Goodman, 1979). These studies raised most of the issues of current concern, such as resistance to workplace innovation by both unions and management, and the importance of having appropriate training and compensation practices. The past few years have seen a wave of innovative case studies, many based on Japanese transplants (Fucini and Fucini, 1990; Graham, 1995; Adler, Goldoftas, and Levine, 1997). These case studies provide insight and suggest hypotheses, but it is difficult to know how well they generalize.

Recently, workplace research has expanded to include surveys (often rather small ones) of firms, lines of businesses, and establishments. By contrast with case studies, surveys cover more than one establishment and their purpose is more often to test theories than to generate them. These surveys can be grouped under three headings.

First are the major government-sponsored British (Millward, Stevens, Smart, and Hawes, 1992) and Australian (Callus, Morehead, Culley, and Buchanan, 1991) surveys of workplace practices, which involve stratified random samples of large and middle-sized workplaces. With high response rates (87% in the Australian case), these provide a wealth of data about the incidence of various practices, but tell us little about their impacts. The closest U.S. equivalents of these studies are a survey conducted by the Government Accounting Office (GAO) with two follow-ups by a University of Southern California group (Lawler et al., 1995), a line-of-business survey by Columbia University researchers (Delaney, Lewin, and Ichniowski, 1988), a study by Osterman (1994), and the two waves of data analyzed by Huselid and Becker. Most of these U.S. studies are based on firms or lines of businesses, permitting analysis of financial performance. At the same time, most of the companies implement a mixture of work practices among their multiple workplaces, making it difficult to determine the particular impact of practices that may be employed in only some of the workplaces. In addition, rather low response rates lead to concerns about these studies' generalizability. (Osterman, 1994, surveys establishments, gaining greater precision in measurement while foregoing most measures of overall organizational performance.)

Each study in this volume has some measure of *incidence* (how frequently a given practice is employed). When incidence studies are repeated, it becomes possible to study the *adoption* and cessation of work practices. For example, Pil and MacDuffie examine the adoption of work practices in the world automobile assembly industry. Adoption studies also provide a weak test of effectiveness; presumably, work practices that managers adopt are those they expect to be successful. Studies of longevity often find that the half-life of many innovations is short, suggesting that their effectiveness is often less than managers had expected

(Drago, 1988; Eaton, 1994). Similarly, Dunlop and Weil found that when innovative work practices in the apparel industry were introduced before related changes in customer relations, the innovations did not last long.

A second set of surveys include matched sets of workplaces in more than one country (e.g., IDE, 1983; Lincoln and Kalleberg, 1990). These studies examine how work practices correlate with employees' attitudes. But they are often based on samples of convenience, leading to concerns about how well the results represent the true incidence of work practices in the economy. In addition, the fact that the establishments covered produce many kinds of products and services precludes common hard measures of outcomes such as productivity.

Three of the studies reported in this volume (those of Kelley, of Dunlop and Weil, and of Berg et al.) represent a third line of research, which focuses on the effects of workplace practice on organizational performance in specific industries. This focus makes it possible to make more precise measurements of performance, work practices, and control variables. In addition, within-industry studies automatically control for factors that differ among industries. This approach also enriches the quantitative analyses with the authors' detailed knowledge of each industry's history, technology, industrial relations, and product market.

Methodological Issues

What kind of studies would provide the greatest confidence about the direction and magnitude of the performance effects of innovative work practices? Case studies may provide rich insights, but one can never be sure if case study results generalize to other settings. While case studies can be very useful for suggesting hypotheses, one must ultimately study larger samples to test those hypotheses. To go beyond case study descriptions, an ideal study would have high internal validity, meaning that explanations (other than the ones being investigated) for an observed correlation between performance and work practices could be ruled out. The ideal study would also have high external validity – that is, its results could be generalized to infer the likely impacts of new work practices were they introduced outside the sample studied.

The ideal design for ensuring high internal validity is an experimental design with the random assignment of innovative work practices. In such a design the best estimate of the effect of high-involvement work practices is provided by the following regression (where Innovative Work Practices is a dummy variable equal to 1 if an organization has innovative work practices):

Organizational Performance$_i$
$$= a + b \text{ Innovative Work Practices}_i + \text{Residual}_i$$

The goal of random assignment is to ensure that on average the treatment and control groups do not differ in terms of other organizational characteristics affecting performance such as management or worker quality. Thus, with random assignment, the mean difference in performance between the two groups (parameter b in the equation) will on average reflect only the impacts of the innovative work practices in question.

The external validity of an experiment depends on how closely the research sites resemble the workplaces we might like to understand. If an experiment is based on college students formed into teams that work together for a single hour, we may be skeptical about whether the findings would apply to long-term employees of real businesses. Thus, we would have greater confidence in the external validity of a design that involved the random assignment of a high-performance intervention to half of a sample of workplaces in a single industry or single firm and left the other half unaffected.

No large-scale studies have used this design and it may be impossible to achieve. Our purpose is not to discourage research in the area, but to lay out this ideal type and use it as a framework for evaluating the research. How close have existing studies come to a true experiment, and what are the directions for future research in this area?

Omitted Variables

The key benefit of an experiment with random assignment is that the innovative work practices are uncorrelated with other worker and organizational characteristics that affect performance. The non-experimental studies described in this volume and elsewhere lack random assignment. Some studies attempt to control for omitted variables by studying a single industry or technology. Others attempt to control for omitted variables by measuring and statistically controlling for variables that affect performance and are correlated with whether or not organizations introduce innovative workplace practices.

For example, organizations that adopt innovative work practices may have "higher-quality" workers. Similarly, those with "higher-quality" management teams may both introduce new workplace practices and pursue more imaginative marketing, finance, and R & D strategies. So to what extent is improved performance due to work practices alone? Self-selection, which occurs when organizations that introduce workplace innovations are more likely to enjoy other good practices as well, implies that the estimated effect of innovative workplace practices will be greater than the true effect.

The opposite form of self-selection processes predicts that less successful organizations are the more likely to innovate. Firms may adopt workplace innovations only because they are in trouble. By contrast, a highly successful organization may develop "competency traps" and be unwilling to depart significantly from existing policies, which the organization believes are responsible for its success (March, 1988). So, when troubled companies are most likely to experiment with new practices, even successful programs may appear to be failures. That is, these forms of self-selection cause the non-experimental estimates to be biased downward relative to the true effect.

If the omitted variables are relatively stable over the study period, then by using longitudinal data to examine whether changes in work practices predict changes in performance, one can control for omitted factors such as workforce or management quality (Huselid and Becker). At the same time, these gains may be offset by greater measurement error of innovative work practices. If the omitted variables are not stable, the only remedy is to identify them from theory, measure them, and attempt to control for them statistically in the analysis.

If the same diffusion process applies across industries and firms, even the average estimate of the performance effect of innovative work practices across a number of industry studies will be biased. Alternatively, if in some industries high-performing firms implement innovative work practices and in other industries low-performing firms are early implementors, the average effect from the studies may not be seriously biased. This observation has two implications for future research. First, in order to better understand the effect of innovative work practices on performance using non-experimental studies, we need more studies like those of Pil and MacDuffie and of Dunlop and Weil that examine the diffusion of innovative work practices and that try to identify the links between past performance and the decision to pursue an innovative work practice strategy. Ideally, this would include both quantitative studies of diffusion and rich case studies that, for example, might contrast an early innovator in an industry and follow this up with a study of a later innovator.

Studying the diffusion process also involves studying the survival of innovative work practices. When firms abandon innovative work practices, does this indicate poor fit with other firm policies (e.g., Dunlop and Weil), poor implementation, or a poorly chosen bundle of work practices? In the absence of experimental control, it is critical that we study the implementation process to improve our understanding of the correlation between innovative work practices and the many variables that affect organizational performance.

Response Bias

Even if an appropriate sample is selected, if survey respondents and non-respondents differ in important ways, the results may be biased. Such response bias can induce a correlation between performance and variables affecting performance that are unobserved by the researcher (the residual in our equation) even where there is no correlation in the population.

Researchers usually rely on data from establishments or firms that voluntarily agree to be observed or agree to complete a phone or mail survey. The need for cooperation introduces the possibility that firms that enjoy above-average success with their workplace innovations are more likely to participate than those less successful. The latter may prefer to remain silent. Thus, the study may overstate program gains.

Longitudinal studies require ongoing organizational participation, something that many organizations are unwilling to provide. Huselid and Becker's study is based on 218 firms (out of about 3,500) that gave usable responses in both waves of their study. This modest response rate is typical of studies of this type, but is clearly a cause for concern. Those who conduct longitudinal studies must not only worry about whether the respondents in the initial wave are a random sample of the population, but also be concerned that attrition between waves may be related to performance. This is almost certain to be a problem, because failing firms by definition do not respond to the second wave.

The best solution is a large random sample with a very high response rate. To date, U.S. researchers have not been able to combine these desirable features. (British longitudinal surveys, by contrast, have response rates of more than 80% [Millward and Stevens, 1986].) Ultimately we need a better understanding of why organizations agree to respond to workplace practice surveys, and the ability to track the history of non-responding organizations as well as respondents.

The Unit of Observation

In the ideal field experiment, innovative work practices are applied to all workers in one randomly selected group of organizations and not to another. Then the performance of workplaces that received the intervention is compared with that of workplaces which did not. An experimentalist would not include in the measure of performance for the treatment group the performance of workplaces that were not subject to the treatment. If not all the workers in the treatment group actually worked in workplaces with innovative practices, the estimated effect of the new work practices would only be less than the true effect. This bias suggests that estimates based on corporate-level performance measures (Huselid and Becker) are likely to be lower-bound estimates of the effect of innovative work practices.

To see the problem, consider the example of a well-run employee involvement program that raises productivity by 10% in those workplaces in which the program is introduced; however, as is the case with most companies studied in this volume, only 20% or so of the employees are involved. Assume further that the kinds of measurement error discussed in the next subsection reduce the estimated impact by one-half, as is likely with such difficult-to-measure constructs as employee involvement. Thus, it would seem, employee involvement increases productivity by only 1%. If some of this productivity gain is split between workers and shareholders, the impact of these innovations on profits and stock market value will be less than 1%.

It is important to study the effects of innovative work practices on financial performance because investors and managers focus on these measures. However, our example shows that the lack of a sizable effect on financial outcomes is likely when a fairly effective innovation affects only a small group of workers while performance is measured over a broader sample of workers. In particular, we should be reluctant to accept the null hypothesis that the work practices have no effect when the unit of observation for the performance measure differs substantially from the treatment unit.

Measurement Issues

In an experiment, the researcher has a well-defined treatment and typically performs a manipulation check to ensure that the implementation of the treatment was effective. Also, because the experimental researcher controls who does and does not receive the treatment, there is typically no measurement error caused by incorrectly measuring whether a subject was in either the treatment or the control group. Non-experimental researchers evaluating innovative work practices lack the luxury of experimental application of the intervention, leading to a number of sources of measurement error.

Many of the constructs central to innovative work practices are based on subjective judgments. For example, a "semi-autonomous work team" may be a totally autonomous group without outside direction, or it may be a traditional work group with a supervisor who held a single team meeting six months ago.

While careful construction of the survey and multiple measures of the same construct can go a long way toward alleviating this problem, it is likely to remain a serious source of error. Eaton (1994), for example, found that managers and union leaders often disagree about whether a specific program actually exists in an establishment. Moreover, as Huselid and Becker show, the effect of this kind of error is magnified when longitudinal data are used to examine changes in work practices – it is often more precise to measure whether something exists now than to measure it twice (each time with error) in an effort to determine how much it has changed.

Many studies measure innovative work practices using only one respondent per firm or establishment, implying that any idiosyncratic opinions or interpretations of the questions can distort the results. Often, the respondent is a top-level manager who may have limited knowledge of what is happening at the workplace. Responses of single corporate-level executives of large companies (as in Huselid and Becker) may be particularly noisy and potentially biased indicators of actual workplace practices.

If the measurement error is random relative to the true value, it biases the estimated effect of innovative work practices on performance toward zero. There are some strategies for dealing with this simple type of measurement error that have not been used in this field. For example, the biasing effect of purely random measurement error could be overcome with just two respondents from each establishment using an instrumental variable technique, as in Ashenfelter and Krueger (1994).

Unfortunately, measurement errors may be systematically related to the true level of performance or of innovative work practices. Some respondents may exaggerate their own success with innovative work practice programs, while others will fail to report unsuccessful efforts at implementing innovative work practices. Such errors may be reduced if there is more than one respondent per organization or if the researcher conducts site visits and interviews with multiple respondents at different levels and in different roles within the organizations.

Four studies described in this volume address the measurement issues by examining multiple plants within single industries and by obtaining rich information on work practices from knowledgeable respondents. Kelley surveyed the managers directly responsible for the activities being measured. Berg et al. visited each plant in their samples, as did Mac-

Duffie and Pil. Dunlop and Weil conducted extensive interviews with experienced industry practitioners before designing their survey.

The intra-industry studies described in this volume that examine performance provide relatively "hard" data (such as the number of hours required to assemble a car) and represent a significant improvement over potentially biased self-reports of the effectiveness of innovations. Unfortunately, it is expensive to make plant visits or to obtain multiple respondents in each plant. Thus, researchers who make intensive surveys of individual plants typically settle for smaller sample sizes. A smaller sample size, in turn, makes it more difficult to estimate precisely the effects of work practices on performance and increases the chances of concluding that a given practice has no effect even when it does. Moreover, if some practices are more effective when used in combination, it is difficult to detect these interaction effects in small samples. Finally, it is unclear how well results from intra-industry studies generalize to other settings.

While it is more difficult to control for the many sources of variation in the performance of heterogeneous firms in cross-industry samples (leading to greater concern with omitted variable biases), studies using these samples can examine important firm-level outcomes such as profits and stock market data (Huselid and Becker).

Identifying "Bundles"

In an ideal experiment, theory would inform us of interesting sets of workplace practices. The researcher would then assign different sets of work practices to different workplaces, and we could easily identify which bundles were effective. In doing so, we could also identify which work practices were substitutes (e.g., when only one of a pair was needed) and which were complements. In non-experimental research, it is difficult to identify which workplaces have introduced a theoretically sound bundle of practices.

One problem is that some practices are substitutes. For example, either employee stock ownership or profit-sharing may create employee identification with employers. Other practices may be complements; as already noted, some work practices may be more effective when introduced as a bundle. For example, it may be far more effective both to train front-line employees in problem-solving and to permit them to solve more problems than it is to make either change alone.

Because bundles are hard to measure, it is difficult to identify which organizations have "the" experimental treatment of being innovative and which have not. In apparel, the change from the assembly-line bundle system to the team-based module system is relatively discrete, facilitating identification of innovative workplaces (Berg et al.; Dunlop and Weil). Unfortunately, even here not all module systems involve cross-training, implying incomplete implementation of the new system (Dunlop and Weil). In other settings, the researcher usually lumps together a number of specific work practices into a smaller number of indicators of work systems. Some researchers rely on theory to identify their indices of workplace practices – for example, ad hoc indices (Pil and MacDuffie) or confirmatory factor analysis (Kelley). Unfortunately, these methods implicitly assume that work practices are substitutes, even though theory suggests that complementarities can be important. Other methods rely more on patterns within the data set to identify workplaces with different bundles of practices (e.g., cluster analysis).

No matter how bundles are measured, the method of identifying workplaces as more and less innovative is always subject to some error. The most convincing results are obtained by multiple methods; they reveal whether different procedures yield similar groupings of work practices and predict similar performance results (Ichniowski and Shaw, 1995).

Longitudinal versus Cross-sectional Designs

With an experiment that has random assignment, one can estimate the effect of innovative work practices on organizational performance with a single cross section of data. In non-experimental studies, cross-sectional data make it very difficult to rule out the possibility that omitted variables affect the result. Thus, as Huselid and Becker argue, longitudinal studies are often preferable. We are pleased to note that five of our studies (those of Dunlop and Weil, Huselid and Becker, Easton and Jarrell [Chapter 7], Hendricks and Singhal [Chapter 8], and Pil and MacDuffie) analyze multiple periods of data.

Longitudinal data raise other important design issues. Huselid and Becker show how measurement error can increase when one is looking at changes in work practices and performance. Another problem: How long should the treatment be applied? And when should the performance measure be taken? If theory predicts that the innovative work practices "treatment" is a complex set of practices designed to influence employees' skills, motivation, and organizational commitment, the complexity of workers' responses may also require that considerable time pass before the treatment alters behavior and performance is measured. This time lag may be even longer if workplace changes are introduced only slowly. As Pil and MacDuffie point out, a plant may still be in transition when the measurement is made and things may get worse before they get better. Moreover, in many cases productivity improvements lead to layoffs, not higher output; thus, innovations that depend on employee initiative may carry the seeds of their own destruction (Sterman, Reppenning, and Kofman, 1997).

The Huselid–Becker results suggest that the lagged effect of workplace changes may be significant, but they cannot say how long the lag might be because they have only two periods of data. The Dunlop and Weil and the Sterman, Repenning, and Kofman (1997) studies suggest that the decision to implement innovative work practices may be "bundled" with other organizational changes that may have their own performance effects, and these other changes may cause or have feedback effects on the original innovations.

These complications do not mean we should not collect longitudinal data; they simply mean we need to collect better measures of innovative work practice policies and information on other organizational changes that may affect performance and that are correlated with innovative work practice policies.

The Effect of Research Design on Confidence in the Results

In short, it is difficult to measure the true effect of work practices, such as employee involvement, on productivity. Measurement problems can lead researchers to find no relationship when there truly is one, or can lead them to believe there is a relationship when there is none. Unfortunately, we cannot even be sure of the sign of the bias – that is, whether estimated results will be unrealistically positive or negative.

Evidence as to Performance

The net result of the problems described in the preceding section is that no single study is likely to be completely convincing. The key to credible results is creating a collage of studies that use different designs with their own particular strengths and limitations.

The studies presented in this volume focus on different levels of analysis, ranging from single production lines, to the establishment, the corporation, and the economy as a whole. They also examine many different performance measures, including employee attitudes, productivity, quality, profitability, and stock prices. They focus on a wide range of work practices. They employ both cross-sectional and longitudinal designs. Moreover, these studies are only a subset of a larger and growing body of research that contains equally diverse samples, measures, and designs.

Taken together, the studies provide a check on the results of any single study, and those results that many studies support are all the more convincing.

In this section, we review several broad themes that emerge from this diverse body of research, considering in turn case studies, single-industry studies, and studies using national cross-industry samples.

Case Studies

Here we examine several methods of learning from case studies: longitudinal studies of manufacturing plants before and after changes to a more participatory work environment; cross-sectional case studies of work groups operating under different sets of work practices within single companies; and a meta-analysis of more than a hundred case studies.

Longitudinal Case Study: NUMMI. The New United Motors Manufacturing Inc. (NUMMI) assembly plant in Fremont, California, represents perhaps the most visible and highly publicized transformation in work practices, labor–management relations, and economic performance during the 1980s. NUMMI provides an early example of a case with documented changes in hard measures of performance after the adoption of new work practices (Shimada and MacDuffie, 1987; Krafcik, 1988; Womack, Jones, and Roos, 1991; Adler, 1992; Adler et al., 1997; Wilms, 1996).

NUMMI is a joint venture between GM and Toyota. In 1982 these companies and the United Auto Workers (UAW) signed an agreement to reopen a closed GM assembly plant in Fremont, California. The GM Fremont plant had a traditional work system and labor–management relationship with high grievance and absenteeism rates. Toyota negotiated a new agreement with the UAW that allowed it to implement the Toyota production system, which emphasized just-in-time inventories, statistical quality control, and an integrated approach to technology and human resource management (Shimada and MacDuffie, 1987).

Eighty-five percent of the employees hired for the new plant came from the laid-off GM workforce. They received training in the Toyota production system, as well as in problem-solving and teamwork processes. Work was organized into teams rather than individual job classifications, traditional work rules were eliminated, a single wage rate was introduced for unskilled hourly workers, and a high priority was given to communications with workers and union leaders.

While the Fremont plant had been one of GM's worst-performing plants with very low levels of productivity (48.5 hours per vehicle), NUMMI achieved, within two years of its startup, the highest productivity and highest-quality performance of any North American assembly plant (19.6 hours per vehicle and 69 defects per 100 vehicles). Though work practices changed dramatically after the new joint venture agreement, Toyota introduced little new technology in the reopened facility that would account for these dramatic performance improvements. Comparisons with other, more automated plants in the GM system showed that in 1987 GM's most automated facility (approximately 40% more automated than NUMMI) required 33.7 hours per hundred vehicles with 137.4 defects per vehicle (Krafcik, 1988). Follow-up studies (Adler et al., 1997) revealed that NUMMI's productivity and quality continued to improve marginally over time and remained among the best of North American auto assembly plants (Womack et al., 1991). NUMMI and the UAW have since renegotiated their labor agreement several times. Union leadership has changed, with considerable internal union debate over aspects of the NUMMI system (Parker and Slaughter, 1988); however, the basic features of the work system and related human resource practices remain in place.

Longitudinal Case Study: A Paper Mill. Ichniowski (1992) documents the change from traditional work practices to a set of innovative human resource management practices at a unionized U.S. paper mill. Previously, jobs were defined narrowly – 94 job classifications covered some 160 employees on a given shift. Wage rates were attached to jobs that were allocated according to employees' seniority. Labor–management communication was channeled through a traditional grievance procedure with a large backlog of cases.

In 1983, during contract negotiations that involved a bitter, three-month strike, management implemented sweeping work practice changes, which it called the "Team Concept." Job classifications were reduced from 96 job titles to 4 work "clusters." Workers received extensive training to become proficient in their new broadened tasks. Old pay rates were eliminated, and all workers received the highest of all the old pay rates now in that cluster. Employment security was guaranteed to all mill workers. Precedents of old arbitration cases were eliminated. The grievance procedure was maintained, but was also supplemented by monthly "listening sessions" between work crews and top mill management. In short, under the Team Concept, the mill adopted a broad set of work practice innovations in the areas of job design, compensation and rewards, communications, and employment security.

Many effects of the change were predictable. Employment levels remained steady during the three-year term of the agreement, in keeping with the employment security pledge. Total labor costs increased 40%, due to the provision by which all employees in the new job clusters were paid the highest pay of any of the old jobs now in the clusters. However, despite becoming a more costly mill under the Team Concept, it became more profitable. First, productivity increased. After maintaining steady levels in 1984, production increased by 5% over the 1983 pre–Team Concept levels. The extra production and sales revenue more than offset the higher labor costs. Second, non-labor costs also declined substantially. As a result, mill profitability more than tripled between 1984 and 1985, from $0.89 million to $2.75 million.

The production increases, savings in non-labor costs, and associated increases in profitability had many specific causes, but the main one was workers' suggestions for improving operations that they had never before offered. For example, downtime was dramatically reduced. One of the two annual shutdowns for major maintenance, the standard practice for the industry, was eliminated. Worker-generated suggestions and modifications identified ways to reduce costs and to increase the speed and efficiency of the machinery – or, as one manager described it, "the workers just made the machines run faster."

Thus, the Team Concept helped transform a marginally profitable paper mill with an adversarial labor relations environment into one of the most productive mills in North America, manned by the highest-paid paper workers and operating at levels of profitability never previously attained. Furthermore, the success of the continuous improvement process achieved by 1985 under the Team Concept contract was not short-lived. Total mill production continued to increase and reached approximately 800,000 tons by 1990 – an additional increase of more than 20% from the output levels in 1985.

Indicators of the quality of the working environment also improved. Grievance filing rates dropped from 80 per month in 1983 to 4 per month in 1984. Accident rates fell from 4.0 per month in 1983 to 1.6 per month by 1985. The rate of absenteeism declined by one-half, from 2.1% in 1983 to 1.0% in 1985. By 1990, labor and management had peacefully renegotiated the original Team Concept labor agreement of 1983 three more times with substantial pay increases for mill employees.

Comparative Case Studies: Apparel. Berg et al. (Chapter 3, this volume) undertook a cross-sectional comparison of the performance of two apparel plants making an identical garment under two very different methods of work organization – one using the industry's traditional "bundle system" and the other the team-oriented "modular production system."

Module work enjoyed a 30% advantage in overall production costs over bundle work, attributable to large savings in warehousing, materials, and direct labor costs. Warehousing and materials cost advantages are expected, given the module system's emphasis on quick turnaround of small orders with minimal work-in-progress inventories. The lower labor costs for modules are more surprising, because bundle manufacturing has the advantage of specialization. Interviews suggest that module operators spend much less time opening and closing work-in-progress bundles, sorting through bundles for necessary pieces, and setting up materials for any given work task.

The difference between bundle production's specialized jobs and module production's multi-skilled work teams, however, is only a small part of a larger set of systematic differences in work practices. Relative to the more traditional bundle system, workers in the module system receive more training in problem-solving and other skills. They are more likely to receive profit-sharing and to be covered by a multi-attribute gainsharing plan that covers more dimensions of performance than the output-based piece-rate pay.

Work Groups at Xerox. Cutcher-Gershenfeld (1991) studied the effects of changes in workplace practices at manufacturing facilities of the Xerox Corporation. In 1981, Xerox and the Amalgamated Clothing and Textile Workers Union (ACTWU) jointly implemented an employee participation and work redesign effort. What started as a narrow quality circle program gradually evolved into changes in many work practices, including the creation of self-managing work teams and special problem-solving task forces, increased flexibility, decentralized decision-making, reductions in status differences among workers and supervisors, and the introduction of methods for resolving grievances informally.

Three Xerox plants that were transformed in this way were compared with plants that retained traditional features. Transformed units exhibited significantly higher productivity and lower scrap, costs, and direct labor hours than traditional units. Xerox and the ACTWU have sustained their commitments to the new work practices and the new labor–management relationship since its inception in the early 1980s.

Work Groups in a Telecommunications Company. Since deregulation and the breakup of the old AT&T Bell System, the telecommunications industry has experienced rapid technological change, substantial product innovation, downsizing, and increased competition. Meanwhile many telecommunications firms have introduced workplace innovations. Examining this trend, Batt (1995) compared work groups operating under different work practices in a regional telecommunications company.

Employees in two different business units of this company were involved. One unit, network service, performs repair and field service operations. The other, customer service, sells new services and responds to customer phone inquiries. During the period of the survey, the units worked under three types of practices. Some work groups retained their traditional work arrangements. Other groups engaged in total quality improvement programs; these groups met periodically to discuss workplace problems, but did so outside of their normal jobs. A final set of work groups were transformed into self-managed work teams. The performances of the work groups under these three types of arrangements were compared.

Compared with traditional work arrangements, the quality program made little difference in performance, while self-managed teams made a lot. In network services, the primary effect of self-managed teams was to reduce the size and costs of middle management. In customer services, self-managed teams achieved sales that were some 20% higher than the sales of traditionally organized work groups. Both sets of self-managed teams reported higher quality and greater improvement in quality.

Apparently the quality program had little impact on workers' attitudes. In contrast, employees in self-managed teams reported significantly higher levels of autonomy, learning, and cooperation within their groups compared with traditionally organized groups. Ninety percent of those in self-managed teams preferred their new work arrangements. Seventy-five percent of those in traditional arrangements expressed a desire to work in teams.

Meta-analysis of Individual Case Studies. The case studies just reviewed strongly suggest that a wide-ranging set of innovative human resource management practices support superior economic performance in a limited group of industries and companies. Still, a broader set of case studies would help provide evidence on whether this pattern of findings applies more generally to U.S. industry.

Macy and Izumi (1993) reported a meta-analysis of published and unpublished case studies on organizational change initiatives that were conducted between 1961 and 1991. These authors considered a broad range of organizational policies, including 31 related to human resources (e.g., fewer job classifications, multi-skilling, different types of work teams, features of compensation systems, and communication procedures), as well as a considerable number of possible outcome measures, including 14 indicators of economic performance (e.g., output and productivity measures, quality indicators, and cost indicators).

Several obvious caveats in interpreting patterns from this overview of case-based research must be kept in mind. First, outcome measures differ across studies and so are not comparable. Second, researchers sometimes have an easier time gaining access to data when an organizational change has been successful (Macy and Izumi, 1993, p. 283). Despite the study's limitations, it details the experiences of a large number of North American businesses with workplace innovations over the past two decades.

Overall, more than three-fourths of the case studies that reported changes in economic outcomes also reported that these were positive. Of particular interest, the number of organizational changes in policies and practices was positively correlated with increased economic performance. No similar correlation was observed with the number of policy changes and worker attitudes (e.g., satisfaction) or behaviors (e.g., turnover). Again, the pattern appears to be that the largest performance changes occur when businesses make sweeping changes in sets of work practices and other related organizational policies.

Studies within a Single Industry

We next review results from studies using broader samples of businesses within four narrowly defined industries – integrated steel making, automobile assembly, apparel manufacture, and metalworking. These studies are noteworthy for their attempts to investigate comprehensive samples of specific types of businesses, for their attention to constructing convincing industry-specific measures of work practices and performance, and for incorporating insights from extensive field research in order to understand how businesses in these industries compete.

Steel Mills. Ichniowski and Shaw (1995) studied the relationship between work practice innovations and economic performance in a sample of steel finishing lines. After conducting on-site investigations in nearly all U.S. production lines of this kind, they assembled detailed longitudinal data on multiple performance measures of the production technology and work practices at these sites. Three main conclusions emerged from their research.

First, work practice innovations are highly correlated. Most mills have one of four basic combinations of work practices. A "traditional" system features narrow job classifications, no work teams, communication confined largely to the grievance procedure, training only through on-the-job learning, and traditional steel industry incentive pay based on tons of steel produced. The "innovative" system is the antithesis of the traditional one: it features extensive screening and orientation at time of hire, broadly defined jobs and problem-solving teams, extensive on- and off-site training in production skills and problem-solving processes, multi-attribute gainsharing-type compensation schemes, employment security policies, and extensive labor–management communication, including sharing of financial information. Between these extremes are two intermediate cases – one with work practice innovations only in the areas of teams and labor–management communications and a second with a more extensive set of innovations.

Second, the different work systems have large effects on productivity and quality outcomes. According to both longitudinal comparisons of production lines that switch their systems of work practices and cross-sectional comparisons of lines with different human resource management (HRM) systems, those lines with the innovative work system always have the highest productivity and quality of output, and traditional systems the lowest.

Third, in contrast to the large effects that different *systems* of work practices have on economic performance, changes in *individual* work practices have no effect on performance.

In sum, the study shows that the adoption of a *coherent and integrated system* of innovative practices, including extensive recruiting and careful selection, flexible job definitions and problem-solving teams, gainsharing-type compensation plans, employment security, and extensive labor–management communication, substantially improves productivity and quality outcomes. The adoption of individual work practice innovations has no effect on productivity.

On the basis of his study of 30 U.S. steel minimills, Arthur (1994) categorizes human resource and workplace environments into "control" and "commitment" systems (a distinction similar to Ichniowski et al.'s [1989] traditional and innovative systems). Like Ichniowski et al., Arthur finds that mills with a system of more innovative workplace practices enjoy higher productivity and quality than do mills employing more traditional practices.

Auto Assembly Plants. MacDuffie (1995) reports on the relationship between various work practices and productivity and quality measures in a sample of 57 auto assembly plants. This sample represents a large proportion of non-luxury car production and includes plants from North

America, Japan, Europe, Australia, Korea, Taiwan, Mexico, and Brazil. Detailed measures of productivity and quality that adjust for production and assembly differences were developed and related to two work practice indices – one based on several variables measuring the design of work (e.g., breadth of job definition, extent of work involvement and team activities) and a second index of a broader range of human resource practices (e.g., pay-for-performance compensation and high levels of training).

In this industry, plants that couple various innovative work practices with production practices representative of "lean manufacturing" (e.g., low buffers and low work-in-process inventories between stages of production) enjoy the highest economic performance. For example, productivity is highest when plants score highest on a combination of the work organization index, the human resource policy index, and the production policy index. In auto assembly plants, systems of innovative work practices are again important determinants of superior performance, but here these policies must be coupled with production methods that are most compatible with this form of work organization.

Apparel Making. Dunlop and Weil (Chapter 2, this volume) investigate the relationship between work practices and performance in a sample of 35 apparel-making business units producing a limited set of garment categories. Like the Berg et al. study of apparel makers, Dunlop and Weil find that module production and bundle production have very different work practices. Module workers perform more tasks and receive more training to accomplish these tasks. Also, they are more likely to be covered by multi-attribute group incentives instead of by piece rates.

Dunlop and Weil show that module production and its particular set of team-oriented work practices go together with more modern product distribution methods, such as direct computer connections between manufacturer and retailer and product bar coding to track shipments and retail sales. Plants that were early adopters of module production's new HRM practices without changing their information-processing and distribution procedures often abandoned the new work practices. In contrast, plants that implemented the new HRM practices together with the new distribution methods continue to operate under these practices and appear to enjoy higher profitability.

Metalworking and Machining Plants. Kelley (Chapter 4, this volume) investigated the effects of problem-solving teams and related HRM practices on performance in a sample of plants in 21 industries engaged in various metalworking and machining operations. This study identifies one set of plants that rely on labor–management committees, autonomous work groups, and contingent pay plans like employee stock ownership plans, and contrasts the performance of these plants with that of others that have more traditional union–management relationships and work rules. Plants with more participative work arrangements typically exhibit higher performance. The main exception to this pattern occurs among single-plant firms where the participative arrangements are not associated with superior performance.

Studies Spanning Many Industries

While the intra-industry studies examine a much larger number of establishments and businesses than do the case studies, the evidence in these studies is confined to four manufacturing industries. Do the empirical patterns showing higher performance for bundles of innovative practices and lower performance for more traditional sets of work practices extend more broadly to other sectors of the economy? Just as important, do the quality and productivity results translate into bottom-line results of high profits and stock market returns?

Huselid (1995) provides evidence based on a large sample of U.S. corporations in many industries. Performance data come from the 1991 Compact Disclosure data base. Of 3,452 firms across all industries in this data base, 28%, or 968 firms, responded to Huselid's survey.

Huselid constructs two indices of work practices – one of elements such as job analysis, attitude surveys, participation programs, skills training, and communication and dispute resolution procedures, and another measuring use of performance appraisals and merit-based pay plans. Higher levels of each index generally correspond to more work practice "innovations" as defined at the outset of this study. In cross-sectional analyses, the second index is significantly correlated with firm productivity, while both the skills and structures index and the motivation index have significant effects on firms' stock market valuation.

Huselid's (1995) national, cross-industry study revealed that annual sales per employee are as much as $100,000 higher in businesses with the "best" work practices than in firms with the "worst." (This calculation assumes that the best and worst work practices differ by four standard deviations of Huselid's index.) This considerable figure is more than half the average value of this productivity measure in these businesses. Differences in work practices affect profits by as much as $15,000 per employee per year, with differences in stock market measures of performance of about equal magnitude.

Huselid and Becker (Chapter 5, this volume) report results from a longitudinal analysis using a second time period of data for Huselid's original sample. Estimated performance effects using these panel data are smaller than the cross-sectional estimates. The authors argue that measurement error in the survey data on HRM practices is a likely cause of the reduced estimates. Their corrections for this measurement error bias suggest that the magnitude of the actual effects of the HRM measures may be closer to cross-sectional estimates.

While these figures may seem implausibly large, research on samples of very similar businesses in which measures of performance and technology are more precise again show very large effects. In their comparison of plants with one very specific steel-making production process, Ichniowski and Shaw (1995) estimate that production lines with a full complement of innovative HRM practices are about 7% more productive than those with more traditional practices. This productivity difference corresponds to a difference in annual revenues of some $2.5 million for this single production area. Improvements in the quality of steel production attributable to the new work practices suggest that the revenue effects are even larger than the productivity effects alone imply. Revenue effects of this magnitude dwarf any reasonable estimates of the direct costs of the work practices themselves.

Case study evidence is consistent with these conclusions. After adopting the Team Concept, the paper mill increased productivity by some 5% and tripled profits. The case study of apparel plants found an overall cost advantage of some 30% for module production over bundle production for an identical garment. Batt's (1995) case study of telecommunications operations revealed that the increase in annual sales revenue associated with self-managed groups in customer service units translated into more than $10,000 per employee, and in network operations, cost savings due to self-managed teams would exceed $200 million per year for the whole division.

Huselid's findings are consistent with the results of an earlier survey-based study of businesses in diverse industry groups. Ichniowski (1990) surveyed COMPUSTAT II business lines for their work practices and related these practices to productivity and stock market performance indicators available from public sources. While this survey yielded a considerably smaller sample of businesses than does the Huselid study, the empirical patterns are similar: HRM practices are highly correlated and businesses that adopt a full complement of innovative practices, including extensive labor–management communication, merit-based rewards, training, and flexible job design, have higher productivity and stock market value.

Finally, evidence of the power of an integrated approach comes from evaluations of total quality management (TQM) programs. While not all TQM programs contain much employee involvement, most successful cases of TQM do empower employees.

While TQM has been credited with much of Japan's manufacturing success, an integrated approach has also been effective in American-run workplaces. A GAO analysis of U.S. companies that won the Baldrige Award for their quality programs concluded:

> Companies that adopted quality management practices experienced an overall improvement in corporate performance. In nearly all cases, companies that used total quality management practices achieved better employee relations, higher productivity, greater customer satisfaction, increased market share, and improved profitability. (1992, p. 2)

Unfortunately, at many private- and public-sector workplaces in the United States, TQM is implemented in ways that do not empower employees. For example, Ken Stockbridge, a GAO expert on TQM, told of a county government quality team that required 10 meetings over 10 weeks to choose a name for the group (personal communication, 1993). Even worse, in many programs, workers are not rewarded for their efforts or ideas, and both middle managers and unions often resist the new programs because they consider them to be poorly conceived and threatening. At its worst, TQM becomes a management speedup that makes workers work harder but does not lead to sustained improvements in the quality of products (Parker and Slaughter, 1988). Thus, many TQM efforts have only modest success.

Because of TQM's relatively recent implementation on a large scale, empirical analyses with large samples remain rare. One of the largest samples comes from a 1991 GAO survey of more than 2,800 federal government installations (GAO, 1992). Two-thirds of the respondents claimed to have some quality program in action, but most programs were less than two years old. As expected, given the newness of the typical program, only 3% of respondents claimed that their installation had achieved "long-term institutionalization" – integration of TQM into all aspects of the organization's operation. All of the latter respondents reported that TQM had a positive impact on customer service, efficiency, customer satisfaction, and timeliness.

In the long run, a high-involvement work organization appears to translate into stock returns as well as high quality and productivity. For example, Jarrell and Easton (Chapter 7, this volume) used a search of companies' annual reports to reveal those with TQM efforts. Follow-up phone calls identified which companies were fairly thorough in their implementation of TQM – that is, those that scored above approximately 500 (out of a maximum of 1,000) on the Baldrige Award evaluation. They found that the companies had 15% excess returns over the five years after the start of the TQM program. No excess returns were evident over the first three years, which was consistent with the stock market failing to observe the quality of the investment in the TQM program until it was already paying off financially.

Similar results were found for companies that won independently administered quality awards (Hendricks and Singhal, Chapter 8, this volume). The companies achieved stock market returns greater than those of similar companies – only about 0.6% in the narrow window of a few days around the announcement of the award but more than 6% in the years leading up to the award (and after the implementation of the quality program).

The fairly recent introduction of most U.S. quality programs makes all conclusions tentative. Researchers also have had difficulty discriminating between typical TQM programs and those that are best practice. Nevertheless, so far all research on the relation between mature TQM programs and corporate performance demonstrates that well-designed TQM programs can increase productivity, quality, and returns to shareholders. These well-designed programs, in turn, rely on, for example, employee involvement, training, and rewards for employees who innovate.

Adopting Workplace Innovations Individually. There are no one or two "magic bullets" that are *the* work practices that will stimulate worker and business performance. Work teams or quality circles alone are not enough. Rather, whole systems have to be changed.

Some studies that investigate the performance effects of workplace innovations estimate much smaller effects of the innovations (see Levine and Tyson, 1990), but these studies focus on individual work practices, such as the use of work teams or quality circles. Without data on sets of work practice innovations, these studies tell us little about whether systems of workplace innovations would have larger effects. Two studies provide evidence on this issue. Katz, Kochan, and Keefe (1987) find that plants that collapsed traditional job classifications into teams without changing other aspects of the labor–management relationship or environment performed worse than traditional systems. Ichniowski and Shaw (1995) include a direct test of relative performance effects of individual workplace innovations and new work systems. In contrast to their finding of large performance effects of new overall work systems reviewed earlier in this chapter, here the adoption of individual innovative work practices does not improve productivity and sometimes is associated with its decline.

In short, the empirical evidence from case studies, samples of plants within specific industries, and broad national samples of firms in different industries tells a consistent story:

Conclusion 1. *Innovative HRM practices can have large, economically important effects on productivity, profitability, and (long-term) stock market value. These positive results rely on the use of systems of related work practices designed to enhance worker participation and flexibility in the design of work and the decentralization of managerial tasks and responsibilities, not on any single innovation.*

Extent of Adoption

While the research shows that work practice innovations have large payoffs, some businesses have adopted these productivity-enhancing practices and others have not. This pattern raises at least two important questions. First, how many businesses have systems of innovative, productivity-enhancing work practices relative to those without them? Second, why have more businesses not adopted them?

National Cross-Industry Survey Data

As to the first question, Osterman (1994) provides the most comprehensive information. He reports on the adoption of various work practice innovations among a sample of some 800 U.S. establishments, designed to be representative of the entire population of private-sector U.S. business establishments with more than 50 employees. Emerging from this survey are two broad conclusions concerning the extent to which various innovations have been adopted. First, a clear majority of U.S. business establishments have adopted at least one work practice innovation. Workplace flexibility, defined as 50% of employees participating in teams, quality circles, or job rotation, is present in 62% of U.S. establishments. Contingent pay, defined as the presence of gainsharing, pay-for-skills, or profit-sharing, is present in 65%. Training, defined by more than 20% of employees in cross-training or off-site training, is present in 81%. And employment security pledges are in effect in 40% of these business establishments.

At the same time, U.S. establishments rarely adopt *bundles* of practices of the kind that, according to the evidence just presented, appears to be responsible for improved economic performance. Only 16% of

U.S. businesses have at least one innovative practice in each of the four major HRM policy areas: flexible job design, worker training, pay-for-performance compensation, and employment security (P. Osterman, personal correspondence; Lawler et al., 1995, report similar results for very large U.S. employers). In short, while individual work practice innovations are quite common, systems of innovative work practices are relatively exceptional.

Adoption in Specific Industries

This pattern in Osterman's national survey is consistent with findings from broad samples of establishments in steel, apparel, and automobile assembly industries. In steel, only 16.7% of the sample of steel production units have no innovative practices at all in the areas of work teams, training, selective screening policies, gainsharing-type incentive pay plans, job flexibility, employment security, or regular labor–management information-sharing (Ichniowski and Shaw, 1995). While the vast majority of steel-making facilities have therefore adopted some new work practices in at least one of these areas, only 11% of these production units had the full system of innovative work practices that is shown to lead to the highest productivity and quality. Put another way, although innovations are spreading and most steel businesses have some innovative work practices, very few have a full complement. In apparel manufacturing, the innovative modular system, which results in better performance along a number of dimensions, is growing in importance. Nevertheless, it accounts for only 9.8% of apparel volume shipped (Dunlop and Weil, Chapter 2, this volume). Similarly, in automobile manufacturing, innovation is spreading and many plants have some experience with some innovative work practices, but only about one-fourth have a full system (MacDuffie, 1995).

The answer to the question concerning how extensively work practice innovations have been adopted by U.S. businesses therefore depends on the definition of "innovations." In particular:

Conclusion 2. *A majority of contemporary U.S. businesses have adopted some forms of innovative work practices aimed at enhancing employee participation such as work teams, contingent pay-for-performance compensation, and flexible assignment of multi-skilled employees. However, only a small percentage of businesses have adopted a comprehensive system of innovative work practices.*

The second part of this conclusion is particularly important, since research on work practice innovations indicates that businesses must adopt a comprehensive system of these innovations to achieve the highest levels of productivity and performance.

Impediments to Broader Diffusion

If systems of innovative work practices stimulate productivity, quality, and other dimensions of business performance, why haven't they diffused more widely through the economy? Why have the experiences of many U.S. businesses with limited forms of workplace innovation not grown into more comprehensive approaches? Unfortunately, we have little hard evidence or good theory to provide a thorough answer to these critical questions. Nevertheless, this section suggests several possible explanations, viewing them as hypotheses in need of further testing.

Limited Performance Gains for Some Businesses

One possible reason for the limited diffusion is that innovative work practices may lead to higher performance only in some industries or firms. The evidence reviewed in the preceding sections is largely confined to a subset of manufacturing industries. New work systems that include participatory team structures, extensive training, and employment security entail costly investments. In industries where turnover is high, firms may not recoup on these investments. In industries where technology determines output, the performance benefits from problem-solving teams may be small.

Still, the research just reviewed compares better- and poorer-performing plants in the same industries. These plants are similar in many respects, but those with innovative practices perform better according to a variety of measures. It is difficult to determine why these systems are not adopted by businesses whose performance presumably would benefit from them.

The answer may in part be that difficulties arise in changing management practices and organizational cultures. New startups ("greenfield sites") are more likely to adopt innovative work practices than are plants that have been operating for longer periods of time (Ichniowski, 1990; Ichniowski and Shaw, 1995; for an opposing view see Osterman, 1994). Low rates of adoption are therefore primarily a concern among older "brownfield" sites. Why have these innovative systems of work practices diffused only slowly to brownfield sites? What advantages accrue to greenfield sites that adopt the new work systems? Current research suggests several answers.

System Inertia

First, the need to change an entire system of work practices – from a traditional set based on narrowly defined jobs, strict supervision, frequent layoffs, and seniority-based pay and promotion rules, to a newer approach involving flexible job design, contingent incentive pay plans, extensive training in multiple skills, and employment security initiatives – will itself limit diffusion. As we have emphasized, economic performance is highest only when firms adopt whole bundles of work practices, and firms that adopt single practices without other necessary changes will not experience improved performance (Katz et al., 1987; Ichniowski et al., 1997).

Levinthal (1994) develops simulations to model various ways that firms might experiment with new practices in their search for more productive forms of organization. He shows that when interaction effects among organizational policies are important determinants of performance, firms do indeed get "locked into" their initial choice of practices. Firms that experiment with individual workplace innovations and see no improvements in performance discard their innovations as failures. These results are consistent with empirical studies which show that many employee participation and quality circle initiatives are abandoned after only a few years (Lawler and Mohrman, 1987; Drago, 1988).

Linkages with Other Organizational Practices

Part of the explanation for limited adoption lies in the fact that in some industries systems of innovative work policies appear to be part of a larger system of production and distribution policies. The magnitude of the economic benefits of adopting new systems in these industries may depend on characteristics of the businesses' product markets and customers.

For example, in apparel, the full benefits of the modular production system require that firms invest in information and order-tracking technologies to streamline the distribution channels. Furthermore, the benefits of adopting the new information technology and module production methods are greater for apparel makers whose customers insist on quick replenishment of stocks and a rapid delivery of new orders (Dunlop and Weil, Chapter 2, this volume). In automotive industries, innovative work practices appear to be complementary to "lean manufacturing" methods such as small work-in-process inventories (Helper, 1995; MacDuffie, 1995).

For firms in these industries, switching to new work practices requires an entirely new set of production and distribution procedures and large investments in new technologies. These costs will be considerably more than the expenses of the new employment policies. Decisions to adopt these policies are not made independently but are part of a larger set of costly choices regarding the manufacturing and marketing strategies of the firm and its key customers.

Labor–Management Distrust

In other industries better-performing plants with innovative practices and poorer performers with traditional work practices employ roughly the same production processes, customers, and distribution practices. In these cases, still other factors must be at work to limit the adoption of productivity-enhancing work systems.

One such factor is a low level of trust between labor and management. Ichniowski and Shaw (1995, pp. 50–52) cite examples at older steel mills of how participation teams were viewed as management "tricks" to cut jobs. Many employees believed management would take away contractual job security guarantees in subsequent contracts after employees offered their ideas to improve operations, and employees also suspected that newly shared financial information was coming from a "second set of books." Union leaders report that one of the biggest barriers to lasting cooperative relations occurs when an employer seeks their cooperation and partnership in existing unionized facilities, while engaging in union avoidance practices at other sites (AFL-CIO, 1994; Commission on the Future of Worker–Management Relations, 1994a).

Winners and Losers

While a firm's productivity may increase with the adoption of new work systems, this improved performance may not translate into better conditions for all of the firm's workers. For example, senior workers in older establishments that tie job assignments and pay rates to length of service may not fare any better under the new arrangements than they do under the more traditional arrangements under which they have worked for many years. These workers may resist changing to new systems (Goodman, 1979). Downsizing and restructuring of businesses that often precede or accompany the adoption of new work systems can create resistance not only among those most at risk of losing their jobs but also

among the "survivors," who may feel overworked or fear they will be the
next to go if productivity improvements outpace business growth (Batt,
1995). Front-line supervisors may also be particularly resistant to new
practices, such as self-directed work teams, that threaten their jobs. Even
if supervisors' jobs are not threatened by the adoption of new work
systems, the kind of work that supervisors would perform under the new
systems would be drastically different from their traditional tasks (Klein,
1984).

Institutional and Public Policy Constraints

Institutional and public policy factors outside the control of individual
firms, workers, or unions may also limit the diffusion of workplace innovations. One institutional constraint lies in the limited options workers
have in acting on their preference for workplace innovations. One survey
found that most workers would prefer to have greater participation in
their jobs but cannot obtain greater participation on their own without
some management initiative (Freeman and Rogers, 1995). This same
majority also recognizes that management cooperation is essential to the
success of participatory processes and may be fearful that the increased
worker voice that unionization would bring might come at the expense
of more adversarial labor–management relations. There is no U.S.
equivalent to the European Works Council, which discusses and con-
sults on human resource practices, including the organization of work
and the division of decision-making responsibilities. Thus, the adoption
of work practice innovations in non-union settings remains an employer
prerogative.

U.S. financial markets and institutions may represent another constraint. To the extent that workplace innovations impose substantial and
easy-to-observe short-run costs while the benefits are less certain and
accrue over a longer term, financial agents may prefer strategies for
improving profitability through short-run cost reductions or investments
in easier-to-monitor assets. Thus, workplace innovations must compete
with alternative strategies for boosting short-run performance not only
among managers with competing preferences and interests within the
firm, but among those who monitor firm performance for shareholders
and large institutional investors. Within U.S. corporations, human
resource managers tend to be among the lowest-paid and least influential of corporate executives, and human resource issues are reported to
be of less interest to investment analysts than are short-term cost and
earning projections (Kochan and Osterman, 1994; Levine, 1995). Taken
together, these features of financial markets and corporate governance

structures may make it difficult for advocates of workplace innovations to attract the resources and support needed to sustain them long enough to achieve their full potential.

Current public policy poses additional constraints. For example, considerable uncertainty exists over the legality of some forms of employee participation in non-union settings. The Commission on the Future of Worker–Management Relations (1994a) concluded that the systemic workplace innovations that have the largest effects on performance are the ones most at risk of violating the National Labor Relation Act's ban on company-dominated unions. While only a few cases have tested this provision, a majority of managers surveyed for the Commission indicated that current government policies make them cautious about broadening existing participation programs or implementing new ones (Commission on the Future of Worker–Management Relations, 1994a, p. 53).

To summarize, though the evidence as to the reasons for the limited diffusion of workplace innovations is only suggestive, it indicates that a number of factors are involved:

Conclusion 3. *The diffusion of workplace innovations is limited, especially among older U.S. businesses. Firms face a number of obstacles when changing from a system of traditional work practices to a system of innovative practices, including the abandonment of organizational change initiatives after limited policy changes have little effect on performance, the costs of other organizational practices that are needed to make new work practices effective, long histories of labor–management conflict and distrust, resistance of supervisors and other workers who might not fare as well under the newer practices, and the lack of a supportive institutional and public policy environment.*

Conclusions

This review of an emerging body of research on the experience of U.S. businesses with workplace innovations marks the considerable progress that has been made in assessing the economic effects of new work practices and the reasons for their adoption. The findings from this research are supported by a broad array of studies employing diverse methodologies. For managers, the implications are clear – systematic innovations in managing organizations appear to offer potentially large payoffs.

Nevertheless, there are several important research gaps that future studies should attempt to address. Nearly all of the research to date focuses on manufacturing businesses, so there is a need for research on the service sector. New research is needed also to address the effects of new workplace arrangements on outcomes of particular concern to workers, particularly their effects on wage structures and income inequality. Do workers share in productivity gains through higher earnings? Are earnings more volatile under work systems that typically include contingent compensation plans? Finally, we need further research to determine whether new work systems work best in certain environments. Do the regular reports of large-scale layoffs by major U.S. businesses indicate that new work systems are less effective in declining product markets? More generally, further research on adoption is necessary to explain the limited adoption of new work systems in many sectors of the U.S. economy. Where unions are present, are the results of new work systems different when the union actively supports the new practices than when the union resists or is passive to the changes?

The research published here has involved quantitative studies. Coupled with past studies and overviews, the balance of the evidence supports the hypothesis that innovative workplace practices work, at least some of the time. These studies find enormous variation, although their above-average attention to providing rigorous controls (case studies such as that of Berg et al. within an industry or technology) helps reduce many sources of error. While additional measures can help, there will always be omitted variables, and quantitative studies will never explain all the variation we observe.

To complement these quantitative studies, we will always need detailed qualitative studies that provide data that are difficult to quantify and that shed light on crucial details of how to implement innovative practices successfully – in other words, we need to get into the "black box" that explains how and why people perform as they do. Ultimately, results will be convincing only if they show up in both qualitative and quantitative studies.

Research to date has identified a number of barriers to the diffusion of successful workplace innovations. Future research must help us better understand these barriers. If they appear to be due to market and government failures (as argued earlier), there might be a national interest in removing government barriers and in actively promoting workplace innovations. In particular, public policies must lower the transition costs that will inhibit some private decision-makers (firms, unions, individuals) from adopting or supporting these innovations even when they improve both the quality of jobs and organizational effectiveness.

REFERENCES

Adler, Paul. 1992. "The Learning Bureaucracy: New United Motors Manufacturing, Inc." In *Research on Organizational Behavior* 13, edited by Barry Staw and Larry L. Cumming, pp. 111–194. Greenwich, CT: JAI Press.

Adler, Paul, Barbara Goldoftas, and David I. Levine. 1997. "Ergonomics, Employee Involvement, and the Toyota Production System: A Case Study of NUMMI's 1993 Model Introduction." *Industrial and Labor Relations Review* 50(3):416–437.

AFL-CIO. 1994. *The New American Workplace: A Labor Perspective.* Washington, DC: AFL-CIO.

Arthur, Jeffrey. 1994. "Effects of Human Resource Systems on Manufacturing Performance and Turnover." *Academy of Management Journal* 37:670–687.

Ashenfelter, Orley, and Alan Krueger. 1994. "Estimates of the Economic Return to Schooling from a New Sample of Twins." *American Economic Review* 84(December):1157–1173.

Batt, Rosemary. 1995. "Performance and Welfare Effects of Work Restructuring: Evidence from Telecommunications Services." Cambridge, MA: Ph.D. Dissertation, MIT, Sloan School of Management.

Callus, Ron, Alison Morehead, Mark Culley, and John Buchanan. 1991. *Industrial Relations at Work: The Australian Workplace Industrial Relations Survey.* Canberra: AGPS.

Commission on the Future of Worker–Management Relations. 1994a. *Fact Finding Report.* Washington, DC: U.S. Departments of Commerce and Labor.

– 1994b. *Final Report and Recommendations.* Washington, DC: U.S. Departments of Commerce and Labor.

Cutcher-Gershenfeld, Joel. 1988. *Tracing a Transformation in Industrial Relations.* Washington, DC: U.S. Department of Labor, Bureau of Labor–Management Relations and Cooperative Programs.

—1991. "The Impact on Economic Performance of a Transformation in Workplace Industrial Relations." *Industrial and Labor Relations Review* 44:241–260.

Delaney, John Thomas, David Lewin, and Casey Ichniowski. 1988. "Human Resource Management Policies and Practices in American Firms." Unpublished manuscript, Columbia University, Graduate School of Business.

Drago, Robert. 1988. "Quality Circle Survival: An Exploratory Analysis." *Industrial Relations* 27:336–351.

Eaton, Adrienne. 1994. "Factors Contributing to the Survival of Employee Participation Programs in Unionized Settings." *Industrial and Labor Relations Review* 47:371–389.

Freeman, Richard B., and Joel Rogers. 1995. *Worker Representation and Participation Survey.* Princeton, NJ: Princeton Survey Research Corporation.

French, Jack R. P., and Lester Coch. 1948. "Overcoming Resistance to Change." *Human Relations* 1:512–532.

Fucini, Joseph, and Suzy Fucini. 1990. *Working for the Japanese.* New York: Free Press.

36   Casey Ichniowski et al.

General Accounting Office. 1992. *Quality Management: Survey of Federal Organizations,* GAO/GGD-93-9BR. Washington, DC: U.S. Government Printing Office.

Goodman, Paul S. 1979. *Assessing Organizational Change.* New York: Wiley.

Graham, Laurie. 1995. *On the Line at Subaru-Isuzu.* Ithaca, NY: ILR Press.

Helper, Susan. 1995. "Human Resource Practices in Automobile Supplier Firms." Paper presented at the Annual Meeting of the International Motor Vehicle Research Program, Toronto, Canada.

Holmstrom, Bengt, and Milgrom, Paul. 1994. "The Firm as an Incentive System." *American Economic Review* 84(4):972–991.

Huselid, Mark. 1995. "The Impact of Human Resource Management Practices on Turnover, Productivity, and Corporate Financial Performance." *Academy of Management Journal* 38:635–672.

Ichniowski, Casey. 1990. "Human Resource Management Systems and the Performance of U.S. Manufacturing Businesses." National Bureau of Economic Research Working Paper No. 3449, Washington, DC.

—1992. "Human Resource Practices and Productive Labor–Management Relations." In *Research Frontiers in Industrial Relations and Human Resources,* edited by David Lewin, Olivia Mitchell, and Peter Sherer, pp. 239–271. Madison, WI: Industrial Relations Research Association.

Ichniowski, Casey, John T. Delaney, and David Lewin. 1989. "The New Human Resource Management in U.S. Workplaces: Is It Really New and Is It Only Nonunion?" *Relations Industrielles* 44:87–119.

Ichniowski, Casey, and Kathryn Shaw. 1995. "Old Dogs and New Tricks: Determinants of the Adoption of Productivity-Enhancing Work Practices." *Brookings Papers on Economic Activity: Microeconomics* (Spring):1–65.

Ichniowski, Casey, Kathryn Shaw, and Giovanna Prenushi (1997). "The Effects of Human Resource Management Practices on Productivity: A Study of Steel Finishing Lines." *American Economic Review* 87(3):291–313.

IDE. 1983. *Industrial Democracy in Europe.* Oxford: Oxford University Press.

Katz, Harry C., Thomas A. Kochan, and Kenneth R. Gobeille. 1983. "Industrial Relations Performance, Economic Performance and QWL Programs: An Interplant Analysis." *Industrial and Labor Relations Review* 37:3–17.

Katz, Harry C., Thomas A. Kochan, and Jeffrey H. Keefe. 1987. "Industrial Relations and Productivity in the U.S. Automobile Industry." *Brookings Papers on Economic Activity* 3:688–715.

Klein, Janice. 1984. "Why Supervisors Resist Employee Involvement." *Harvard Business Review* 62:87–95.

Kochan, Thomas A., Harry C. Katz, and Robert B. McKersie. 1986. *The Transformation of American Industrial Relations.* New York: Basic Books.

Kochan, Thomas A., and Paul Osterman. 1995. *The Mutual Gains Enterprise.* Boston: Harvard Business School Press.

Krafcik, John. 1988. "Triumph of the Lean Production System." *Sloan Management Review* 30:41–52.

Lawler, Edward E., and Susan A. Mohrman. 1987. "Quality Circles: After the Honeymoon." *Organized Dynamics* 15(4):42–55.

Lawler, Edward E., Susan A. Mohrman, and Gerald Ledford. 1995. *Creating High Performance Organizations*. San Francisco: Jossey-Bass.

Levine, David I. 1995. *Reinventing the Workplace: How Business and Employees Can Both Win*. Washington, DC: Brookings Institution.

Levine, David I., and Laura D'Andrea Tyson. 1990. "Participation, Productivity, and the Firm's Environment." In *Paying for Productivity: A Look at the Evidence*, edited by Alan S. Blinder, pp. 183–236. Washington, DC: Brookings Institution.

Levinthal, Daniel. 1994. "Adaptation in Rugged Landscapes." Unpublished manuscript, University of Pennsylvania, Wharton School.

Lincoln, James, and Arne Kalleberg. 1990. *Culture, Competence, and Commitment: A Study of Work Organization and Work Attitudes in the U.S. and Japan*. Cambridge University Press.

MacDuffie, John Paul. 1995. "Human Resource Bundles and Manufacturing Performance: Organizational Logic and Flexible Production Systems in the World Auto Industry." *Industrial and Labor Relations Review* 48:197–221.

Macy, Barry A., and Hiroaki Izumi. 1993. *Organizational Change, Design, and Work Innovation: A Meta-Analysis of 131 North American Field Studies, 1961–1991*. Research in Organizational Change and Development, Vol. 7. Greenwich, CT: JAI Press.

March, James G. 1988. *Decisions and Organizations*. New York: Blackwell.

Marrow, Alfred Jay, David G. Bowers, and Stanley E. Seashore. 1967. *Management by Participation*. New York: Harpers.

Milgrom, Paul, and John Roberts. 1990. "The Economics of Modern Manufacturing." *American Economic Review* 80(3):511–528.

—1993. "Complementarities and Fit: Strategy, Structure, and Organizational Change in Manufacturing." *Journal of Accounting and Economics* 19(3): 179–208.

Millward, Neil, and Mark Stevens. 1986. *British Workplace Industrial Relations, 1980–1984*. Dartmouth, UK: Aldershot.

Millward, Neil, Mark Stevens, David Smart, and W. R. Hawes. 1992. *Workplace Industrial Relations in Transition*. Dartmouth, UK: Aldershot.

Osterman, Paul. 1994. "How Common Is Workplace Transformation and Who Adopts It?" *Industrial and Labor Relations Review* 47:173–187.

Parker, Mike, and Jane Slaughter. 1988. *Choosing Sides: Unions and the Team Concept*. Boston: South End Press.

Shimada, Haruo, and John Paul MacDuffie. 1987. "Industrial Relations and Humanware." MIT, Sloan School of Management Working Paper.

Sterman, John D., Nelson P. Repenning, and Fred Kofman. 1997. "Unanticipated Side Effects of Successful Quality Programs: Exploring a Paradox of Organizational Improvement." *Management Science* 43(4):503–521.

Whyte, William F., et al. 1955. *Money and Motivation*. New York: Harpers.

Wilms, Wellford. 1996. *Restoring Prosperity*. New York: Random House.

Womack, James, Daniel Jones, and Daniel Roos. 1991. *The Machine That Changed the World*. New York: Rawson/Macmillan.

CHAPTER 2

Diffusion and Performance of Modular Production in the U.S. Apparel Industry

John T. Dunlop and David Weil

The apparel industry is no stranger to discussions of "high-performance work systems," team or "modular" assembly, and innovative human resource practices. Modular assembly alters the traditional method of production, which relies on individual operators to perform one or two tasks repetitively, by substituting teams of workers to sew and assemble parts or all of a garment. Throughout the 1980s, team-based assembly was heralded by the garment industry trade press, the major apparel manufacturing association, major fiber and textile producers, the non-profit Textile Clothing Technology Corporation, and the Amalgamated Clothing and Textile Workers Union as a means of reducing costs and enhancing workforce performance.

Despite the advocacy for modular assembly, these practices have not diffused to a significant degree in the U.S. apparel industry to date. In 1992, about 80% of garments were sewn and assembled by the traditional Tayloristic progressive bundle system. Only 9% utilized the modular system.[1]

Drawing on a unique set of data, this chapter examines the determinants of the diffusion of modular production and the impact of these systems on firm performance relative to traditional assembly systems in

This chapter is a slightly revised version of an article that originally appeared in *Industrial Relations* 35:3 (July 1996); reprinted by permission of Blackwell Publishers.

The study described here was supported by funds from the Alfred P. Sloan Foundation. We are indebted to our colleagues on this project, Frederick Abernathy and Janice Hammond, for their comments. We are grateful to Catherine George and Igor Choodnovskiy for research assistance. For a complete discussion of these issues, see Abernathy et al. (1999: chaps. 8–10).

[1] These results are taken from the industry data set underlying this chapter and described in detail in a later section. The estimates are consistent with those of the American Apparel Manufacturers Association (1992).

the apparel industry. The data set allows the modeling of different classes of adoption determinants, particularly those related to the product market. The data also permit assessment of how modular systems affect firm performance relative to other managerial innovations.

Our empirical results demonstrate that the adoption of modular systems arises from the same product market forces driving the adoption of manufacturing practices related to new forms of apparel retailing. In particular, modular systems have been adopted by those business units that have adopted information systems increasingly required by apparel retailers. The impact of modular assembly on business unit performance arises from its interaction with these information systems, enabling adopting apparel suppliers to respond to more stringent retail delivery standards while reducing their own need to hold large work-in-process and finished product inventories.

Data

This study draws from a larger data set providing comprehensive information on a wide range of apparel manufacturing practices in 1988 and 1992 at the business unit level.[2] The sample consists of 42 business units in the men's shirt, suit, and pants sectors, and in men's and women's jeans and undergarment product lines. These product categories rely on in-house manufacturing and have relatively large production runs.

The detailed and confidential information requested in our 60-page questionnaire meant that a random, stratified sample of the whole apparel industry was not feasible. Instead, in order to secure such detailed responses, the survey effort required sponsorship and support from industry participants. This survey procedure was successful in ensuring responses by major manufacturers in certain targeted product segments (particularly on the men's side of the industry). As a result, the sample is biased toward larger firms and business units.

The sample provides for considerable homogeneity in product market characteristics and manufacturing practices among business units. The survey response rate for these product categories was about 50%, result-

---

[2] A business unit is defined as the lowest level of a firm that has responsibilities for the formulation of annual policies dealing with merchandising, planning, manufacturing, distribution, and related activities for a product line or lines and that collects financial data for those activities. For some organizations, the business unit may be the overall corporation. For others, a number of business units might operate within a single corporate umbrella. A business unit may rely on one (or more) in-house plant(s) to manufacture its products and/or may rely on a network of contractors (with either domestic or foreign operations) to produce its products.

ing in a sample that represents 30% of the total volume shipped by U.S. producers in 1992 for the five product categories.[3] The findings presented here were also tested against a larger sample of business units that did in-house manufacturing regardless of product category. Analysis of this larger data set yields results consistent with those presented here and are available from the authors.

Apparel Assembly: Progressive Bundle and Modular

Producing a garment in large quantities presents a set of operating problems. A typical jeans manufacturer, for example, can have upward of 20,000 different items in its collection at a particular time (arising from different size, style, and fabric combinations). The manufacturer is faced with the task of assembling each of these product variations from a large number of separate cut pieces. Individual sewing processes vary considerably for a given garment, from relatively simple operations requiring little skill to operations that can require more than a year to learn. The limp character of fabric has thwarted attempts to automate the assembly process to any major extent. Even today, only a limited number of sewing operations have been successfully automated.

Thus, apparel manufacture is labor intensive. For example, nearly three-quarters of all production workers in the dress shirt industry are involved in sewing room assembly.[4] Sewing room work[5] is currently undertaken by one of two major methods: progressive bundle and modular systems.[6]

[3] More detailed information on response rates and sample representativeness by product category are available from the authors.
[4] The distribution of production workers in the men's shirt industry is indicative of overall patterns in the apparel industry. In 1990, the distribution of production workers by department was as follows: cutting room, 2,075 (5.5%); sewing room, 27,303 (72.5%); finishing department 5,830 (15.5%); miscellaneous (e.g., maintenance, shipping clerks), 2,463 (6.5%). See U.S. Department of Labor (1992, Table 7).
[5] Organization of work in the cutting room raises questions that are fundamentally different from those that apply to the sewing room; these questions concern technology, investment, material costs, and access to skilled workers and are not addressed in this chapter.
[6] The unit production system is a third assembly method that has been widely discussed over the past decade. This system has a great degree of similarity to progressive bundle systems: sewing operations are broken down to minimize direct labor content, and each operator works independently rather than in teams on her assembly step. It differs from the progressive bundle system, however, in that work-in-process is transferred between operators through automated material handling systems rather than through the use of large buffers in the form of bundles.

Progressive Bundle System

Since the emergence of mass markets for apparel, the dominant production method chosen for garment assembly has been the bundle system. While bundle systems date back to before 1900, the progressive bundle system (PBS) represents a refinement of the bundle system originated in the 1930s (Dunlop and Weil 1994). In PBS, each individual sewing task is specified and then organized in a systematic fashion. PBS entails engineering specific sewing tasks to reduce the amount of time required for each task. It also requires laying out shops to reduce the time required to shuttle a bin of garment bundles from operator to operator.

In PBS, each operation is done by a single worker operating at a stationary sewing machine. Each worker receives a bundle of unfinished garments. She (seldom he) then performs a single operation on each garment in the bundle. As the operator finishes a bundle, it is placed in a buffer with other bundles that have been completed to that point. The bundles in the buffer are then ready for the next operator in the sequence.

Each task in the assembly process has a target "standard allocated minutes" (SAM), which represents the total amount of direct labor time required for each task. The SAM for an entire garment is therefore calculated as the sum of the number of minutes required for each operation in the garment production process, with adjustments for worker fatigue, break times, and related factors.[7] Compensation is based on the operator's rate of production relative to the SAM.

Refinement of PBS over time has led to high levels of pace and labor productivity in terms of direct labor content per assembled apparel product. Productivity in specific apparel segments measured as constant-dollar value of output per employee hour rose steadily over the past quarter century. In men's and boys' suits and coats, for example, output per employee-hour increased 60.7% in the period 1973–1995, or 2.8% a year (U.S. Department of Labor 1998). As a result, a typical men's dress shirt in 1992 required about 18 minutes of direct labor, a pair of trousers 24 minutes, knit pants 3 minutes, and a T-shirt 1.5 minutes. Given average hourly earnings in 1989 for these garments, the dollar value of direct labor for shirts was about $1.71, for pants $2.24, for knit pants $0.33, and

---

[7] A SAM is based on rates of speed for a fully trained worker. As a result, new workers in a production line will perform below the SAM estimate on their operation, while some experienced workers achieve rates of production far above the established SAM. For a discussion of this system of measurement, see Gomberg (1955) and Abruzzi (1956).

for a T-shirt $0.17. Even the most complex garment among men's collections, suits, had only about $12.50 of direct labor inputs (Dunlop and Weil 1994).

A major by-product of PBS arises from its dependence on buffers between assembly operations to minimize the downtime of workers given uneven assembly time requirements for different operations. Standard practice is a one-day buffer between operations. As a result, a pair of pants that requires roughly 40 operations to assemble results in a large amount of work-in-process inventory. More important, a *given* pair of pants requires 40 days or more to move from cut pieces to final product.

Modular System

Modular production is based on a fundamentally different notion than bundle assembly. Rather than breaking sewing and assembly into a long series of small steps, modular production entails grouping tasks (e.g., the entire assembly of a collar) and assigning each task to members of a module (i.e., a team of workers). A module, ranging in size from 5 to 30 operators, works together to produce part or in some cases all of a garment (81% of the business units using modular assembly in our sample indicate that at least some modules in the business unit assemble an entire product). While most operators in the module still spend the majority of their time on a single assembly task, operators move to other tasks if work is building up at some other step in the module. Compensation is based primarily on the module's output. Modules are partially self-directed in that operators determine task assignments, pace, and output targets in most cases on the basis of incentives provided by the group compensation system.[8]

Focusing production at the group level means that modular lines rely on far smaller buffers between assembly steps than under PBS.[9] Since

---

[8] Manager descriptions of modular activities from our sample indicate that workers in modules focus primarily on these matters directly related to production, as well as scheduling hours, breaks, and planned absenteeism for team members. Modules on average report "some or little" influence on the selection of team leaders and members, training, performance evaluation, and dispute resolution, while reporting "little or no" influence on the introduction of new technologies and capital investments. These results are available from the authors.

[9] However, buffers are not usually eliminated even in modular assembly. There is an average buffer of 60 apparel items between production steps in modular lines in the sample. Only 30% of the business units using modular systems in the sample responded that workers directly hand off garments to other team members (implying a zero buffer). See Lowder (1991) and George (1998) for related discussions.

Table 2.1. *Human Resource Practices by Assembly System, 1992*

	% of Business Units Drawing on Human Resource Practices		
	Overall[a]	PBS	Modular
Compensation practices			
Individual piece rates	91.4	98.1	30.0
Straight hourly rate – target output	2.0	0.0	20.0
Straight hourly rate – skill or quality	3.5	0.0	20.0
Group incentive – target output	8.2	0.0	80.0
Group incentive – skill or quality	7.8	0.0	80.0
Split incentive (individual and group)	23.3	20.4	50.0
Penalty for rework	34.3	31.5	60.0
Other compensation system	1.7	1.9	0.0
Training practices			
Workers trained for one job only	54.1	58.9	10.0
Workers trained for two jobs	31.7	28.6	60.0
Workers trained for three jobs	6.8	5.4	20.0
Workers trained for four jobs	7.4	7.1	10.0
% of Volume shipped by business unit using assembly system	88.9[b]	80.0	8.9

[a] Based on weighting reported incidence of practices by the overall percentage of volume shipped by business unit using each assembly system. Overall incidence includes unit production system.
[b] Remaining volume shipped using unit production system (2.2%) (see text) and other systems related to PBS.

sewing operators are compensated at the group level, production activities are geared to ensure that the sequence of steps delegated to the module is completed, thereby reducing the amount of work-in-process inventory in the module. By substantially reducing work-in-process buffers, throughput time for a given garment can be dramatically decreased: average throughput time for sewing operations on modular lines was 1.7 days versus 9.2 days for PBS lines.

As the foregoing description would suggest, modular systems entail considerable modification of the human resource practices associated with assembly. The relation of the assembly method to human resource practices can be seen in Table 2.1. By breaking down assembly operations into discrete operations undertaken by individual operators, PBS relies solely on piece-rate compensation and draws on line supervisors and – where present – union stewards to deal with problems and disputes on the line. Modular assembly shifts the focus of incentive structure away from the individual and places it on the group. As a result, only one-third of assembly workers on modular lines are paid by piece rates, with the majority of operators receiving some type of group incentive. Training requirements differ as well, given the need for modular operators to perform multiple assembly tasks. Table 2.1 suggests, however, that modular production relies on training for a more limited number of jobs (a median of two jobs vs. one for PBS) than popular industry accounts might suggest.

The tight linkages between human resource practices and production systems indicate that the diffusion of innovative practices like group incentives, team-based supervision, and multi-skilling will be fundamentally linked to the diffusion of the underlying production systems. In this sense, innovative human resource practices are more usefully described as a set of complementary practices associated with an underlying manufacturing system rather than as separable decision-variables for the firm.[10] The complementary relation between assembly method and human resource practices also illustrates why business units are often reluctant to innovate in the sewing room. Introducing modular production requires far more than rearranging plant layout; it requires changing the incentive system and training requirements for production workers along a number of dimensions.

Diffusion of Modular Production

Early advocates of modular assembly (such as the American Apparel Manufacturers Association [AAMA] and the Amalgamated Clothing and Textile Workers Union) argued for its wide-scale adoption because of its positive impacts on job characteristics, human resources, and in turn labor costs (e.g., AAMA 1988; Bailey 1993). In response to persistent problems in finding and retaining a skilled workforce, these advocates argued that modular assembly improves the desirability of apparel employment by increasing task variety and decreasing the isolation of individual operators in PBS. Since more interesting work attracts a more stable and dedicated workforce, modular assembly is a response to labor shortages and can also decrease absenteeism and turnover.

An alternative argument for modular adoption relates to the "external fit" between larger competitive forces and assembly methods. Com-

---

[10] The link between work organization and human resource practices is particularly tight in apparel in this respect. See Ichniowski, Shaw, and Prennushi (1997) for a contrasting analysis of these linkages in steel making.

petitive dynamics in many segments of the apparel industry are being transformed as a result of technological innovations that allow the low-cost collection, processing, and dissemination of consumer sales data (Abernathy et al. 1995, 1999). These innovations set the foundation for a new retailing strategy directed at reducing a retailer's exposure to demand risk by adjusting the supply of products at retail outlets to match consumer demand on the basis of daily, point-of-sale information. These retailers require, in turn, that their suppliers compete not only on the historic basis of price, but also on the basis of their replenishment speed, flexibility, and services.

These industry changes have direct implications for the adoption of modular systems. A central advantage of modular systems over PBS is their impact on throughput times for garments (Cole 1992; Hill 1992). By reducing the amount of time required to assemble a given product, an apparel supplier can become more responsive to retail requirements for rapid product replenishment. Thus, the emergence of lean retailing in the late 1980s gave a competitive premium to systems that minimized throughput, much as PBS's impacts on direct labor content led it to dominate given price- or cost-based competition.

In our sample, 16 business units used modular systems at some point during the past decade. These business units can be divided into two groups: "experimenters" – business units that tried but abandoned modular systems at some point *before* 1992; and "adopters" – which adopted modules after 1988 and continued to use them up to 1992. Table 2.2 provides characteristics of both groups in addition to those of business units that did not adopt modules throughout the entire period.[11]

The most commonly cited reason that modules were abandoned by experimenters (after an average eight-month trial period) concerns the perceived costs of modular systems in terms of lost labor productivity and the consequent inability of modules to provide a sufficient payback to justify continuation of their use.[12] Given that the majority of experimenters adopted before or around 1988, these responses suggest that these business units adopted modules primarily because of their impact on direct internal costs, associated with the "job characteristic" arguments described earlier.

The adopter group of business units, in contrast, introduced modules in more recent years. (No business units in our sample had modules in

---

[11] Two of the business units that abandoned modular systems reintroduced them by 1992 and therefore fall in both groups.

[12] These factors were cited by all eight of the business units that had dropped modular assembly. Only two business units cited additional factors (such as workforce or management disruptions caused by modular systems) as reasons for dropping modules.

Table 2.2. *Characteristics of Modular Adopters and Non-adopters*

Business Unit Characteristics	Overall	Non-adopters	Modular Users	
			Experimenters, pre-1992[a]	Adopters, 1992[b]
Number of business units[c]	42	26	8	10
Replenishment pressure,[d] 1988	41.5 (39.2)	44.5 (39.8)	24.9 (31.9)	39.2 (40.0)
Replenishment pressure,[d] 1992	44.6 (36.2)	44.0 (37.6)	30.4 (32.4)	53.2 (32.0)
% of Volume in basic product lines, 1988	54.3 (30.3)	56.2 (32.8)	57.5 (25.2)	44.6 (23.2)
Work-in-process inventories held in sewing operations, 1988	3.6 (2.3)	3.3 (1.6)	5.0 (3.6)	3.1 (2.3)
Size (1988 $million sales volume)	151.9 (267.4)	82.0 (89.8)	144.4 (161.2)	356.2 (469.8)
Average length of modular trial (years)[e]	—	—	0.7 (1.0)	1.8 (0.6)

Note: Standard errors are in parentheses.
[a] Business units that adopted and then abandoned modular systems before 1992.
[b] Business units that adopted modular systems after 1988 and continued to have them in operation in 1992.
[c] Two business units adopted, abandoned, and readopted modular systems and therefore are classified in both "experimenters" and "adopters" categories.
[d] Percentage of volume shipped to national chains and mass merchants.
[e] Length for "experimenters" indicates the average reported time for those who abandoned modular assembly; length for "adopters" measures the average length of time between adoption and 1992.

1992 that had been in continuous operation before 1989.)[13] Survey responses by business unit managers suggest that "external fit" played a greater role in the adoption decisions of this group than in those of experimenters. Table 2.3 presents business unit respondents' rankings of the reasons for their adoption of modular assembly systems.

Ability to meet retailer standards on product delivery was cited as the most important reason for adoption. This was followed by reduction in

[13] Of the 10 business units in the adopters group, 1 introduced modules in 1989, 6 in 1991, and 3 in 1992.

Table 2.3. *Reasons for Modular Adoption by Business Units*

Reasons for Modular Adoption[a]	Ranking[b] Mean (SD)
Improves ability to meet retailer standards on product delivery	2.8 (0.4)
Reduces work-in-process inventories	2.6 (0.7)
Improves first-pass product quality	2.5 (0.7)
Reduces throughput time for product assembly	2.5 (0.7)
Improves worker safety and health	2.3 (0.8)
Decreases turnover and absenteeism	2.2 (0.7)
Improves job satisfaction of workforce	2.2 (0.8)
Reduces number of material handlers and support workers	2.0 (0.7)
Reduces number of supervisors	1.7 (0.8)
Helps attract new workers	1.1 (0.9)
Reduces direct labor content required for garment assembly	0.9 (1.3)
Reduces amount of space needed for assembly operations	0.9 (1.0)
Number of business unit observations	10

[a] Based on business unit managers' responses for those business units that adopted modular systems between 1988 and 1992.
[b] Based on a scale of 1 to 3, where 0 = "not important"; 1 = "somewhat important"; 2 = "important"; and 3 = "extremely important."

work-in-process inventories, quality, and throughput time. Attributes related to the impact of modular production on human resource factors (e.g., impact on satisfaction, turnover, and safety and health[14]) are ranked next. Managers ranked at the bottom reasons related to modular's potential impact on reducing the number of support workers and supervisors, increasing space availability, and improving the attractiveness of assembly jobs.

Modeling Modular Adoption

Tables 2.2 and 2.3 suggest that the motivations of recent modular adopters differ significantly from those of non-adopters and experimenters. In order to assess the comparative impact of these factors, the adoption of modules by business units between 1988 and 1992 can be expressed as a function of the degree of replenishment pressure and other product market factors before adoption (measured in 1988) as well as the other potential correlates discussed in the following subsections.

Product Market Factors. If the adoption of modular systems is linked to the competitive pressures faced by adopting units, one would expect higher probability of adoption among those units facing the greatest degree of pressure from retailers to provide products on a rapid replenishment basis. Retailer rapid replenishment programs emerged and remain concentrated in two retail segments: national chains and mass merchants.[15] Table 2.2 indicates that the recent modular adopters experienced the greatest increase in shipments to mass merchants and national chains between 1988 and 1992 (from 39% to 53% of total volume shipped) and therefore replenishment pressure. The volume shipped to these retailers by both non-adopters and experimenters remained relatively unchanged. This would suggest a relation between the propensity to adopt modular systems and the volume shipped to this category of retailers.

---

[14] Repetitive-motion injuries arising from PBS have been a major problem for business units in many apparel sectors. Reducing these costs by increasing each operator's task variety can therefore be a motivation for introducing modular assembly.

[15] Examples include Wal-Mart among mass merchants and J. C. Penney's among national chains. The link between these retail segments and rapid replenishment demands can be seen in the following. In 1992, daily or weekly replenishment shipments constituted less than 30% of total wholesale dollar volume shipped to department stores by business units. In contrast, 65% of total volume was shipped on a daily or weekly basis to mass merchants and 74% to national chains (Abernathy et al. 1995: 187–188).

Replenishment requirements also potentially change the cost of work-in-process (WIP) inventories associated with PBS. Higher WIP inventories imply a larger burden on business units facing a demand for rapid replenishment and therefore a greater incentive to introduce modules. As a result, business unit WIP inventory in 1988 is used as a second product market predictor of 1992 modular adoption.

Finally, rapid replenishment can be defined as the ability to restock products within a selling season. Basic (rather than fashion) products are therefore the focus of most replenishment programs. The percentage of basic products in a business unit's collection should therefore be related to the incentive to adopt modular systems.[16]

Other Business Unit Practices. The degree to which business units were prepared to offer rapid replenishment may have also affected the rate of modular adoption. In order to test for this, we use the presence of information linkages with retailers in 1988 as a control variable (see the section titled "Linking Modular Adoption to Information Investment"). In addition, we control for the presence of previous experiments with modular systems.

Control Variables. Business unit size must be controlled for, since larger business units may also be more able to afford investments in modular systems. The ability of a business unit to manage its plants' assembly operations efficiently – independent of the factors already described – may also affect adoption. We employ estimated unit labor costs[17] for a typical garment item in the business unit as a proxy to control for these business unit fixed effects. Mean values for all variables are found in the first column of Table 2.4.

Findings

Table 2.4 presents the results of logit regression models of the determinants of modular adoption. Since the shift toward rapid replenishment

---

[16] Rapid replenishment programs are still relatively uncommon for fashion products because of the difficulties of providing in-season replenishment of these goods. Even women's apparel retailers like The Limited that have incorporated replenishment principles have a narrow product line with a lower level of product turnover than is typical for the fashion end of the women's apparel business.

[17] Unit labor costs are calculated using the reported average number of minutes to assemble a typical garment in the business unit's collection and the reported average hourly earning to calculate the direct costs of labor for a typical garment produced by the business unit.

Table 2.4. *Logit Model of Modular Adoption Determinants: Change in Use of Modules, 1988 and 1992*

Determinant	Mean (SE)	Model (1) Coefficient (SE)	Model (1) Prob. Effects[a]	Model (2) Coefficient (SE)	Model (2) Prob. Effects[a]
Replenishment pressure, 1988 (% of volume shipped)[b]	41.45 (39.17)	0.083* (0.047)	12.3	—	—
Replenishment pressure, 1992 (% of volume shipped)[b]	44.62 (36.24)	—	—	0.127* (0.071)	14.4
Work-in-process inventories, 1988 (weeks of supply)	3.57 (2.26)	−0.499 (0.439)	−5.2	0.076 (0.563)	0.0
% of volume in basic product lines, 1988	54.25 (30.26)	−0.089* (0.043)	−13.0 (0.018)	−0.102* (0.057)	−10.9
Previous experiment with modular assembly (= 1 if yes)	0.19 (0.39)	3.11 (2.33)	1.9	2.68 (2.22)	1.3
Information system investments, 1988 (= 1 if present)	0.26 (0.45)	−0.711 (1.52)	0.7	−1.73 (2.07)	0.9
Size (in 1988 $million sales volume)	4.09 (1.48)	2.93* (1.33)	9.7	3.60* (2.10)	6.8
Unit labor cost for typical garment (ln 1992 $)	1.02 (1.33)	0.968 (0.925)	2.9	0.405 (0.961)	0.9
Log likelihood	—	22.55	—	24.51	—
Predicted modular adoption probability at means	—	.31	—	.22	—
Sample size	42	42	—	42	—

*Significant at the .05 level; t-tests are one-tailed.
[a] Impact of a 10% increase in independent variable on the probability of adoption, all other variables held constant at their mean values.
[b] Percentage of volume shipped to mass merchants and national chains.

occurred between 1988 and 1992, Model (1) includes the variables just described and uses 1988 replenishment pressure as an independent variable, while Model (2) uses replenishment pressure in 1992. χ^2 tests of the collective significance of the variables in both logit equations are significant at the .01 level.

The replenishment pressure coefficients in Models (1) and (2) confirm that firms shipping a high percentage to mass merchants and national chains are more likely to adopt modular systems than those with lower shipments. The coefficients imply that a 10% increase in shipments increases the probability of adoption by 12% in Model (1) and 14% in Model (2), all other factors being held at their mean. The coefficients are significant in both models and imply that replenishment pressure raises adoption probabilities more than any other factor (except for percent basic in Model (1)).[18]

While WIP inventories in 1988 show a weak negative relation to adoption in Model (1), and virtually no relation in Model (2), the percentage of volume produced in basic product lines by the business unit is negatively (and significantly) associated with adoption.

The logistic results provide little evidence that previous experience with modular systems or the presence of information linkages in 1988 affects later adoption. The former result is consistent with the notion that the first group of modular adopters was motivated by factors very different from those motivating the more recent adopters. The lack of connection between 1988 information investments and recent adoption is more puzzling, but may arise from greater heterogeneity in the motives of early bar code / electronic data interchange adopters relative to those who adopted in the period after 1988, when rapid replenishment emerged as a major retail strategy.[19] The other major factor affecting adoption is business unit size: the larger the business unit, the more likely it is to have adopted modular systems.

Performance Effects of Modular Assembly

Despite the strong association between module adoption and replenishment pressure, modular assembly is used by a small percentage of the industry. The 10 business units classified as adopters in Table 2.2 draw on

---

[18] Among the 10 business units using modules, the 3 units using the highest percentage of modular systems for assembly shipped about 52% of their products to mass merchants and national chains in 1988. In contrast, the 3 business units using modules least for assembly in 1992 had supplied only 26% to these retailers in 1988.

[19] Lagged replenishment pressure is a strong determinant of bar code and EDI adoption in 1992, but is only weakly related to their adoption in 1988.

it for an average of 36% of total volume assembled (ranging from a low of 10% to a maximum of 70%). As a result, by 1992, only 8.6% of the volume shipped by business units in the sample was assembled via modular systems versus 80% by PBS.

There are several possible explanations for the lack of more widespread use. First, limited diffusion may reflect the fact that modular systems do not have the expected impacts on throughput and replenishment speed. Second, modular systems may yield benefits, but high "switching costs" may inhibit their adoption (as found by Ichniowski and Shaw [1995] in the case of innovative human resource practices in the steel industry). Third, the benefits of modular assembly may accrue only given the presence of other business unit investments also associated with lean retailing. Without these investments, the comparative benefits of modules may be small (or unattainable). All three explanations require analyzing the relation of modular investments to other business unit practices related to retail replenishment, and then measuring the impact of modular systems and other potentially complementary investments on performance.

Linking Modular Adoption to Information Investment

Retailer demand for rapid replenishment itself requires investment in information systems to transmit detailed sales and order information. Suppliers must adopt an electronic common language for identifying products and provide a means to transmit this information efficiently to and from retailers on a daily or weekly basis. Specifically, a business unit must invest in two basic information linkages with retail partners: (1) uniform bar codes for each of the products provided to the retailer, which enable them to track sales at the individual product level; and (2) electronic data interchange (EDI), which provides sales information in real time. Overall investments in the two basic components of information transfer increased dramatically between 1988 and 1992. In 1988, 26% of all business units were shipping at least some volume through the use of these systems, while by 1992, 81% utilized them.

Modular adoption must therefore be understood as part of a set of sequential decisions necessary to adapt to changing retailing requirements. Meaningful changes in the method of production make little sense if one has not made investments in information regarding product demand. Similarly, if one is unable to ship products efficiently to retail distribution centers, there will be little to gain from throughput reductions arising from modular assembly.

Case studies of sophisticated apparel manufacturers support this notion of sequential manufacturing investments. Levi Strauss and Haggar – two of the largest manufacturers of jeans and men's trousers – invested heavily in developing methods for uniquely identifying products and exchanging information electronically well in advance of any changes in design, cutting room, sewing, or relations with textile manufacturers. In contrast, two of the earliest adopters of modular assembly in the men's separate trouser and dress shirt sectors abandoned their modular lines by 1992. Neither manufacturer had EDI with their retail customers at that time.

The relation between investments in information systems and the adoption of modular systems can be seen in the sample. In 1992, *every* business unit that had modular manufacturing also had the basic information investments necessary to deal with lean retailers (vs. an incidence of 75% for non-adopting business units). There was no such link between the presence of basic information investments and modular manufacturing before 1992. Only two of the eight experimenter business units that adopted and abandoned modular systems before 1992 also had information linkages with retailers in 1988. This corresponds to the overall incidence of information investments in 1988 (which comprised about 26% of business units), once again suggesting that motivation for modular adoption before 1988 arose from other causes.

Modeling Performance Effects

Two types of business unit performance outcomes will be examined. First, we look at the impact of modular adoption on lead times. Lead time is the total time required in the apparel production process, from the time fabrics are ordered to the time finished products are ready for shipment by the business unit. It therefore represents a critical measure of the ability of a business unit to compete in a market increasingly dominated by rapid replenishment retailing principles.

Second, we look at the impacts of modular assembly on operating profits as a percentage of sales. If lead times capture a unit's external performance, operating profits are a key measure of its internal performance: A unit can reduce lead times by holding large inventories and be judged externally as successful, but this strategy could adversely affect its bottom line. A unit that engages in internal restructuring to reduce lead times (including the introduction of modular assembly) could both reduce lead times and enhance profitability.

Since our concern is with performance at the business unit level, we do not consider here the direct impact of modules on unit labor costs in the sewing room per se. A comparison of labor costs in the subsample reveals that business units with modular lines have average unit labor costs about 4% to 5% lower than those with only PBS lines. In a case study of three apparel companies, Berg et al. (1996) found that modules outperformed PBS lines in quality, costs, and responsiveness. A detailed study using direct comparisons of modular and non-modular lines in a single company by George (1998) indicated that modular lines have slightly higher productivity levels, although neither type of line dominates in regard to its ability to provide multiple products.

Performance is modeled as a function of modular assembly as well as other factors associated with performance. Given that all business units that adopted modular assembly also had made basic information investments, we cannot measure the independent effect of modules on those outcomes. We can, however, measure the degree to which modules improve performance above and beyond the benefit conferred by information investments by themselves.

Bar Code and Electronic Data Interchange Investments. The sequential investment discussed earlier suggests that the ability of a business unit to benefit from modular adoption would presumably be affected by the presence or absence of these investments.[20] Business unit use of bar codes *and* EDI is employed as the measure of information investment.

Modular Assembly Variables. Rather than using a dichotomous variable to capture modular effects, we use the percentage of business unit volume assembled in modular lines. This provides a means of capturing the comparative impact of modular assembly in business units that rely heavily upon it versus those that use it for only a small percentage of assembly. Performance regressions using this variable are presented in Table 2.5.

Control Variables. The analysis controls for business unit size and the percentage of basic products shipped in order to control for other factors correlated with performance and modular assembly practices.

Findings

The first four columns of Table 2.5 present the estimated impact of the percentage assembled via modular systems, information investments, and

---

[20] Analysis of the entire data set (including all 118 business units) has demonstrated large and positive relationships between these investments and apparel supplier performance (Abernathy et al. 1995; Hwang and Weil 1997).

Table 2.5. *Regressions of Business Unit Performance, 1992*

	Lead Time – Standard (Days), 1992[a]		Lead Time – Shortest (Days), 1992[b]		Operating Profit, 1992 (% of $ Shipments)	
	(1)	(2)	(1)	(2)	(1)	(2)
Dependent variable: mean (standard error)	83.0 (65.83)	83.0 (65.83)	44.87 (41.01)	44.87 (41.01)	9.07 (6.34)	9.07 (6.34)
Model Use of UPC bar code standards and EDI, 1992 (= 1 if yes)	−92.52** (26.52)	−89.06** (26.62)	−53.47** (16.87)	−50.26** (17.21)	6.53** (2.72)	6.06** (2.66)
Modular assembly (% of total volume assembled)[c]	—	−0.630 (0.574)	—	−0.700 (0.679)	—	0.098* 0.057
Size (1988 $million sales volume)	−0.022 (0.036)	0.004 (0.043)	0.040 (0.054)	0.051 (0.055)	0.002 (0.004)	−0.002 (0.004)
% of Volume in basic product lines, 1988	0.202 (0.351)	0.209 (0.350)	0.070 (0.226)	0.068 (0.226)	−0.058* (0.033)	−0.056* (0.032)
Adj. R^2	.31	.336	.276	.304	.196	.261
Sample size	42	42	42	42	42	42

*Significant at the .05 level; **significant at the .01 level. *t*-tests are one-tailed.
[a] Lead time measured in elapsed calendar days for "standard" or average product manufactured domestically.
[b] Lead time for "shortest" or best performance for product manufactured domestically.
[c] For business units that adopted modular assembly between 1988 and 1992 only.

other factors on lead time performance (measured as standard and shortest reported lead times for a business unit). Model (1) (which excludes the modular variable) indicates pronounced and significant effects of information investments on both types of lead time. The negative coefficients (not significant) on the modular assembly variables in both standard and shortest lead time equations indicate that modular systems lower lead times, as predicted. These coefficients imply relatively small modular effects for the sample as a whole: for standard lead times, Model (2) coefficients imply that a 1% increase in modular assembly leads to a 0.6 day decrease in lead time, which represents less than a 1% decrease in average lead times. However, for the typical modular adopter, which draws on modules for 36% of assembly, these coefficients imply lead time reductions of about 23 (standard) and 25 days (shortest). These modular effects, however, diminish dramatically if the log values of lead times are employed as the dependent variable.[21]

The amount of performance variation accounted for by the models (as measured by adjusted R^2) changes little with inclusion of the modular assembly variable. A great deal of the variation in lead time performance is therefore explained by information investments, while relatively little lead time performance can be attributed to variation in modular assembly volumes. The results with regard to shortest lead time performance are parallel to those just discussed.

Information investments are also associated with higher operating profits. Business units using bar codes and EDI in 1992 earn average operating profits as a percentage of sales that are 6.5% higher than those of business units lacking information investments.

Business unit operating profits are raised further by modular production, as shown in the last two columns of Table 2.5. The coefficient implies that a 1% increase in modular production would increase operating profits as a percentage of revenues by 0.098%. For a typical modular adopter, this estimate implies increased profits of 3.5% (or about a one-third increase in average operating profit levels). This effect is about one-half the size of the bar code and EDI effect, and is also statistically significant at the .05 level.

The larger and more significant impacts of modular assembly on operating profits versus lead times are consistent with the earlier distinction between "internal" and "external" performance. A business unit may improve lead times by a variety of means other than altering production strategies (most directly by simply holding more inventory for retail cus-

---

[21] However, bar codes and EDI continue to have a large impact on the log value of both lead time measures. The estimated coefficient on the information system variables for log(standard lead times) is −.85 (significant at a .01 level), implying that a 10% increase in the use of bar codes and EDI results in an 8.5% lead-time decrease. In contrast, the coefficient for modular assembly is −.009 (not significant), implying less than a 1% reduction in standard lead times for a 10% increase in modular assembly by business units.

tomers). However, production strategies (including modular assembly) that increase a supplier's responsiveness can enable that business unit to achieve lead time targets while decreasing its costs from holding more WIP and finished goods inventory. By reducing throughput times, this impact of modular systems may best explain the relatively large and significant profitability results found in Table 2.5.

The performance results are also consistent with the more general findings on complementarities in modern manufacturing (Milgrom and Roberts 1990; Ichniowski, Shaw, and Prennushi 1997): Major performance effects arise from the investment in bundles of manufacturing practices, particularly those associated with information linkages. Having the set of practices required to send and receive sales and order information at this point in apparel industry development dramatically changes the external and internal performance of business units. The marginal impact of other manufacturing innovations in the cutting or sewing room or in distribution operations is small in comparison.[22] While this dynamic may change as more and more apparel firms adopt baseline practices, understanding the sequential nature of investments in response to product market changes is central to interpreting the potential impacts of human resource innovations specifically and other manufacturing changes more generally.

The foregoing analysis can be illustrated by developments at Levi Strauss Associates. The partnership agreement reached between Levi and the Union of Needletrades, Industrial, and Textile Employees (UNITE!) in 1994 represented a landmark in labor relations for the apparel industry and other industries in the joint role of both parties in introducing modular and other innovative workplace practices and in giving UNITE! a role in implementing these practices even in non-union plants (and providing the union with an open invitation to organize those plants). It would be inaccurate, however, to assess the agreement without understanding the larger context of decisions made by Levi over time.[23]

Levi was one of the first companies to invest in information linkages with retailers. In fact, Levi helped create one of the early systems for information exchange before an industry standard had been put in place. Levi also invested heavily in setting up state of the art logistic opera-

---

[22] Using the full data set, Hwang and Weil (1997) found that the use of sales information for production forecasting in tandem with the minimum standard practices described here has additional positive impacts on performance.

[23] See "Partnership Agreement Levi Strauss & Co. / Amalgamated Clothing and Textile Workers Union." For recent accounts, see Uchitelle (1994) and Bureau of National Affairs (1994).

tions, consolidating a large number of traditional warehouses into four distribution centers that rapidly process shipments from plants to retail customers. Levi's understanding of the critical nature of information and time for competitive performance has therefore motivated much of its strategy, including its most recent announcement of a program to provide individual customers with customized jeans.

Levi's strategy in short is premised on providing customers with the right product, when they want it, without holding large inventories in the process. The partnership agreement is a necessary extension of this effort in making its union and non-union production facilities capable of responding rapidly and with flexibility to retailer and ultimately consumer demand.[24]

Conclusion

Innovative human resource practices in the apparel industry – those linked primarily to modular assembly systems – have diffused slowly in the U.S. apparel industry. Modular systems, and the accompanying cluster of compensation, training, worker involvement, and supervisory practices, account for less than 10% of all assembly. These practices have been adopted in apparel workplaces with close relationships to retailers and inventory management, including investment in information technology. Where this suite of investments and relationships has been implemented, business units have improved performance along a number of dimensions. To set apart modular adoption as either the impetus of change or normatively as the savior of the industry is to misunderstand fundamentally the dynamics of the product market driving the apparel industry and the relation of those systems to larger manufacturing decisions.

The modest impact of modular assembly suggests that the attention this innovation has received in the trade press is misplaced relative to other human resource changes arising from product market changes. For example, the advent of lean retailing is having more pervasive effects on the growing strategic role of distribution center workers (who can powerfully affect time-based outcomes for retailers and their suppliers) in the retail–apparel–textile channel. Just as the skilled cutter was once the focal point of leverage in the industry, lean retailing implies significant

---

[24] The Levi partnership has not been without its problems, including the decision by the company to close eleven production plants, which resulted in a loss of 6,395 jobs in 1997 (Rutberg and Socha 1997). In addition, the company has had difficulties in implementing teams in many of its plants and has encountered resistance among workers who favor PBS methods of assembly and related rewards (King 1998).

leverage for distribution workers on wages and other labor market outcomes. With lean inventories in retail stores and in apparel supplier plants, the prompt, efficient, and uninterrupted operation of the distribution center is decisive to retailers' operations. It should not be surprising that unions have clearly realized this strategic role. For example, in 1997 UNITE! organized distribution centers of Marshall's acquired by TJX Company, in Georgia and Virginia, each with 600 to 700 employees. In 1998, the union organized an additional center in Massachusetts that employs 900 workers. Distribution workers now represent some 25,000 of UNITE!'s 300,000 members. Lean retailing has also severely diminished the role of the traditional buyer, whose "feel" for the market (and the compensation and career paths associated with that art) is being replaced by the real time sales data and advanced forecasting methods of the merchandise manager.

The growing importance of replenishment has also improved the viability of assembly operations closest to the U.S. consumer market. This implies shifts in employment away from the Far East and back to North America. In a related vein, replenishment requirements provide insight into the problem of sweatshops in some U.S. urban centers. Although one reason that government labor standards continue to be flouted is the ever-present pressure to reduce the labor-cost component of garments, the growing importance of replenishment also explains the recent reemergence. Sweatshop operations offer the dual "advantage" of low labor costs and proximity to the U.S. market. Suppliers relying on contractors who violate wage and hour laws can achieve timely replenishment without incurring the risk associated with holding large inventories and can still pay low wages.[25]

Our findings also have broader implications for the study of human resources. First, analysis of human resource systems must be embedded in an understanding of the environmental factors facing adopting business units, fundamentally those concerning products markets, labor markets, and regulatory regimes (Dunlop 1993; Kochan, Katz, and McKersie 1986; Weil 1994). Second, the underlying production technology constrains the degree of choice in alternative human resource practices. Third, human resource innovations made in response to evolving competitive dynamics cannot be separated from the larger set of choices undertaken by business units. In many sectors, the movement toward greater responsiveness to demand conditions fosters a need to innovate along dimensions described here for the retail–apparel channel. To

---

[25] The growth of sweatshops has received recent attention by the U.S. Department of Labor. See Abernathy et al. (1999): chap. 15 for a detailed discussion of these efforts.

60   John T. Dunlop and David Weil

regard human resource innovation separate from other practices necessary to adapt to new market conditions is potentially to overstate the
impact of these innovations. From a policy and applied viewpoint it may
also distract decision-makers (management and labor) from looking into
the larger set of choices to be made.

REFERENCES

Abernathy, Frederick, John T. Dunlop, Janice Hammond, and David Weil. 1995.
"The Information Integrated Channel: A Study of the U.S. Apparel Industry
in Transition." *Brookings Papers on Economic Activity: Microeconomics*
(Spring):175–246.
Abernathy, Frederick, John T. Dunlop, Janice H. Hammond, and David Weil.
1999. *A Stitch in Time: Lean Retailing and the Transformation of Manufactur-
ing – Lessons from the Apparel and Textile Industries.* New York: Oxford Uni-
versity Press.
Abruzzi, Adam. 1956. *Work, Workers, and Work Measurement.* New York: Colum-
bia University Press.
American Apparel Manufacturers Association. 1988. *Flexible Apparel Manu-
facturing: The Coming Revolution.* Report of the AAMA Technical
Advisory Committee. Arlington, VA: American Apparel Manufacturers
Association.
—1992. *Survey of Apparel Manufacturing.* Report of the AAMA Technical
Advisory Committee. Arlington, VA: American Apparel Manufacturers
Association.
Bailey, Thomas. 1993. "Organizational Innovation in the Apparel Industry."
Industrial Relations 32 (Winter):30–48.
Berg, Peter, Eileen Appelbaum, Thomas Bailey, and Arne Kalleberg. 1996. "The
Performance Effects of Modular Production in the Apparel Industry." *Indus-
trial Relations* 35(3):356–373.
Bureau of National Affairs. 1994. "Levi Strauss, ACTWU Announce New Part-
nership Arrangement." *Daily Labor Report*, Oct. 14.
Cole, William. 1992. "Modular's True Colors." *Bobbin* (July):64–67.
Dunlop, John T. 1993. *Industrial Relations Systems*, rev. ed. Boston: Harvard Busi-
ness School Press.
Dunlop, John T., and David Weil. 1994. "Diffusion of Human Resource Innova-
tions: Historic and Current Lessons from the Apparel Industry." Working
paper, Harvard Center for Textile and Apparel Research.
George, Catherine. 1998. "The Impact of Product Variety on Production Effi-
ciency: A Comparison of Alternate Production Systems in the Apparel Indus-
try." Ph.D. dissertation, Harvard University.
Gomberg, William. 1955. *A Trade Union Analysis of Time Study*, 2d ed. New York:
Prentice-Hall.
Hill, Ed. 1992. "Flexible Manufacturing Systems." *Bobbin* (April):48–50.
Hwang, Margaret, and David Weil. 1997. "The Diffusion of Modern Manufac-

turing Practices: Evidence from the Retail-Apparel Sectors." Center for Economic Studies Working Paper 97-11.

Ichniowski, Casey, and Kathryn Shaw. 1995. "Old Dogs and New Tricks: Determinants of the Adoption of Productivity-Enhancing Work Practices." *Brookings Papers on Economic Activity: Microeconomics* (Spring):1–63.

Ichniowski, Casey, Kathryn Shaw, and Giovanna Prennushi. 1997. "The Effects of Human Resource Management Practices on Productivity." *American Economic Review* 87(3):291–313.

King, Ralph T. 1998. "Jeans Therapy: Levi's Factory Workers Are Assigned to Teams, and Morale Takes a Hit." *Wall Street Journal*, May 20:A1, A6.

Kochan, Thomas, Harry Katz, and Robert McKersie. 1986. *The Transformation of American Industrial Relations*. New York: Basic Books.

Lowder, Robert. 1991. "Balance: A Delicate Word in Modular Manufacturing." *Bobbin* (November):132–138.

Milgrom, Paul, and John Roberts. 1990. "The Economics of Modern Manufacturing: Technology, Strategy, and Organization." *American Economic Review* 80 (June):511–528.

Rutberg, Sid, and Mile Socha. 1997. "Levi's Cutting Back Production: 11 Plants to Shut." *Women's Wear Daily*, November 4:2.

Uchitelle, Louis. 1994. "A New Labor Design at Levi Strauss." *New York Times*, Oct. 13.

U.S. Department of Labor, Bureau of Labor Statistics. 1992. *Industry Wage Survey: Men's and Boys' Shirts (Except Work Shirts) and Nightwear, September 1990*. Bulletin 2405. Washington, DC: U.S. Government Printing Office.

—1998. "Annual Indexes of Output per Hour for Selected Industries." *Monthly Labor Review*, 21(3):132–133, Table 42.

Weil, David. 1994. *Turning the Tide: Strategic Planning for Labor Unions*. New York: Lexington Books/Macmillan.

CHAPTER 3

Modular Production: Improving Performance in the Apparel Industry

Peter Berg, Eileen Appelbaum, Thomas Bailey,
and Arne L. Kalleberg

Introduction

In the apparel industry, module and bundle production are two distinct methods of work. The module system is a team-based strategy that relies on the involvement of multi-skilled workers. In contrast, the progressive bundle system is a traditional approach to production that is based on the accumulation of in-process inventories and in which work is highly fragmented and "deskilled."

Our study differs from other studies of work organization because it uses a unique multi-level research design. Our conclusions are based on data and information obtained from several sources, including company records and interviews with corporate officials; plant, human resource, and training managers; and union officials (for the two unionized plants). In each plant, we also interviewed a random sample of approximately 100 employees, stratified by occupation. These half-hour interviews were conducted by telephone after work hours.[1] The data presented in this chapter are from four U.S. plants of two companies in the basics segment of the apparel industry.[2]

This chapter is a slightly revised version of an article that originally appeared in *Industrial Relations* 35:3 (1996); reprinted by permission of Blackwell Publishers.

The authors thank the Alfred P. Sloan Foundation for its support of this project, as well as the editors and reviewers of *Industrial Relations* for their helpful comments. We also acknowledge the assistance of Terrel Hale of the Economic Policy Institute and Carola Sandy of Columbia University.

[1] The sampling and interviewing procedures are described in detail in Appelbaum et al. (1994). The response rate was 69%.

[2] We also studied a third firm. Its innovative plant used a unique form of work organization that differs significantly from the innovative production systems used by the first two firms. That system, referred to as "mini-lines," is also less ambitious than the approaches used in the other two firms. For a detailed discussion of mini-lines see Appelbaum et al. (1994).

In the next section, we briefly review the literature on the effects of human resource innovations on performance. We then provide a brief overview of the apparel industry. After discussing our research design, we examine the extent of workplace transformation across our sample of plants. In the following section, we present a variety of performance data, and conclude with a discussion of the causes of differences in performance.

Theoretical Issues

In the past ten years there has been a wide variety of research on the effects of human resource innovations on firm performance (Eaton and Voos, 1992; Levine and Tyson, 1990; MacDuffie, 1995). Studies of individual practices associated with innovative work organization, such as employee involvement, the use of teams, training, group-base pay, or profit sharing, tend to show either positive or at least neutral effects (Bartel, 1991; Cooke, 1994; Holzer et al., 1993; Lawler et al., 1992; Weitzman and Kruse, 1990). Recently, scholars have argued that while individual practices may not have much effect, a comprehensive and coherent system of innovative work organization, human resource, and industrial relations practices is more likely to have positive results (Bailey, 1993a; Ichniowski, Shaw, and Prennushi, 1997; Huselid, 1995; Appelbaum, Bailey, Berg, and Kalleberg, forthcoming).

Another stream of research has sought to explain *how* innovative work organization affects performance (Cotton, 1993; Cotton et al., 1988; Locke and Schweiger, 1979). Cohen (1993) identifies two main theoretical explanations for the effectiveness of work teams – job characteristics theory and sociotechnical theory. Job characteristics theory argues that task attributes influence team effectiveness through their impact on motivation and job satisfaction. In contrast, sociotechnical theory views team self-regulation as the primary mechanism through which the design of the work group's tasks influences outcomes (Cohen, 1993). The empirical evidence for these theories is mixed (Cordery et al., 1991; Kemp et al., 1983; Miller and Monge, 1986; Wall et al., 1986). Our data provide stronger support for the sociotechnical than for the job characteristics theory.

Characteristics of the Industry and Its Workers

Employment in the U.S. apparel industry numbered 1.3 million people from the mid-1960s through the 1970s. Since 1979 employment in the industry has declined steadily. Nevertheless, nearly 1 million people are

64   **Peter Berg et al.**

still employed in this industry, more than 600,000 of them women. The moderate skill requirements and its easily copied and cheap technology leave the industry vulnerable to competition from plants in countries where wages are much lower. The trade deficit in apparel reached $20.1 million in 1991 (U.S. Department of Commerce, 1993:32–37) despite the imposition of tariffs and volume quotas. Competitive pressure increased further for domestic apparel producers during the 1980s as mergers and acquisitions among U.S. retailers resulted in larger, more powerful firms with exorbitant debt levels. The high debt service made retailers more cost conscious, while their larger size and smaller numbers increased their market power and enabled them to make new demands on manufacturers. In an effort to achieve cost savings, retailers have focused on reducing the cost of carrying inventories at all stages of production. The potential cost savings in this area is large (Office of Technology Assessment, 1987:26–27), and retailers have stepped up their demand that domestic apparel manufacturers make just-in-time deliveries when stocks are low. In order to meet these demands, manufacturers either must hold large inventories, which is expensive and risky, or must develop more flexible and responsive production systems. Thus demands by retailers since the mid-1980s have increased the pressure on apparel manufacturers to abandon their traditional approaches to production (American Apparel Manufacturers Association, 1988:1–2; Bailey, 1993b; Dunlop and Weil, Chapter 2, this volume).

Work Organization in Apparel

Production workers comprise a much higher percentage of employees in apparel than in other manufacturing industries. As a result, apparel manufacturers have traditionally tried to cut costs and improve productivity by reducing the amount of direct labor in garments.[3]

The Progressive Bundle System

The progressive bundle system, still the most widely used production system in this industry, is designed to maximize the output of individual operators. This is done by fragmenting the overall assembly process into many operations, each of which can be carried out in a few seconds (e.g., sewing a hem or attaching a pocket). Substantial amounts of inventory

---

[3] Productivity growth in apparel products has slightly outpaced overall productivity growth in manufacturing. Between 1975 and 1985, productivity in apparel grew at 2.7% per year compared with 2.4% in manufacturing (Office of Technology Assessment, 1987).

are (literally) tied up in the bundles of about 60 cut garment parts. These bundles move from operator to operator, and two or more bundles are often waiting at each station. There can be between 15 and 20 days of work-in-process in plants producing garments requiring no more than 20 minutes of labor (American Apparel Manufacturers Association, 1988:12). The system is designed to minimize the total amount of direct labor and labor cost for each garment. Furthermore, the bundle system isolates each worker and prevents problems in one operation from spreading to others, thus improving the utilization of equipment. This also allows the use of a compensation system based on piece rates, which many see as the motivational basis of productivity in the industry.

While labor productivity and utilization of machines are maximized at each stage, the traditional system has many weaknesses. The accumulation of inventories adds time to the production cycle; maximizing the productivity of individual workers may not maximize the productivity of the system; and the minute engineering of each small step makes it more difficult to change styles. Innovative firms are developing systems that seek to increase flexibility, speed production times, improve quality, and promote cooperation between apparel firms and retailers.

The Modular Production System

As managers have become convinced that it is difficult to bring about a more responsive and flexible production system based on the progressive bundle system, some managers have begun experimenting with a more team-based organizational technique known as modular production. In modules, groups of operators work together to assemble an entire garment. In the plants in our study, operators complete a task or series of tasks on bundles of up to 10 cut pieces or on a single garment and pass the bundle or garment directly to the next operator. Thus, modules drastically reduce in-process inventory.

Although the actual sewing tasks carried out by workers in modules do not differ from the tasks performed by bundle workers, the module system requires important changes in the industry's human resource practices. Supervisors and engineers must consider how the actions of each worker affect the functioning of the group. Workers must become involved in the quality and pace of production of their co-workers. Operators must help other team members who fall behind. In well-functioning modules, imbalances in the production process are corrected without any intervention by the supervisor. This requires operators to be able to do a variety of sewing tasks and to operate several different types of sewing machines. Operators may be given instructions in some of the basics of machine maintenance and repair. Group members may have some role in setting and meeting group goals, in organizing the flow of work, and in deciding the physical arrangement of the sewing machines. Peer pressure may play an important role in maintaining the pace of work and in reducing absenteeism. Finally, individual piece rates are replaced in modules by compensation schemes in which operators are paid a straight hourly rate or an hourly rate with a group bonus. In some instances, group piece rates are substituted for individual piece rates, with the pay of team members tied to the team's daily output.

Management of the interactions among group members is important in a module, and a high degree of communication, cooperation, and coordination is required among the operators as they set team goals, solve problems, and resolve conflicts. These types of activities are completely absent in a traditional bundle plant. Moreover, the high turnover rates typical of operators in this industry are a greater barrier to successful operations in modules.

In addition to the new demands on human resources, there are also high up-front costs associated with transforming a plant from the bundle to the module system. Management must supply each team with a full complement of machines required to produce finished garments. In the plants in this study, this raised the machine per worker figure from 1.1 in traditional bundle plants to between 2 and 2.5 for teams. Training costs also rise with modules. While bundle workers can be productive as soon as they learn one operation, module workers must be trained to carry out several before they can be fully integrated into the team.

Research Design

Our multi-level research design consists of worker surveys and manager interviews at two apparel companies. Through our worker survey, we are able to distinguish between the human resource policies of companies as reported by managers and as perceived by workers. The worker survey also enables us to determine whether the workers in innovative work systems differ in significant ways from those in more traditional workplaces. Were this the case, any findings that suggest that innovative work organization is associated with superior performance may reflect a more selective hiring system. For example, in their study of work organization in the steel industry, Ichniowski and Shaw (1995) found that the most innovative and successful production lines were in greenfield plants (new plants built and staffed with the needs of the new work organization in mind). Yet their data did not enable them to compare the characteristics of the labor force employed in different work systems. Greenfield plants may be able to select workers who would have been more productive in more traditional operations as well. Alternatively, innovative work organization may indeed be potentially more productive, but only with particular types of workers. Therefore, when analyzing the effects of different work systems on firm performance, it is important to determine whether and to what extent differences in employee characteristics affect the outcomes.

Both companies in the study were from the basics sector of the apparel industry and therefore faced similar competitive pressures and demand conditions. Two plants were selected from each company. In one company (Company 1), all of the workers in Plant A worked in modules and all of the workers in Plant B were in the bundle system. In Company 2, bundles and modules were mixed in each plant – two-thirds of the workers in Plant C worked in modules and two-thirds of those in Plant D worked in the bundle system. This research design avoids the situation in which plants with innovative work systems and human resource practices are drawn from companies in which unmeasured attributes (e.g., work–family policies or management training programs) are generally superior to those of the companies from which the traditional plants are drawn and, in general, minimizes variation between transformed and traditional work systems in unobserved variables that may correlate with the variables of interest in this study. Both companies were multi-nationals with plants in the United States and in Third World countries.

How Human Resource Practices Interrelate

For the plants in the study, bundles and modules are diametrically opposed forms of work organization. Modules are part of a comprehensive and coherent system of innovative practices. The work process in modules exhibits technical and strategic complementarities among employment security, trust, flexibility in job assignments, and participation in problem-solving activities. Module workers have more influence over the way the garment is assembled, are more likely to know how to adjust their machines, have greater opportunity to learn new things and be creative, and are more likely to find their work challenging. Workers in modules also have more influence than those in bundles over specific tasks or work assignments and over product quality improvement. In addition, module workers have the ability to regulate and coordinate their own work processes. Workers in modules are more likely than those in the bundle system to have responsibility for setting production goals, selecting work methods, and stopping production to deal with quality problems. They are also more likely to get adequate time to meet and solve problems (Appelbaum et al., forthcoming).

Performance

Managers in the companies in this study concluded that they had to move away from the bundle system. The events and pressures that led to the introduction of modules differed for the two firms, but in each case the desire to improve delivery and response time and increase flexibility was at the center of the decision. Cost was always an issue, but in both cases lower cost could have been, and often was, achieved with offshore production. Initially, managers simply hoped to achieve the quality and delivery time benefits of modules without a significant increase in labor costs.[4] In this section, we discuss the development of modules and their performance in the two companies.

Company 1

During the three years before our fieldwork, Company 1 had begun to respond to increasing competitive pressure by offering more styles and changing styles more often. The company initially tried to increase the number of styles using traditional methods. The manager of Plant A became convinced that modules were most effective for this new strategy and was given the resources to introduce them. In the view of corporate officials, this approach proved more flexible, and the company now uses Plant A to produce many short-run items such as samples, products in which styles change more frequently, and some standardized goods in high demand.

As a result of this new role, the volume of goods produced at Plant A increased dramatically between 1989 and 1993. The value added per

---

[4] Despite the conviction among managers that modules would improve their competitive position, the up-front costs and risks of the transition led managers to maintain traditional capacity in some of their plants or even within the same plant as they introduced changes in work organization. In one case, corporate officers chose not to experiment with their most productive plants. In another case, the initiative for change came from a particular plant manager, who persuaded headquarters to implement changes in this plant first. The resulting sequenced process of change allowed us to compare different production techniques within the same company. In some cases, companies produce the same item in both bundle and module systems.

worker in Plant A also increased 26 percent over this time period, and throughput time (time from receipt of cut goods to the shipment of finished products) fell from eight days in 1989 to five days in 1993. In contrast, the throughput time for Plant B, a bundle plant at Company 1, was 9 to 11 days in 1993. Plant A also reduced work-in-process inventory, as a percentage of shipments at wholesale price, by 62 percent over the same time period, which reduced the costs associated with carrying this inventory. The company attributes these improvements to the change in work organization. In addition, the reorganization of the plant floor as a result of modular production and the reduction of work-in-process inventory freed up space within the plant for alternative uses. This reduced overhead costs such as rent, heat, electricity, and insurance, which are allocated to particular styles on the basis of space required to produce the style. Quality also was slightly better at Plant A – the percentage of irregulars at Plant A in 1993 was 2.1 percent, compared with 2.9 percent for the bundle Plant B. Finally, the most striking difference between the two plants was the number of styles produced by each. Over the course of one year, Plant A produced more than a hundred styles, while Plant B produced essentially one style with some small variations.

Company data are not sufficient to make a direct comparison between the costs or productivity of production of a similar product using the two different production systems.[5] In general, the two plants play different roles within the overall corporate strategy. Plant A produces short runs of many styles, while Plant B produces long runs of one style. Although this appears to be a reasonable division of labor, company managers are beginning to plan for innovations at Plant B. Even with the standardized garments produced there, managers want to increase the plant's potential flexibility.

Managers at Company 1 are convinced that modules improve flexibility and quality, and they are moving toward broader implementation of team organization. Our worker survey enables us to determine whether workers agree with the managers' perceptions. Workers were asked to rate the quality of work produced by their work group on a scale of 1 to 5 (1 = "not good at all" to 5 = "excellent"). Table 3.1 displays the results of an ordered logit regression in which the workers' rating is the dependent variable and whether they worked in a bundle or module is the primary independent variable. (The table also includes

---

[5] All inventories (including in-process inventories), capital equipment, buildings, and warehousing costs are kept on company-wide accounts. Plant-specific data on these variables are not available.

Table 3.1. *Correlates of Workers' Perceptions of Work Team Quality*

	Company 1	Company 2	Company 2
Module	1.3154***	1.1830***	1.4033***
	(0.38005)	(0.37891)	(0.41191)
% Producer	−0.0031	−0.0076	−0.0096
	(0.0074)	(0.00854)	(0.00866)
Experience	−0.0169	0.0056	0.0038
	(0.02026)	(0.01821)	(0.01828)
Gender	−0.7281	1.4704	1.4437
	(0.54075)	(1.13755)	(1.13889)
Race	−1.7120	0.4196	0.4461
	(1.33575)	(0.46254)	(0.46172)
Education	−0.1104	0.0090	−0.0079
	(0.08686)	(0.10496)	(0.10572)
Firm tenure	0.0047	0.0424	0.0602*
	(0.03583)	(0.03462)	(0.03666)
Plant 4	—	—	0.6079
			(0.42439)
	$n = 131$	$n = 117$	$n = 117$
	$\chi^2(6) = 16.16$	$\chi^2(6) = 15.97$	$\chi^2(6) = 18.04$
	Prob $> \chi^2 = .0237$	Prob $> \chi^2 = .0254$	Prob $> \chi^2 = .0209$
	Pseudo $R^2 = .0556$	Pseudo $R^2 = .0605$	Pseudo $R^2 = .0684$

Note: The dependent variable in these equations is the worker's assessment of the overall quality of the work performed by the work team. The variable takes five values: 1 = "not good at all"; 2 = "below average"; 3 = "average"; 4 = "above average"; 5 = "excellent." Standard errors are in parentheses.
*** Significant at the 1% level.
* Significant at the 10% level.

a similar analysis for Company 2, which will be discussed later.) In order to take into account the possibility that workers have different perceptions of the same quality level, we also controlled for personal characteristics that might influence those perceptions. For example, workers with more experience, firm tenure, education, or higher individual productivity levels might have more demanding standards. In addition to these four variables, we also controlled for gender and race. The results show that modules have a positive and significant effect on perceived performance of the work group after controlling for the variables that may affect these perceptions.[6]

Data from company records and managerial perceptions indicate that, in Company 1, modules outperform the traditional progressive bundle system. Workers' perceptions of the quality of the work of their work groups also support this conclusion.

One explanation for the better performance of module relative to bundle production might be that more productive workers have been assigned to the modules. We examined this possibility with a logit regression that predicts whether a worker in Company 1 will be assigned to a module or a bundle operation. The regressors included a measure of individual productivity.[7] The results (available from the authors) show that the difference in performance between modules and bundles in this company cannot be explained by differences in individual productivity levels.

Company 2

Company 2 has also faced increased competitive pressure. In 1989, in order to save labor costs, it began to shift production to the Caribbean Basin and to reduce employment at Plant C. But the cheaper offshore production was not able to meet the increasingly demanding delivery schedules of the large U.S. retailers the company wanted to supply. In 1992, the company decided to switch production at Plant C to modules, enabling the plant to respond to domestic retailers' demands for quick response and high-quality garments. By 1993, two-thirds of the operators in this plant worked in modules. The company found that modules enabled it to compete effectively for orders from such domestic retail-

---

[6] We have shown elsewhere that modules have a strong and significant effect on a worker's perception of the quality of the work done in the work group, even after controlling for the effects of other variables, such as job design characteristics and a full array of human resource and employment relations practices (see Appelbaum et al., 1994; Batt and Appelbaum, 1995).

[7] The workers were asked to report their normal productivity level. In a piece-rate system, engineers set a target for what they consider to be normal, or "100%" production levels. A worker who typically produces 20% above the quota is considered a 120% producer. Since their pay is based on their production level, workers who have worked in a bundle system usually can report their production level defined in this way. This concept does not have a well-defined meaning for individual module workers, so the module workers were asked what their production level had been the last time they worked in the bundle system. Bundle workers reported their current production level.

ers as Wal-Mart, Sears, and Lane Bryant. As a result of new orders, shipments increased dramatically, rising from 750 dozen units a week in 1989 to 3,500 dozen in 1993 and nearly 4,000 dozen units per week in 1994. Value added per worker increased by nearly 200 percent for the same period.

The plant's quick response capability increased rapidly. In February 1994 it was just able to meet Wal-Mart's demand that orders be shipped within five days of receipt, but by October 1994 Plant C was able to meet Wal-Mart's even more demanding three-day shipment policy. Quality levels were high for both module and bundle plants of this company (Plants C and D) – less than 0.2 percent of the output was rated as "irregular" – but according to monthly data from both plants, modules in Plant C had zero defects and "rework" (fixing correctable errors) in 1993 and 1994.[8]

The executives of Company 2 were convinced that modules allowed them to meet the demanding delivery schedules of companies like Wal-Mart without holding costly inventories. Modules had allowed them to remain in business. This is clearly more than managerial hyperbole, since in the past two years, the company has moved some of its capacity from the Caribbean to the United States. Employment at Plant C increased from 98 employees in 1989 to 140 in 1993. The company opened Plant D in 1992 with 80 workers and increased employment to 180 workers in 1993, one-third of them in modules. The company now plans to move both plants entirely to module production, although the capital and training costs associated with the introduction of modules have slowed their progress.

While reducing production costs was not the motive for adopting modular production, detailed comparisons between the costs of production of the same item (although the fabric was different) also reveal significant cost savings. Table 3.2 compares the actual production costs for similar women's undergarments produced at the two plants. The garments in Plant C are produced by modules, and the garments in Plant D are produced on a bundle line. Although the material used for the two items is different, the two fabrics are of similar weight and have similar handling and sewing properties. As a result, the manager attributes differences in direct labor costs to the differences in work organization and not in fabric.

Modules are believed to save cost through reductions in inventory levels, space requirements (and therefore rent and utilities), supervisory

---

[8] Errors were made within the modules, but they were all corrected by the modules before they released the items.

Table 3.2. *Comparison of Cost per Dozen of Two Similar High-Volume Styles*

	Plant C	Plant D
	(Produced by Modules), 200 Dozen per Day in 1993	(Produced by Bundles), 200 Dozen per Day in 1993
Cutting	$2.25	$1.88
Overhead	$9.85	$12.40
Direct wage cost	$4.92	$6.20
Attachment of label	$0.00	$0.30
Warehouse	$0.73	$2.18
Machine parts	$0.34	$0.44
Miscellaneous costs[a]	$1.45	$1.54
Production cost (net of material costs)	$19.54	$24.94

[a] Miscellaneous costs include those for label, hanger, selling aid (picture), packaging, outside carton, design, repair, return, premium freight, premium labor, and electronic data interchange.

and service functions, quality inspections and rework. All of these are reflected in the lower overhead costs – $12.40 per dozen for bundle production and $9.85 per dozen for modular production. Modules need fewer supervisors, fewer quality inspectors, fewer service workers to move bundles around, and less space on the factory floor (to store the bundles of work-in-process). Since it is easier to produce on demand with modules, there is less need to hold inventories of finished goods (to allow fast delivery); thus there is less need for warehouse space and labor associated with warehousing. Traditional warehousing functions such as packaging are also done within the modules. Thus bundle production requires $2.18 per dozen for warehousing, while the equivalent cost for warehousing for apparel produced in modules is only $0.78.

Managers at Company 2 were surprised to find that modules also led to direct savings in production wage costs. The traditional view has been that the highly engineered bundle system driven by piece rates would result in lower direct production labor costs, when compared with modules, but would lead to higher overhead, slower throughput, and inferior quality. But the data from Company 2 show a $4.92 direct labor cost per dozen for modules compared with $6.20 for bundles.[9] Indeed, labor costs for bundles should be considered $6.50, since module workers attach the labels within the module, while it is considered an extra cost in the bundle operation.

As was the case with Company 1, module workers reported higher quality of work produced by their work group than bundle workers (see Table 3.1). The coefficient for the module dummy variable is positive and significant after controlling for personal characteristics that might account for differences in perception. In this case, we were able to control for plant-specific effects (with a dummy for Plant 4), since there were bundle and module workers at both plants. The coefficient for the Plant 4 variable is not significant, and introducing the plant dummy increases the size of the coefficient for modules. Therefore, company data (in this case including detailed cost comparisons) and managerial perceptions indicate that modules outperform the bundle system in Company 2. And workers also perceive that module production results in higher quality.

To what extent can the differences in the performance of module and bundle production be attributed to differences in worker characteristics? The results from logit regressions on Company 2 indicate that individual productivity does not significantly predict whether one is assigned to a module or a bundle operation. The joint likelihood ratio test of the overall model, including a control variable generally related to productivity such as education and experience, is not statistically significant for Company 2.

Explaining the Superior Performance of Modules

The results that we have presented so far suggest that modules, when compared with bundles, improve quality, reduce throughput time, and lower inventory levels and delivery times. In addition, Company 2 experienced a significant cost reduction attributable to the use of modules. As discussed earlier, there are two broad explanations for superior team performance. The job characteristics argument suggests that job redesign improves performance by enhancing motivation and promoting job satisfaction, while sociotechnical theory suggests that the design of the work promotes more effective production through design efficiencies and

[9] This difference in labor cost between the module and bundle production cannot be attributed to differences in the base wage rates between operators in the two plants. Both plants are unionized, and the base wage rates are slightly higher in Plant C, the module plant.

economies of self-regulation. The worker survey enables us to examine these competing views.

Workers were asked, "All in all, how satisfied would you say you are with your job?" (1 = "very dissatisfied" to 4 = "very satisfied"). They were also asked to respond to the following statement: "The amount of stress you feel at work has increased over the last two years" (1 = "strongly dis-agree" to 4 = "strongly agree"), as well as a battery of questions to gauge their commitment to the firm.[10] The answers to this battery were used to create an index of organizational commitments ranging from 1 to 4, with 4 representing higher commitment.

Table 3.3 presents worker responses at the two companies combined with the questions about satisfaction, commitment, and stress. There is no statistically significant difference in the mean values for the satisfac-tion and commitment variables between bundle and module workers. Module workers are neither more satisfied by their jobs nor more com-mitted to their companies than are bundle workers. Moreover, module workers report more often than bundle workers that their jobs have become more stressful in the past two years.[11] These results contradict the job characteristics argument that job redesign promotes improved performance by increasing job satisfaction and commitment.

In contrast, our study suggests that it is the design of work and the communication and learning that it promotes that improve performance. For example, the manufacturing vice president at Company 2 attributes the higher direct labor costs of bundle production to the time wasted handling bundles that must be untied and retied, setting out the cut pieces, and picking pieces up as they are needed. By contrast, modules make one garment at a time, eliminating bundles entirely, and both set-out and pickup times have been drastically reduced. Further, in modules, workers have incentives from group targets and bonuses to improve the

---

[10] The workers were asked to agree or disagree with the following statements: "I am willing to work harder than I have in order to help this company succeed"; "I feel very little loyalty to this company"; "I would take almost any job to keep working for this company"; "I find that my values and this company's values are very similar"; "I am proud to be working for this company"; "I would turn down another job for more pay in order to stay with this company." These are standard measures of organizational com-mitment and have been widely used by other researchers. A factor analysis which indi-cated that these items represent a single underlying attitude of workers toward their companies is consistent with previous studies of organizational commitment using these measures (Lincoln and Kalleberg, 1990; Marsden et al., 1993). The scale we formed using these items has an internal consistency reliability (Cronbach's alpha) of .75.

[11] These results hold for an analysis of these variables for each company separately. They also are not changed in a regression that controls for personal characteristics as well as individual job characteristics (Appelbaum et al., 1994).

Table 3.3. *Measures of Satisfaction, Commitment, and Stress for Workers in Modules and Bundles*

	Bundle	N	Module	N	Combined	N
Satisfaction[a]	3.10	140	3.01	162	3.05	362
	(0.627)		(0.692)		(0.663)	
Commitment[b]	2.56	138	2.55	160	2.55	298
	(0.334)		(0.322)		(0.327)	
Stress[c]	2.78	138	3.23	163	3.03	301
	(0.808)		(0.806)		(0.837)	

Note: Standard errors are in parentheses.
[a] "All in all, how satisfied would you say you are with your job?" (1 = "very dissatisfied" to 4 = "very satisfied"). H_0: Mean (bundles) = mean (modules). $t = 1.23$ with 300 d.f.; Prob > |t| = .2205.
[b] See note 9 in the text for an explanation of this variable. H_0: Mean (bundles) = mean (modules). $t = 0.21$ with 296 d.f.; Prob > |t| = .8342.
[c] "The amount of stress you feel at work has increased over the last two years" (1 = "strongly disagree" to 4 = "strongly agree"). H_0: Mean (bundles) = mean (modules). $t = -4.83$ with 299 d.f.; Prob > |t| = .0000.

overall process of apparel assembly, while bundle workers have only an incentive to increase their own output.

One of the design features that enhances the productivity of modules is the integration of learning and problem solving into the production process for modules (Table 3.4). The employee survey asked workers: "Have other workers informally taught you shortcuts, problem solving, or other ways to improve your work?" (0 = "no," 1 = "yes") and "To what extent have you acquired skills by doing different tasks or jobs at this plant?" (1 = "not at all" to 4 = "to a great extent"). Almost 90 percent of module workers have learned ways to improve their work through informal training, compared with 71 percent of bundle workers, and module workers also reported significantly more learning through job rotation.

Conclusion

Modular production organizes workers to achieve (1) horizontal coordination in the assembly of complete garments and (2) continuous communication and adjustment in work methods to share shortcuts, reduce bottlenecks, and eliminate defects. As in Aoki's (1990) "J-mode" organi-

Table 3.4. *Measures of Informal Learning for Workers in Modules and Bundles*

	Bundle	N	Module	N	Combined	N
Informal training[a]	0.714 (0.453)	140	0.896 (0.307)	163	0.812 (0.391)	303
Skills acquisition through job rotation[b]	2.729 (0.912)	140	3.301 (0.738)	163	3.036 (0.870)	303

Note: Standard errors are in parentheses.
[a] "Have other workers informally taught you shortcuts, problem solving, or other ways to improve how you work?" (0 = "no"; 1 = "yes"). H_0: Mean (bundles) = mean (modules). $t = -4.13$ with 301 d.f.; Prob > |t| = .0000.
[b] "To what extent have you acquired skills by doing different tasks or jobs at this plant?" (1 = "not at all' to 4 = "to a great extent"). H_0: Mean (bundles) = mean (modules). $t = -6.03$ with 301 d.f.; Prob > |t| = .0000.

zations, innovative apparel firms sacrifice some of the economies of specialization associated with the progressive bundle system – both high utilization rates for individual pieces of equipment and, in many cases (though not in Company 2 in this study), lower production wage costs per garment. In a team production system, some part of the time and effort of sewing operators must be diverted to acquiring multiple skills (learning) as well as to communicating with each other. Team production also requires large investments in equipment and results in idle machines. This pays off provided that the gains from learning and coordination are greater than the productivity losses due to reduced specialization.

In apparel, opportunities for horizontal coordination exist at the point where the garment is assembled. While workers in modules must complete certain operations to make a garment, the order in which they do those operations as well as the combinations of operations that each team member performs can be unique to each module. The gains from modular production depend on the ability of modules to continuously balance the flow of production and regulate work among themselves.

Our research suggests that many of the gains in modular production in the basics segment of the apparel industry come from economies associated with this self-regulation. Self-regulation in modular production allows work teams to realize economies from the coordination of work and the elimination of bottlenecks and of buffers of work-in-process inventories. As a result, module production leads to large savings in overhead costs, savings from reductions in rework and irregulars, savings in warehouse costs, and savings in indirect labor costs as teams take over scheduling and as they do their own routine maintenance. Managers also expect the movement of workers among machines and tasks and the reduction of repetitive-motion and other injuries to reduce workers' compensation costs.

More important even than any cost savings, reductions in turnaround time, measured as the amount of time it takes a *particular* garment to go from cut fabric to finished product ready for shipment, improves a firm's ability to provide just-in-time delivery to retailers and to deliver precisely the colors, sizes, and styles required by the retailer at that moment. This confers a competitive advantage on firms able to respond in a timely fashion to the whims of the market and the requirements of individual retailers. Retailers are able to carry much smaller inventories of products and to achieve significant savings by avoiding markdowns or stockouts. As a result, retailers may be willing to pay a premium to the manufacturer who can deliver products on time and on short notice. Alternatively, retailers may simply demand faster delivery. For producers, innovative work organization is the key to better performance and competitive success.

REFERENCES

American Apparel Manufacturers Association. 1988. *The Coming Revolution: Flexible Apparel Manufacturing.* Washington, DC: American Apparel Manufacturers Association, Technical Advisory Committee.

Aoki, Masahiko. 1990. "Toward an Economic Model of the Japanese Firm." *Journal of Economic Literature*, 28(March), pp. 1–27.

Appelbaum, Eileen, Thomas Bailey, Peter Berg, and Arne Kalleberg. Forthcoming. *Manufacturing Competitive Advantage.* Ithaca: Cornell University Press.

Bailey, Thomas. 1993a. "Discretionary Effort and the Organization of Work: Employee Participation and Work Reform since Hawthorne." Technical paper, Columbia University, Institute on Education and the Economy, Teachers College.

—1993b. "Organizational Innovation in the Apparel Industry." *Industrial Relations*, 32(1), pp. 30–48.

Bartel, Ann P. 1991. "Productivity Gains from the Implementation of Employee Training Programs." National Bureau of Economic Research Working Paper No. 3893.

Batt, Rosemary, and Eileen Appelbaum. 1995. "Worker Participation in Diverse Settings: Does the Form Affect the Outcome?" *British Journal of Industrial Relations*, 33(3), pp. 353–378.

Cohen, Susan G. 1993. "Designing Effective Self-Managing Work Teams." CEO Publication G 93-9 (229). Los Angeles: University of Southern California, Center for Effective Organizations.

Cooke, William N. 1994. "Employee Participation Programs, Group-Based Incentives, and Company Performance: A Union-Nonunion Comparison." *Industrial and Labor Relations Review*, 47(4), pp. 594–609.

Cordery, J. L., W. S. Mueller, and L. M. Smith. 1991. "Attitudinal and Behavioral Effects of Autonomous Group Working: A Longitudinal Field Study." *Academy of Management Journal*, 34(2), pp. 464–476.

Cotton, J. L. 1993. *Employee Involvement: Methods for Improving Performance and Work Attitudes*. Newbury Park, CA: Sage.

Cotton, J. L., D. A. Vollrath, K. L. Froggatt, M. L. Lengnick-Hall, and K. R. Jennings. 1988. "Employee Participation: Diverse Forms and Different Outcomes." *Academy of Management Review*, 13, pp. 8–22.

Eaton, Adrienne E., and Paula B. Voos. 1992. "Union and Contemporary Innovations in Work Organization, Compensation, and Employee Participation." In Lawrence Mishel and Paula B. Voos, eds., *Unions and Economic Competitiveness*. Armonk, NY: Sharpe, pp. 175–215.

Holzer, Harry, Richard Block, Marcus Cheatham, and Jack Knott. 1993. "Are Training Subsidies for Firms Effective? The Michigan Experience." *Industrial and Labor Relations Review*, 46(4), pp. 625–636.

Huselid, Mark. 1995. "The Impact of Human Resource Management Practices on Turnover, Productivity, and Corporate Financial Performance." *Academy of Management Journal*, 38, pp. 635–670.

Ichniowski, Casey, and Kathryn Shaw. 1995. "Old Dogs and New Tricks: Determinants of the Adaptation of Productivity-Enhancing Work Practices." *Brookings Papers on Economic Activity: Microeconomics* (Spring), pp. 1–65.

Ichniowski, Casey, Kathryn Shaw, and Giovanna Prennushi. 1997. "The Effects of Human Resource Management Practices on Productivity: A Study of Steel Finishing Lines." *American Economic Review*, 87(3), pp. 291–313.

Kemp, Nigel J., Toby D. Wall, Chris W. Clegg, and John L. Cordery. 1983. "Autonomous Work Groups in a Greenfield Site: A Comparative Study." *Journal of Occupational Psychology*, 56, pp. 271–288.

Lawler, Edward, Susan Mohrman, and Gerald Ledord. 1992. *Employee Involvement and Total Quality Management: Practices and Results in Fortune 1000 Companies*. San Francisco: Jossey-Bass.

Levine, David I., and Laura D. Tyson. 1990. "Participation, Productivity, and the Firm's Environment." In Alan S. Blinder, ed., *Paying for Productivity*. Washington, DC: Brookings Institution, pp. 183–243.

Lincoln, James R., and Arne L. Kalleberg. 1990. *Culture, Control, and Commitment: A Study of Work Organization and Work Attitudes*. Cambridge University Press.

Locke, E. A., and D. M. Schweiger. 1979. "Participation in Decision-Making: One More Look." In Barry M. Staw, ed., *Research in Organizational Behavior*, vol. 1. Greenwich, CT: JAI Press, pp. 265–339.

MacDuffie John P. 1995. "Human Resource Bundles and Manufacturing Performance: Organizational Logic and Flexible Production Systems in the World Auto Industry." *Industrial and Labor Relations Review*, 48(2), pp. 197–221.

Marsden, Peter V., Arne L. Kalleberg, and Cynthia R. Cook. 1993. "Gender Differences in Organizational Commitment." *Work and Occupations*, 20, pp. 368–390.

Miller, K. I., and Peter R. Monge. 1986. "Participation, Satisfaction, and Productivity: A Meta-Analytic Review." *Academy of Management Journal*, 29, pp. 727–753.

Office of Technology Assessment. 1987. *U.S. Textile and Apparel Industry: A Revolution in Progress*. Washington, DC: Congress of the United States, Office of Technology Assessment.

U.S. Department of Commerce, International Trade Administration. 1993. "Apparel and Fabricated Textile Products." In *U.S. Industrial Outlook, 1993*. Washington, DC: U.S. Government Printing Office, pp. 32–1 to 32–9.

Wall, Toby D., Nigel J. Kemp, P. R. Jackson, and Chris W. Clegg. 1986. "Outcomes of Autonomous Workgroups: A Long-Term Field Experiment." *Academy of Management Journal*, 29(2), pp. 280–304.

Weitzman, Martin L., and Douglas L. Kruse. 1990. "Profit Sharing and Productivity." In Alan S. Blinder, ed., *Paying for Productivity: A Look at the Evidence*. Washington, DC: Brookings Institution, pp. 95–139.

CHAPTER 4

The Participatory Bureaucracy:
A Structural Explanation for the Effects
of Group-Based Employee Participation
Programs on Productivity in the Machined
Products Sector

Maryellen R. Kelley

Collaborative problem-solving involving groups of workers organized in committees or teams has been heralded as a superior method for addressing problems of coordination within complex organizations, permitting more rapid diagnosis and resolution of production problems affecting quality and productivity than do traditional bureaucratic systems (Adler, 1993; Tjosvold, 1986). The new participatory structures operate on the premise that specific knowledge about technical operations and how to improve them is fragmentary and distributed unevenly among workers in different occupations at multiple levels in an organization's hierarchy. Indeed, a central feature of organizational reform programs such as total quality management, continuous improvement, and re-engineering is their reliance on formal group-based problem-solving processes (Hackman and Wageman, 1995). In a *participatory bureaucracy*, a formal system of employee participation in group problem-solving activities provides the opportunity to re-examine old routines and to take advantage of informal shortcuts that employees have worked out on their own. An important goal of such a process is the establishment of better procedures that retain the advantages of bureaucracy

This chapter is a slightly revised version of an article that originally appeared in *Industrial Relations* 35:3 (1996); reprinted by permission of Blackwell Publishers.

The author acknowledges the generous support of the Alfred P. Sloan Foundation (Grant 92-10-2) and research asssistance by Grant Emison. For their comments, criticisms, and suggestions for revisions, the author is grateful to Cynthia Cook, Mauro Guillen, Bennett Harrison, Sue Helper, Casey Ichniowski, Arne Kalleberg, David Levine, Craig Olson, and George Strauss. The author is solely responsible for any remaining errors.

associated with a highly specialized division of labor, formalization and standardization.

In this chapter, I am concerned with how widespread group-based participatory practices are in an important sector of manufacturing, that of machined durable goods. Using factor analysis, I assess the interdependency among group-based problem-solving and incentive schemes and their distinctiveness from traditional systems for organizing and rationalizing production work. Which types of enterprises tend to rely on multiple group-based participation mechanisms more than on other forms of work organization? Are enterprises in more competitive markets or more customized markets more likely to rely on these mechanisms? Or is the reliance on participatory structures related to greater demands for closer coordination among firms in collaborative customer–supplier networks?

Recent quantitative research showing a direct link between participatory practices and objective measures of manufacturing performance at the establishment level has been confined to high-volume operations that make the same or a standardized product (Arthur, 1994; Ichniowski, Shaw, and Prennushi, 1995; MacDuffie, 1995). Yet, if participatory structures provide a more flexible and speedy avenue for resolving coordination problems, performance should be particularly enhanced in settings where the demand for flexibility is high and coordination problems are particularly complex. In manufacturing, these are the normal conditions of multi-product batch process settings, where there are frequent changeovers in the products made (or services delivered), a large variety of tasks to be performed, and variability in the type of technology used. Do group-based participatory practices have the expected effects on productivity in such demanding environments?

My study of the multi-product batch process known as machining is the first to evaluate the effects of participatory structures on productivity among a large sample of workplaces with high demands for technical flexibility. Instead of restricting my analysis to a common or standardized product, as has been done in other studies of this type, I explicitly model the quality dimensions of the product that make it difficult (i.e., costly) to produce. By allowing product attributes to vary, I am able to evaluate how participatory structures and other aspects of the organization of work affect performance across industries with different technical requirements. This approach is an adaptation of the method of hedonic regression that is commonly used by economists to evaluate the contribution to prices of quality-related differences in products. Moreover, since this analysis is conducted using survey data with a high response rate (84 percent) from a size-stratified, randomly selected sample, I avoid the sample bias problems that Appelbaum and Batt (1994) identified among earlier studies of employee participation focused exclusively on the practices of large firms. This study is therefore also the first to compare the effects of multiple participatory structures on the operations of large and small enterprises.

In prior research, I found that in 1987 one type of group-based participatory structure – that of joint labor–management committees – was associated with *poorer* manufacturing performance, on average, in the machining process, especially among branch plants of large enterprises (Kelley and Harrison, 1992). These negative effects were attenuated by the application of information technology in the form of programmable automation (Kelley, 1994). In the current study, I use 1991 data from the sample of establishments I previously surveyed in 1987 to determine whether, with the passage of time and the accumulation of experience, organizations with *multiple* participatory structures outperform those that rely on few or no group-based forms of employee participation. Moreover, I ask how the performance effects in the new group-based participatory structures compare with those associated with traditional systems of work rationalization achieved through unionization and seniority-based promotion schemes or through craft-type internal labor market structures.

The Persistence of Bureaucratic Structures: Obsolescence, Inertia, or Adaptation?

Traditional industrial bureaucracies rely on systems that strongly reflect the principles of "scientific management" as first promulgated by Frederick Taylor at the turn of the twentieth century. In organizations that adhere to Taylorist principles, managers depend on conformance to rules and procedures as a device to ensure that work is carried out in expected and predictable ways, in what Edwards (1979) has characterized as a system of bureaucratic control. Specialization and standardization – the hallmarks of bureaucratic organization – allow repetitive, routine tasks to be carried out with a high degree of efficiency. However, the technical conditions favoring Taylorist bureaucratic structures – that is, stable, expanding product markets and economies of scale – are widely believed to be disappearing at the dawn of a new post-industrial era, in which flexible technologies and work systems will provide competitive advantages (Kern and Schumann, 1984; Piore and Sabel, 1984). Powerful new technologies, particularly in the application of computers and micro-electronic controls, are expected to open new vistas for small-volume producers (and small-size employers), providing the opportunity to achieve performance improvements through automation that will reduce or eliminate entirely the productivity advantages of high volume (standardized, repetitive work) and large size (specialization). In this context, we should expect new, more egalitarian forms of work organization to be superior to traditional Taylorist bureaucracies and to dominate the industrial landscape among enterprises in highly competitive markets in which customized small-volume production is important.

The functionalist view of bureaucratic structure has also been questioned by organizational theorists who see inertia, rather than rationality, as the main explanation for the persistence of certain organizational forms. Crozier (1964), for example, asserts that in complex organizations there evolves an elaborate maze of rules that are dysfunctional and inefficient. According to Carroll and Hannan (1995), complex organizations are not very adaptable to changing environments, but tend to retain the routines and procedures established at the time of their founding, even if these practices are ill-suited to the demands and conditions of a later age. During a transitional period when new organizational forms are being introduced, we should therefore expect to find diversity in structural arrangements and these differences should be related to the age of the organization. Older organizations will tend to rely on forms that dominated an earlier period, and younger organizations will be more apt to display the new structures. Hence, if the adoption of group-based participatory structures is related to a shift from one techno-economic regime to another and such structures are particularly advantageous to the new regime, we should expect to find younger organizations displaying a greater reliance on participatory structures.

More generally, the persistence of heterogeneity of organizational structures may be explained by differences in the external environment. These differences may arise from changes in technology, the behavior of customers, the behavior of competitors, or the firm's ability to shape the environment of other organizations through barriers to entry and to exert power as a customer (or provider) of goods and services procured from (or provided to) upstream (or downstream) firms. Group-based participatory structures may be particularly advantageous for addressing the problems of enterprises operating in certain kinds of environments but not others. In particular, employee participation mechanisms may enhance an organization's responsiveness to new demands for close coordination of the firm's operations with those of other enterprises in the same production network. A number of studies suggest that contemporary manufacturing systems depend increasingly on joint technology development activities between ostensibly independent firms and on the coordination of technical and production operations of companies that belong to the same subcontracting network (Harrigan, 1988; Harrison and Kelley, 1993; Mowery, 1988). Such close collaborative ties among firms require greater coordination of their respective internal operations and place new demands on organizations to develop internal capabilities for information-sharing and coordination. Hence, if group-based participatory structures enhance an organization's capacity to engage in collaborative relations with other firms, we should expect to find the reliance on such structures to be greater for organizations with these types of relationships.

Forms of Employee Participation and Their Measurement

Group discussion mechanisms of an instrumental problem-solving nature are a central feature of all participatory schemes. The main purpose of these discussion mechanisms is to draw on the collective wisdom of the group in diagnosing problems, formulating plans of action, and, in some cases, assigning tasks to group members and evaluating their performance. The members of such problem-solving groups may include individuals from different positions in the organization's hierar-chy, as in labor–management committees, or may be confined to the same level, as in work teams. The issues considered may be broad and com-prehensive, or narrowly focused on specific topics, such as methods for reducing defects in a particular production process.

Participatory structures also affect the compensation system. In a tra-ditional industrial workplace, pay is tied solely to an individual's job clas-sification and productivity. In a group-based participatory structure, rewards to the individual employee are at least partly contingent on the collective performance of the work group or organizational unit. These are designed to reinforce cooperation among organizational members. Group-based reward systems vary in how closely (or distantly) the reward is tied to the performance of a work group and whether the com-pensation comes in the form of wages or stock (Kruse, 1993). Some of these group-based compensation schemes are tied to the achievement of specific performance targets in a product line. More common are systems that tie compensation to the overall organization's profitability.

Rather than attempt to isolate a specific constellation of "best" prac-tices, defined in terms of some ideal model of participation or displayed by leading companies in an industry, I ask: To what extent do employers in this sector rely on a common set of group-based participatory prac-tices distinct from other aspects of the organization of work? I consider two kinds of practices as indicative of a new type of participatory structure: group-based discussion mechanisms and compensation practices that tie individual employees' rewards to the organization's financial success. I choose to ignore labels such as "total quality management" and "re-engineering," focusing instead on the basic structure of the arrangements through which employees exert influence and share in the financial success of the enterprise. In this study, I follow Osterman (1994) and treat training and job design as separate aspects of the organization of work. Unions are treated as a unique representative form of employee participation for negotiating work rules.

Data Description and Methodological Issues

The data come from an original 1991 national telephone survey of a size-stratified random sample of manufacturing establishments selected from 21 industries. Whatever else they may do, all the workplaces are engaged in a common technical process known as *machining*, which is applied to the manufacture of a wide variety of metal products, including aircraft engines, elevators, automobiles, machine tools, precision instruments, and hand tools. I label the population of industries represented by my sample the *machining-intensive durable goods* (MDG) sector.[1]

Responses were obtained from 84 percent of the sample plants originally surveyed in 1987 that survived to 1991 and were still engaged in the machining production process in that later year. At each surveyed plant, the same manager or engineer identified as most knowledgeable about the machining production process in 1987 (or his or her replacement) was interviewed again in 1991. In addition to information on work practices, the survey also sought information on technology, production operations, aspects of the competitive environment, and attributes of selected products manufactured in the machining process at each plant. For each plant that I surveyed, the production manager directly responsible for supervising machining operations at the plant provided information on one or two products made by that process. There are 973 plants in the size-stratified 1991 sample. Unless otherwise stated, all population estimates are weighted averages.[2]

[1] Machining involves the use of precision tools to cut and shape metal, and includes grinding, drilling, milling, planing, boring, and turning operations. Using the U.S. Bureau of Labor Statistics' industry-occupational matrix for 1985, I identified 21 three-digit industries specializing in this production process. Collectively, these industries accounted for virtually the entire capital goods sector (except for computers) and approximately one-fourth of all U.S. manufacturing output and employment during the late 1980s. See Kelley (1995) for further details on the sample characteristics and sampling procedures.

[2] For each observation, the sample weight is calculated as the reciprocal of the probability of selection into its size stratum.

Patterns of Employee Participation in the
Machining-Intensive Durable Goods Sector

In the 1991 survey, I asked about seven practices, including group-based discussion mechanisms for employee participation, compensation packages that provide workers the opportunity to own stock or to share the profits of the enterprise, unionization, and employer-provided skill development and training programs. Table 4.1 displays the incidence of these practices among the plants in the MDG sector, and the extent of the sector's employment and output concentrated in plants displaying these practices.

The most common form of employee participation involves committees made up of groups of production workers and managers who focus on problems concerning the introduction of new technology, quality control, or other production issues. In addition to these *joint labor–management problem-solving committees*, respondents reported on the practice of allowing groups of production workers to meet by themselves to discuss problems in *autonomous work-group meetings*. This practice is more common than *union representation*. However, with respect to total sector employment and employment in machining, unions affect a larger share of the sector's workforce than do autonomous work-group meetings.

Compensation practices that are specifically designed to allow workers to share economic rewards include a *profit-sharing plan* in which all employees participate or an *employee stock ownership plan* (ESOP) (when production workers are included). More employers have adopted profit-sharing plans than ESOPs. However, ESOPs are disproportionately found among large employers; plants with ESOPs employ nearly 35 percent of all workers, even though they are found in less than 5 percent of all workplaces.

Group-based participatory practices are not independent of one another, nor should we expect this to be the case. Other studies have also found that these practices tend to be introduced in clusters (Appelbaum and Batt, 1994; Ichniowski, Shaw, and Prennushi, 1995; Levine, 1995; MacDuffie, 1995). For example, among plants that allow autonomous work-group meetings, 75 percent also have joint labor–management committees (LMCs). Eighty-three percent of plants with ESOPs and 60 percent of plants with profit-sharing plans also have LMCs, providing further support for the view that LMCs serve as an anchoring practice for participatory structures. Moreover, for a majority of plants, group-based forms of employee participation are relatively new. Fully 85 percent of plants with LMCs in 1991 had adopted such committees

Table 4.1. *Selected Attributes of the Organization of Production Work in the Machining-Intensive Durable Goods Sector, 1991*

	Percentage of All Plants	Percentage of Total Sector Employment	Percentage of Sector's Total Annual Sales (1990)	Percentage of Total Machining Employment
Forms of employee participation				
Joint labor–management problem-solving committees	46.9	89.1	95.3	84.5
Autonomous work-group meetings	19.5	31.7	66.8	54.2
Union representation	8.9	62.7	83.1	56.0
Profit-sharing plan	29.0	27.2	18.1	28.0
Employee stock ownership plan	4.5	34.9	66.1	50.3
Skill development and training				
Employer-provided technical classes	22.3	68.5	80.8	66.4
Craft apprenticeship program	15.8	39.9	23.4	16.7

within the last 10 years. Similarly, 63 percent of profit-sharing plans and 70 percent of ESOPs were introduced between 1981 and 1991.

With respect to skill development and training policies, I asked questions that were technically relevant to the machining production process. *Employer-provided technical classes* includes instruction in any of the following: the interpretation and analysis of blueprints and drawings; "shop" mathematics, such as algebra and trigonometry; principles of metallurgy; or programming for numerical control (NC) or computer numerical control (CNC) machine tools. A *craft apprenticeship program* provides at least three years of training for such well-defined, traditional high-skill occupations as all-around machinist and tool and die maker. More than one-fifth of all workplaces offer employer-provided technical classes in one or more subjects. These opportunities were potentially available to two-thirds of all workers employed in machining jobs in the sector. Fewer than 16 percent of all workplaces had craft apprenticeship programs, affecting an equally small percentage of the machining workforce. Certain training policies are also correlated with employee participation programs. Nearly three-fourths (74 percent) of plants with employer-provided technical classes also have LMCs.

To determine whether group-based participatory practices constitute a separate dimension and to assess the degree to which these practices are aligned with certain bureaucratic structural elements, I conducted a confirmatory factor analysis on nine dummy variables. In addition to the seven measures listed in Table 4.1, I included two indicators for bureaucratic structure: whether seniority rules were routinely used by managers in making decisions about promotion and job assignments, and the reliance on formal, written procedures and methods in performing production tasks in the machining process. The purpose of the factor analysis was to confirm the hypothesis that group-based participatory practices (i.e., LMCs, autonomous work-group meetings, employee stock ownership, and group-based profit-sharing plans) align on a single dimension – that is, are more correlated with one another than with other practices – and, further, to establish that this dimension is distinguishable from the tendency of organizations to rely on a traditional craft-type internal labor market structure (as evidenced by a craft apprenticeship training program) or a traditional union-based bureaucratic structure. The results of the factor analysis appear to confirm these hypotheses.

I employed the maximum likelihood method of extracting factors. The results of χ^2 tests indicate that there is at least one common factor ($p < .001$), and three factors are probably sufficient ($p < .11$). The rotated factor pattern for the three retained factors is displayed in Table 4.2. The

Table 4.2. *Factor Pattern of Work Organization and Bureaucratic Structure*

	Participatory Bureaucracy	Union/Seniority-Based Bureaucracy	Traditional Craft Apprenticeship
Joint labor–management problem-solving committees	.66	.00	-.06
Employer-provided technical classes	.44	.03	.11
Formalization and standardization of work methods	.33	.03	-.01
Autonomous work-group meetings	.31	-.07	.05
Employee stock ownership plan	.29	-.04	-.08
Union representation	-.01	.94	.02
Seniority rules in promotion and job assignment	.17	.31	-.01
Craft apprenticeship program	-.02	-.04	.72
Profit-sharing plan	.16	-.27	.08
Squared multiple correlations of variables with each factor	.59	.88	.54

Note: Factor analysis was conducted on unweighted data. The results displayed are for the PROMAX oblique rotation of the maximum likelihood solution.

scores generated for each factor are based on all of the variables used in the analysis. As the table shows, the first factor, *participatory bureaucracy*, has relatively high loadings on five variables: joint labor–management problem-solving committees, worker-run work-group-based problem-solving committees, ESOPs, classroom instruction in specific technical subjects for the production workforce, and conformance to formal procedures and standardized methods in carrying out machining tasks. If a plant has none of these practices but is unionized or has a craft apprenticeship program, then, as the loadings indicate (–.01 and –.02, respectively), it will have a low score on this scale. The factor pattern indicates that the set of participatory practices not only cluster together but are also distinct from traditional craft and industrial-type internal labor market structures. Moreover, organizations that rely on multiple participatory mechanisms also tend to rely on a well-known bureaucratic control mechanism, standardization.

The second factor distinguishes organizations in which the production workforce is represented by a union, and in which a worker's seniority (i.e., years of experience on the job) is an important criterion in promotion and job assignment decisions within the plant, from those that do not have seniority systems or union work rules. I call this the *union/seniority-based bureaucracy*, which is otherwise recognizable as the traditional industrial-type internal labor market structure with experience-based promotion ladders composed of narrowly specialized jobs. High scores on the third factor are plants with a craft apprenticeship training program of at least three years' duration, indicating craft control over machining skills, which is labeled *traditional craft apprenticeship*.[3]

Considering the correlations shown in Table 4.3 of the factor scores with establishment size (as measured by number of employees) and indicators of the potential market power of the enterprise (as measured by whether or not the plant manufactures a product of its own design, the number of competitors in its markets for machined products, and dependence on sales to its largest customer), I find the tendency toward a participatory bureaucratic structure to be strongly associated with larger plants operating in product markets where the enterprise enjoys some degree of market power (i.e., has a proprietary product and is significantly less dependent on sales to a single customer). These are also fea-

---

[3] The factors are relatively independent of one another, with a correlation of only .24 between the *participatory bureaucracy* factor and the *union/seniority-based bureaucracy* and .19 between the *traditional craft apprenticeship* factor and the two bureaucracy factors.

Table 4.3. *Correlations of Selected Establishment and Product Market Characteristics with Work Organization Factors*

	Work Organization Factor		
	Participatory Bureaucracy	Union/Seniority-Based Bureaucracy	Traditional Craft Apprenticeship
Establishment characteristics			
Number of employees (log)	.556**	.451**	.166**
Average wage of machine operators (log)	-.017	.201**	.118**
Age of plant (years)	.107**	.363**	.058
Product market characteristics			
Proprietary product line (yes, no)	.191**	.116**	-.059
Percentage of output in small batches	-.239**	-.019	.030
Number of competitors (log)	.033	-.031	.132**
Percentage of total sales revenue from largest customer	-.167**	-.092**	.010**
Number of years in business with largest customer	.059	.232**	.109**
In the past two years, did your largest customer			
provide technical assistance to your plant? (yes, no)	.180**	.032	.067*
receive technical assistance from your plant? (yes, no)	.149***	.048	.001
jointly develop new products with your plant? (yes, no)	.184***	.060	.020

** Statistically significant at $p < .01$.
* Statistically significant at $p < .05$.

tures associated with the tendency toward a union/seniority-based bureaucracy.[4]

As noted earlier, Carroll and Hannan (1995) have persuasively argued the case for entropy in organizational systems. However, age-related organizational inertia does not consistently explain the persistence of traditional practices. Although there is a significant correlation between the age of a plant and its tendency to rely on a traditional union/seniority-based bureaucratic structure, there is no relationship between the age of a plant and its tendency to rely on a craft-type internal labor market structure. Moreover, contrary to what we would expect from this theory, *older* organizations are more likely to have adopted multiple participatory structures.

Looking at the evidence of a relationship between participatory structures and the technical demands of the environment, I find no support for the hypothesis that customization (i.e., the tendency to produce very small batches) is related to the tendency to rely on multiple participatory practices. However, organizations facing external demands from important customers for closer cooperation and coordination in technology development and information exchange *are* more likely to rely on multiple group-based participatory internal structures. For all three indicators of a close collaborative tie to important customers (providing and receiving technical assistance, and joint development of new products), there is a significant correlation with the participatory bureaucracy factor.

Participatory structures are taking hold among relatively large, old, and powerful organizations that also have a tendency to rely on traditional bureaucratic control mechanisms. Taken together, these correlations provide support for the view of the new group-based forms of employee participation as mechanisms for reforming existing structures, rather than being indicative of an entirely new, non-bureaucratic way of organizing authority relations within the workplace. Moreover, evidence suggests that the emergence of the new participatory bureaucracy form of organization is related to new demands for closer coordination by customer firms that are dependent on the technical capabilities of their suppliers. In the next section, we turn to the question of how the tendencies to manifest these different forms of work organization – participatory bureaucracy, union/seniority-based bureaucracy, and craft-controlled

---

[4] One important difference that distinguishes these two bureaucratic forms is their relationship to wages. I find no correlation between wages and the tendency to rely on a participatory structures, whereas higher wages are significantly correlated with high scores on the traditional *union/seniority-based bureaucracy* factor and the *craft apprenticeship* factor.

apprenticeship – are related to manufacturing performance in the machining process.

Work Organization and Manufacturing Performance

New practices and structures are adopted and spread among enterprises for a variety of reasons. The emergence of a dominant pattern of practices among organizations operating in the same field or referent organizational community indicates the popularity of these practices among managers, but not necessarily their superiority over competing forms in all circumstances (DiMaggio and Powell, 1983). Hence, even if group-based participatory structures become widely diffused in U.S. industry, we should not expect all enterprises that employ them to reap a performance advantage. If the main *function* of participatory structures is the rapid resolution of coordination problems and the reformation of rules and standards of bureaucratic organizations, then we should expect to find the productivity of the operations of large enterprises to be improved by participatory structures, but to find little advantage among small firms that have relatively simple internal coordination problems.

More generally, to what extent is manufacturing performance a function of the tendency toward a participatory bureaucratic structure or other forms of work organization? Here we examine the impact of the three work organization factors on performance, as measured by the number of hours it takes to complete key operations in the machining process, making allowances for differences among establishments in the kinds of products manufactured, in investments in new technology, and in the specialization of production operations.

Methodological Issues

In batch processes, a number of products are made using the same technology with the same workforce. For each product, the respondent provided detailed specifications on the complexity of tooling, precision requirements, and the cost of specialty materials, the amount produced, and the hours involved in making the product. For plants where both conventional mechanically controlled machines and the programmable forms of automation (PA) control known as CNC and NC technology were used, the manager provided a detailed description of a product made with each technology. If only one technology was used at the plant, the respondent provided information on only one product specific to that technology.

In industries where batch production processes are the norm, there is no such thing as a "standard" product. In the machining process, all products have some common features; that is, they are all metal parts requiring the removal of some material in order to fit a certain shape and function in relation to other mechanical components of a machine. However, there are also important differences in the properties of the product, related to its shape, type of material, and function. These quality-related differences affect the length of time that would normally be required to complete the machining process. How to control for these differences and their effects on performance is a critical methodological question.

I use the hedonic regression technique, which has been applied to analyzing the effect of quality and other product differences on prices.[5] According to the hedonic approach, any good can be described as "a bundle, or package of characteristics." Moreover, "individual products vary according to the presence or absence of characteristics, and also by the amount of each characteristic they embody" (Kokoski, 1993, p. 36). I adapt this method to the problem at hand by specifying a vector of quality-related attributes of machined products that are well known and normally taken into account in production planning and scheduling.

Key Variables

In all regression models, the dependent variable is defined as the total hours required in the machining process to produce one item of a given product type. With conventional mechanically controlled technology, two basic operations contribute to production time: hours of "setting up" by workers, which consists of time spent preparing tools, fixtures, and jigs, and positioning the workpiece in the machine; and the hours that machines are utilized in completing the cutting operations. For PA technology, a third operation occurs: "programming," in which the instructions for each cutting operation are coded and entered onto computer tape or disk. These instructions control the operation of NC or CNC tools or flexible manufacturing systems automatically during their "run" cycle. For each new part or product to be machined, a program must be written and tested. Once the program has been written and used to make the first batch, the same program can be used again for subsequent batches of the same product on the same programmable machine.[6]

---

[5] There is an extensive literature on hedonic regression in analyses of productivity (see Griliches, 1990).

[6] The time spent on any reprogramming of subsequent batches manufactured during the year is also included in this measure.

I use the composite measure *machining production hours per unit of output* to compare the relative efficiency of machining production operations across the sample plants. After taking into account the quality and complexity of the product and controls for industry,[7] I expect three types of variables to influence the efficiency with which machining operations are performed: work organization attributes, the technology and operations strategy of the enterprise for the machining process at the plant, and educational requirements and wage policies pertaining to the machining workforce. Variable definitions, means, and standard deviations for the entire sample are contained in Table 4.4.

Product Quality and Complexity

Geometric complexity is a proxy measure for the complexity and intricacy of the geometric shape of a product. The more complex the geometry, the greater is the variety of operations and tool motions that have to be performed and the greater is the number of tool changes. The indicator *specialty materials costs* measures the influence of expensive materials on production time. The speed at which a machine tool can cut metal is determined, in part, by the type of material being machined (Xue, 1991). Unusually hard and costly materials, such as special alloy steels, are more difficult to machine. The tighter the tolerance requirements (i.e., the higher the *precision standards*) to which a part or product must conform, the smaller the latitude for error in making a part. Allowing for more intermediate steps for inspection, by making repeated cutting actions at closer and closer tolerances, reduces the likelihood that a finished product will fail to meet tolerances. This practice increases the amount of time it takes to make a finished product.

Technology and Operations Strategy

Programmable automation acquires flexibility by incorporating the instructions controlling machine operation into the software rather than the hardware, thereby reducing the costs of both large- and small-batch operations. Fully 58 percent of the plants surveyed in 1991 employ this technology to some degree. The direct effect of choosing to make a product of given attributes with PA technology is measured by the dummy variable. Because this technology makes it possible to run

---

[7] Six industry dummies are entered in all equations.

machines at faster speeds and also reduces the amount of time required to set up the equipment, I expect that products made with PA can be manufactured in less time than products made on non-programmable machines, all else constant.

Productivity increases arise both from radical shifts to a new, more effi-cient technology and from continued, incremental improvements in a mature technology (Dewar and Dutton, 1986). Whatever the technology, we should expect plants that rely to a greater extent on a newer gener-ation of equipment to be more efficient than those that use mostly older machinery. *Percentage of new machinery* is an indicator of the vintage of the capital stock. It is defined in relation to the type of technology used in the product's manufacture (either PA or conventional machines) as the percentage of the total machine tools in use at the plant that are less than five years old.

In batch manufacturing processes, production is punctuated by fre-quent changes in the type of product being made. Hence, the learning process related to the accumulation of experience in making the same product is discontinuous. Thus, learning-based increases in efficiency derive from the frequency with which the same setup tasks are repeated on subsequent batch orders. The higher the number of repeated orders for the same product over the course of a year (as measured by *batches of product*) – holding differences in other variables constant – the greater is the short-term learning advantage and the fewer are the production hours per unit of output.

Engineering studies (Ayres and Miller, 1983) suggest that there is a trade-off between having a high degree of flexibility from specializing in very small batch production and production costs. Hence, the more that a plant specializes in very small batch operations, and the higher the *percentage of total output in small batches* (which I define as fewer than 10 units per batch), the less efficient it will be, compared with plants with less diverse needs. I also include an indicator for estimating the productivity advantage stemming from the degree to which a plant specializes in relatively high volume production (*percentage of total output in large batches*, defined as a batch size of more than 500 units).

Plants with a relatively large number of machine tools are expected to enjoy a scale advantage over smaller operations. These may derive from more highly specialized division of labor, from greater capacity, or from logistic advantages achieved by dedicating groups of machines to spe-cific product lines – all of which are related to size. *Size of machining operations* is an indicator of scale effects, measured by the number of machine tools of the same technology type.

Table 4.4. *Definitions, Means, and Standard Deviations for Regression Variables*

Variable	Definition	Mean	Standard Deviation
Machining production hours per unit of output	For selected product, log{[hours of setup per batch/no. of units in a batch) + (machining hours per unit) + (hours to write and revise program/no. of units produced in the year)]	−0.56	2.44
Participatory bureaucracy	See Table 4.2 for a description of the factor scale	−0.40	0.74
Union/seniority-based bureaucracy	See Table 4.2 for a description of the factor scale	−0.38	0.60
Traditional craft apprenticeship	See Table 4.2 for a description of the factor scale	−0.13	0.67
Percentage of operator programming	Percentage of all programmable machine operators in the plant who regularly write new programs for the machines they tend ($n = 549$)	37.94	26.54
Geometric complexity	For selected product, log(number of tool changes) per unit	1.67	0.91
Precision standards	For selected product, log(1 ÷ ltolerance limit in fractions of inches|)	6.46	1.59
Specialty materials costs	For selected product, log(specialty materials costs, in cents)	6.62	2.93
PA technology	For selected product: = 1, if made using computer-controlled machines = 0, if made using conventional machines	0.31	0.46

Percentage of new machinery	If PA technology = 1, then = percentage of all computer-controlled machines <5 years old if PA technology = 0, then = percentage of all conventional machines <5 years old	24.68	29.76
Size of machine operations	if PA technology = 1, then = log(no. of computer-controlled machines) if PA technology = 0, then = log(no. of conventional machines)	2.14	1.09
Batches of product	For selected product, log(number of batches made during the entire year)	2.06	1.40
Percentage of total output in large batches	Percentage of total machining output (all products made in the year) produced in batch sizes >500 units	17.02	28.48
Percentage of total output in small batches	Percentage of total machining output (all products made in the year) produced in batch sizes <10 units	47.06	38.11
Average machine operator wage	log(estimated average wage paid to machining workers)	2.34	0.26
Technical education: 2 years post HS	= 1, if 2 or more years of post–high school technical education required of all those newly hired in machine occupations = 0, if less (or no) post–high school technical education required	0.24	0.43

Work Organization

The work organization factor scales *participatory bureaucracy, union/ seniority-based bureaucracy,* and *traditional craft apprenticeship* are included in all models. To the extent that the combination captured in the participative factor scale adds up to a superior "system," we should expect to find that the higher a plant scores on this scale, the more efficient its machining operations are likely to be.

There are two ways to view plants with high scores on the *union/ seniority-based bureaucracy* scale and their expected relationship to manufacturing performance. These plants may represent the traditional hierarchically organized work system predicated on narrow job ladders, which provides a productivity advantage through a high degree of specialization and informal (unmeasured) on-the-job training (Althauser and Kalleberg, 1981; Doeringer and Piore, 1971). However, to the extent that plants with high scores on this factor scale have rigid work rules, we may find no productivity advantage associated with union/seniority-based bureaucratic structures.

With respect to the *craft* factor, it seems reasonable to assume that high-scoring plants have special needs for a highly skilled workforce. Whether or not craft control of skills translates into higher productivity is likely to depend on the type of technology employed in the plant. The transition from conventional to PA technology requires new skills. Hence, the traditional system of training for craft skills associated with this form of work organization may be in the process of becoming obsolete and may fail to provide a productivity advantage with the new technology.

Attaching program-writing responsibilities to the jobs of machine operators is a type of "job enrichment" strategy that may have substantial productivity payoffs. I include the indicator *percentage of operator programming* as a regressor in models of "high-tech" machining operations – that is, those involving the exclusive use of PA technology.

Wages and Hiring Policies

Two variables measure inter-plant differences in labor policies. *Average wage* is a measure of the average wage paid to workers in machining occupations at the plant. *Technical education: 2 years post HS* is an indicator of a high technical education requirement for people newly hired into machining occupations at the plant (i.e., two or more years of formal technical education beyond high school is required of all newly hired workers). Both of these variables are proxy measures for the quality of the workforce.

Specification and Estimation Issues

Because their distributions are right-skewed, the log transformation is specified for the dependent variable and the following continuous variables: *geometric complexity, precision standards, specialty materials costs, size of machining operations*, and *average wage*. The variables controlling for quality-related attributes of products were all statistically significant in every regression model. OLS estimation is used throughout.

Table 4.5 presents the regression results for all plants (first and second columns), for branch plants (third and fifth columns), and for single-plant firms (fourth and sixth columns). There are 1,301 observations in the overall sample, since some plants were able to provide information on two products (with their respective conventional and PA technologies). The first column shows the effect on unit production hours of the three work organization factors when only the controls for product attributes and industry are included in the model.[8] In the second column, the variables measuring differences in technology use and other aspects of the plant's operations strategy are included along with wage and hiring policy variables. The parameters on the *craft* and the *union/seniority-based bureaucracy* factors are relatively stable. However, for the *participatory bureaucracy* dimension, when technology and operations variables are included, I find no independent effect on machining performance. Moreover, the coefficient measuring the effect of this factor becomes much smaller. This result is surprising, suggesting that much of the impact of participatory practices is associated with differences in technology and operations strategy.

To determine whether a small number of unusually influential cases was responsible for these findings, I employed a variety of influential point diagnostics, including the DFFITS statistic developed by Belsley, Kuh, and Welsch (1980).[9] From the regression results for the fully specified model (second column, Table 4.5), I identified 118 cases with

---

[8] Due to space limitations, the parameter estimates for the six industry dummy variables are not shown.

[9] The DFFITS statistic is a measure of the change in predicted value identified with a particular observation and is calculated by deleting that observation. A large value of DFFITS indicates an influential observation. An absolute value of DFFITS in excess of $\pm.248$ exceeds the size-adjusted cutoff of $2*\sqrt{(p/n)}$, where p is the number of parameters (20) and n is the sample size (1,301).

Table 4.5. *Regression Results for Machining Production Hours per Unit of Output, All Plants, Branch Plants, and Single-Plant Firms*

	All Plants: with Product Quality and Industry Controls	All Plants: Fully Specified Model	All Branch Plants	All Single-Plant Firms	PA Technology Only	
					Branch Plants	Single-Plant Firms
Intercept[a]	-6.371*** (0.519)	-6.445*** (0.621)	-8.144*** (0.831)	-6.302*** (1.022)	-6.972*** (1.661)	-7.430*** (1.580)
Work organization						
Participatory bureaucracy	-0.293*** (0.073)	-0.017 (0.068)	-0.312*** (0.121)	0.025 (0.090)	-0.265* (0.165)	-0.225** (0.127)
Union/seniority-based bureaucracy	-0.203*** (0.090)	-0.155** (0.081)	-0.057 (0.083)	-0.185* (0.129)	-0.096 (0.112)	-0.243* (0.184)
Traditional craft apprenticeship[a]	0.168** (0.080)	0.256*** (0.071)	0.246** (0.111)	0.250*** (0.094)	0.474*** (0.140)	0.238* (0.130)
percentage of operator programming	n.a.	n.a.	n.a.	n.a.	-0.005* (0.004)	-0.004 (0.003)
Product quality						
Geometric complexity	0.821*** (0.058)	0.834*** (0.055)	0.637*** (0.090)	0.867*** (0.074)	0.415*** (0.118)	0.241** (0.110)
Precision standards	0.124*** (0.032)	0.181*** (0.029)	0.132*** (0.050)	0.185*** (0.039)	0.182** (0.083)	0.238*** (0.068)
Specialty materials costs	0.402*** (0.018)	0.310*** (0.017)	0.427*** (0.028)	0.293*** (0.022)	0.382*** (0.043)	0.413*** (0.032)

Technology and operations					
PA technology	—	−0.888*** (0.129)	−1.023*** (0.199)	−0.803*** (0.174)	n.a.	n.a.
Percentage of new machinery	—	0.000 (0.002)	−0.002 (0.003)	0.000 (0.002)	−0.007** (0.003)	0.001 (0.002)
Size of machining operations	—	−0.193*** (0.053)	−0.316*** (0.072)	−0.132* (0.074)	−0.162 (0.120)	0.269** (0.126)
Batches of product	—	−0.197*** (0.033)	−0.064 (0.050)	−0.216*** (0.045)	−0.260*** (0.073)	−0.479*** (0.090)
Percentage of total output in large batches	—	−0.008*** (0.002)	−0.008*** (0.003)	−0.009*** (0.003)	−0.007** (0.004)	0.001 (0.004)
Percentage of total output in small batches	—	0.017*** (0.002)	0.009*** (0.002)	0.018*** (0.002)	0.008*** (0.003)	0.007** (0.004)
Wage and hiring policies					
Average machine operator wage[a]	—	0.478*** (0.189)	1.093*** (0.332)	0.393 (0.248)	0.765 (0.506)	0.588 (0.439)
Technical education: 2 years post HS	—	0.090 (0.110)	0.117 (0.191)	0.064 (0.143)	0.192 (0.263)	0.048 (0.203)
Adjusted R^2	.465	.586	.596	.589	.589	.554
Number of parameters	12	20	20	20	20	20
Number of observations	1,301	1,301	555	744	247	301

Note: All models include six industry dummy variables as controls for SICs 34, 35, 36, 37, 38, and 39. A negative sign for a coefficient indicates that the effect of the variable is to *lower* the number of hours per unit of output, implying an *increase* in productivity. Standard errors are shown in parentheses.

[a]Two-tailed statistical test.

*** Statistically significant at $p < .01$.

** Statistically significant at $p < .05$.

* Statistically significant at $p < .10$.

DFFITS values that exceeded the size-adjusted cutoff recommended by Belsley, Kuh, and Welsch for identifying influential cases. All but 10 of these cases were small, single-plant firms with fewer than 50 employees.[10] None were unusually efficient or had especially high scores on the work organization factors. It is possible that there are systematic differences in the effects of the predictor variables on unit production hours between the subsample of generally small, single-plant firms and that of all branch plants of multi-unit companies. I therefore ran separate regression models for branch plants of multi-unit enterprises (third column) and for single-plant firms (fourth column), as well as the subsets of cases of high-tech operations involving the use of PA technology within branch plants (fifth column) and single-plant firms (sixth column). The results of Chow tests show that the regression parameters estimated for the sample of single-plant firms are indeed different from those estimated for branch plants.[11]

Discussion of Findings

Group-based participatory structures do not have beneficial effects on productivity for all types of enterprises engaged in the machining process in the MDG sector. Nor are traditional union/seniority-based bureaucratic structures universally inferior to this new form of employee participation. Instead, I find that branch plants derive a significant productivity advantage from a participatory bureaucratic structure that is not generally available to small, single-plant firms that emulate this participatory bureaucracy form of organization. In contrast, a small firm that has rationalized the structure of production jobs with internal promotion ladders associated with union work rules and a seniority system gains a significant productivity advantage that is not apparent among branch plants. Moreover, for all subsamples, reliance on a traditional craft apprenticeship form of work organization is consistently associated with *less* productive machining operations, on average. Some additional (unknown and unmeasured) aspect of product quality differences related to an organization's tendency to rely on a craft form of work organization may be responsible for this unexpected result.[12] In addition,

---

[10] The average single-plant firm employed only 22 workers in 1991. By contrast, the average branch plant of a multi-unit company employed 461 workers.

[11] F-value = 2.04, d.f.$_{20,1259}$, is statistically significant at $p < .01$.

[12] This seems an especially plausible explanation, since the scores on the traditional *craft* factor scale are positively and significantly correlated with the available indicators of product quality: *geometric complexity* (.13), *precision standards* (.10), and *specialty materials costs* (.17).

aspects of the technology and production operations strategy of an enterprise consistently contribute to the efficiency with which machining operations are performed. For both single-plant firms and branch plants, the use of PA technology provides a substantial savings in the hours required to produce a machined product. And for both types of plants, product-specific learning effects are associated with the frequency of repeated batches. For all single-plant firms and the high-tech operations in branch plants, no productivity improvements are associated with differences among establishments in the wages or educational requirements of the machining workforce.[13]

When branch plants are compared with single-plant firms, some key differences in the effects of different bureaucratic forms on performance are evident. Among branch plants, those with high scores on the *participatory bureaucracy* factor are substantially more efficient, independent of the technology and operations strategy of the enterprise. For single-plant firms, in contrast, there is no overall productivity advantage from increasing the types of formal group-based participatory structures. Only with the use of PA technology (sixth column) do small firms derive significant benefit from group-based participatory structures.[14] Surprisingly, I find that the *union/seniority-based* factor provides no significant productivity advantage for branch plants in 1991, but that combination appears to be beneficial for single-plant firms.[15] Among large enterprises,

---

[13] Wages are correlated with higher demands for product quality: *geometric complexity* (.22), *precision standards* (.10), and *specialty materials costs* (.21). Among branch plants, I find higher wages to be associated with significantly longer hours per unit of output. This unexpected result may reflect the greater willingness of large employers with unusual requirements to pay a premium to workers to ensure conformance to higher-quality standards.

[14] Tests for a synergistic interaction between work organization factors and the use of PA technology confirm that there is a significant interaction effect between the deployment of PA and the *participatory bureaucracy* factor, but this effect is evident only among single-plant firms.

[15] This result for the 1991 sample is in sharp contrast to the findings from an analysis on earlier data from the same sample. I estimated separate regression models on the 1987 sample and the 1991 sample using only two features of the organization of work that were available from both waves of the survey: the presence/absence of a union and the presence/absence of joint labor–management problem-solving committees. For all other variables, the specification was the same as shown in the second column of Table 4.5. Among branch plants in 1987, unionized plants were significantly *more* efficient than non-union plants, and plants that relied on LMCs were significantly *less* efficient, on average. When the same specification is applied to the 1991 data, I find that LMCs provide a significant productivity advantage, but no independent effect associated with unionization for branch plants. By 1991, it is no longer possible to separate out a union effect from the influence of collaborative problem-solving through LMCs in unionized workplaces, for two reasons. The incidence of unionization has declined between the two

at least, group-based participatory structures are emerging as a superior form, whereas rationalization of internal promotion ladders and union work rules provides a productivity advantage over the ad hoc structures that predominate among small firms.

The introduction of PA technology is accompanied by changes in the skill structure of machining jobs. Compared with workplaces that employ a more specialized division of programming labor, an organization that relies on a high percentage of operator programming allows a greater proportion of its machining workforce autonomy in carrying out new skill-enhancing tasks. A flattening of the occupational hierarchy and a more dispersed distribution of control over the use of the new technology are also a consequence of a high dependence on operator programming. I find that a significant productivity advantage is gained from operator programming for high-tech branch plants that is not apparent among single-plant firms.[16] For large organizations with high technical flexibility requirements, not only does a more dispersed distribution of control over programming flatten the occupational hierarchy, but, as expected, it also contributes to providing the enterprise a productivity advantage in the form of an overall reduction in machining production hours per unit of output.

Conclusions

In this chapter, I have argued that a number of group-based employee participation mechanisms are being combined in a new organizational form, the participatory bureaucracy, that may provide a better "fit" with industrial environments in which collaborative ties among enterprises belonging to the same production network are important for innovation and the achievement of system-wide productivity advantages. I have shown that establishments relying on group-based participatory mechanisms tend to retain some of the features associated with bureaucratic organizations. Moreover, enterprises with closer collaborative ties to important customers are more inclined to exhibit highly participatory bureaucratic structures, suggesting that this form of work organization

periods, and too few unionized branch plants adhere strictly to the traditional model. Fully 87.9 percent of unionized branch plants have LMCs in 1991, whereas only 70 percent of unionized branch plants had such committees in 1987. There was no change in the overall incidence of LMCs among the sample plants between 1987 and 1991. Note that the other group-based participative practices, such as workers meeting by themselves and profit-sharing plans, are not strongly associated with unionization. For single-plant firms, I find no significant effects on machining performance related to LMCs or unionization per se for either period.

[16] A one-tailed t-test just fails a significance test at the threshold level $p < .10$.

may be particularly useful in addressing the difficulties arising from closer coordination of an enterprise's operations with those of its customer.

Large, complex (multi-location) organizations are far more likely than small, single-plant firms to rely on formal participatory structures. The high incidence of these practices among large enterprises is accompanied by a high degree of reliance on such traditional means of bureaucratic control as occupational specialization and standardization. Employee participation in one domain – through group-based problem-solving, stock ownership, and so on – does not necessarily imply a flattening of hierarchy and a devolution of decision-making responsibility to the individual worker in the domain of technology. Indeed, among branch plants, the *participatory bureaucracy* factor is *inversely* correlated with *percentage operator programming* (–.32). Large employers tend to rely on a high degree of involvement of workers in formal group-based participatory structures, whereas they tend to rely more on traditional bureaucratic structures (through occupational specialization) for maintaining centralized control over such core tasks as programming in new technical systems.

Although new forms of group-based participation are widely diffused in the MDG sector, they do not provide productivity advantages for all types of enterprises that have adopted them. Among the branch plants of large companies, I find a consistent pattern showing that reliance on multiple participatory structures leads to a reduction in the per unit machined production hours, independent of the type of technology used. For single-plant firms, the circumstances in which these mechanisms provide a similar performance advantage are limited to high-tech operations, where programmable machines are employed. For small enterprises, it appears that group-based participatory structures facilitate the adaptation of traditional authority relations and organizational routines necessary to reap additional productivity advantages from the new technology.

The failure of low-tech single-plant enterprises to gain a productivity advantage from participatory structures may arise from a number of sources. Changes in organizational routines and the behavior of more cohesive work groups, rather than the participatory process itself, are presumably the main source of the productivity gains enjoyed by more technically sophisticated small firms. Participatory structures that do not involve such changes are not likely to yield much productivity improvement. Small, low-tech firms may simply be poor imitators, adopting employee involvement programs but not using them very effectively. Another explanation is that employee participation is *complementary* to the use of information technology, augmenting the productivity benefits from programmable machines but providing little advantage to small firms that do not use the new technology. This effect may be more pronounced for smaller enterprises because of their relatively simple intra-organizational coordination problems. It is not evident among large enterprises, perhaps because the multiple purposes for which participatory structures are employed – for example, as a means of coordinating groups in complex production systems and as a substitute for collective bargaining negotiations about changes in work rules – confound these effects and reduce the synergy between the new technology and participatory structures.

Instead of proving to be dinosaurs, large, bureaucratically structured organizations are demonstrating a capacity for adaptation and change, employing group-based participatory structures along with standardization to achieve new productivity advantages. Moreover, the branch plant operations of organizations continue to be able to exploit economies of scale, as evidenced by the productivity advantages from specialization in large-batch production and from the size of their machining operations.

REFERENCES

Adler, Paul S. 1993. "The New 'Learning Bureaucracy': New United Motor Manufacturing, Inc." In *Research in Organizational Behavior*, edited by Barry Staw and L. L. Cummings, pp. 111–194. Greenwich, CT: JAI Press.

Althauser, Robert P., and Arne L. Kalleberg. 1981. "Firms, Occupations, and the Structure of Labor Markets: A Conceptual Analysis." In *Sociological Perspectives on Labor Markets*, edited by Ivar Berg, pp. 119–149. New York: Academic Press.

Appelbaum, Eileen, and Rosemary Batt. 1994. *The New American Workplace: Transformation of Work Systems in the United States.* New York: ILR Press.

Arthur, Jeffrey. 1994. "The Effects of Human Resource Systems on Manufacturing Performance and Turnover." *Academy of Management Journal* 37(3): 670–687.

Ayres, Robert U., and Steven M. Miller. 1983. *Robotics: Applications and Social Implications.* Cambridge, MA: Ballinger.

Belsley, David A., Edwin Kuh, and Roy E. Welsch. 1980. *Regression Diagnostics: Identifying Influential Data and Sources of Collinearity.* New York: Wiley.

Carroll, Glenn R., and Michael T. Hannan. 1995. *Organizations in Industry: Strategy, Structure and Selection.* New York: Oxford University Press.

Crozier, Michel. 1964. *The Bureaucratic Phenomenon.* Chicago: University of Chicago Press.

Dewar, Robert D., and Jane E. Dutton. 1986. "The Adoption of Radical and Incremental Innovations: An Empirical Analysis." *Management Science* 32 (November) 11:1422–1433.

DiMaggio, Paul J., and Walter W. Powell. 1983. "The Iron Cage Revisited: Institutional Isomorphism and Collective Rationality in Organizational Fields." *American Sociological Review* 48:147–160.

Doeringer, Peter B., and Michael J. Piore. 1971. *Internal Labor Markets and Manpower Analysis.* Lexington, MA: Heath.

Edwards, Richard. 1979. *Contested Terrain: The Transformation of the Workplace in the Twentieth Century.* New York: BasicBooks.

Griliches, Zvi. 1990. "Hedonic Price Indexes and the Measurement of Capital and Productivity." In *Fifty Years of Economic Measurement: The Jubilee of the Conference on Research in Income and Wealth,* edited by Ernest R. Berndt and Jack E. Triplett, pp. 185–202. Chicago: University of Chicago; Cambridge, MA: National Bureau of Economic Research.

Hackman, J. Richard, and Ruth Wageman. 1995. "Total Quality Management: Empirical, Conceptual, and Practical Issues." *Administrative Science Quarterly* 40(2):309–342.

Harrigan, Kathryn R. 1988. "Joint Ventures and Competitive Strategy." *Strategic Management Journal* 9:141–158.

Harrison, Bennett, and Maryellen R. Kelley. 1993. "Outsourcing and the Search for Flexibility: The Morphology of 'Contracting Out' in U.S. Manufacturing." *Work, Employment, and Society* 7(June):213–235.

Ichniowski, Casey, Kathryn Shaw, and Giovanna Prennushi. 1995. "The Effects of Human Resource Management Practices on Productivity in the Steel Industry." Working Paper No. 5333. Cambridge, MA: National Bureau of Economic Research.

Kelley, Maryellen R. 1994. "Information Technology and Productivity: The Elusive Connection." *Management Science* 40(November)11:1406–1425.

—1995. "Methodological Issues in Panel Surveys of Organizations." Proceedings of the 47th Annual Meeting, Industrial Relations Research Association, Madison, WI, pp. 142–151.

Kelley, Maryellen R., and Bennett Harrison. 1992. "Unions, Technology, and Labor–Management Cooperation." In *Unions and Economic Competitiveness,* edited by Lawrence Mishel and Paula B. Voos, pp. 247–286. Washington, DC: Economic Policy Institute.

Kern, Horst, and Michael Schumann. 1984. *Das Ende der Arbeitseilung? Rationalisierung in der industriellen Produktion.* Munich: Beck.

Kokoski, Mary F. 1993. "Quality Adjustment of Price Indexes." *Monthly Labor Review* 116(12):34–46.

Kruse, Douglas L. 1993. *Profit Sharing: Does It Make a Difference?* Kalamazoo, MI: W. E. Upjohn Institute.

Levine, David I. 1995. *Reinventing the Workplace: How Business and Employees Can Both Win.* Washington, DC: Brookings Institution.

MacDuffie, John P. 1995. "Human Resource Bundles and Manufacturing Performance: Organizational Logic and Flexible Production Systems in the World Auto Industry." *Industrial and Labor Relations Review* (48):197–221.

Mowery, David C. 1988. *International Collaborative Ventures in U.S. Manufacturing.* Cambridge, MA: Ballinger.

110 Maryellen R. Kelley

Osterman, Paul. 1994. "How Common Is Workplace Transformation and Can We Explain Who Adopts It?" *Industrial and Labor Relations Review* (47):173–188.
Piore, Michael J., and Charles Sabel. 1984. *The Second Industrial Divide: Possibilities for Prosperity*. New York: BasicBooks.
Tjosvold, Dean. 1986. *Working Together to Get Things Done: Managing for Organizational Performance*. Lexington, MA: Lexington Books.
Xue, Lan. 1991. "Technology Choice and Manufacturing Performance: An Empirical Analysis of the Implementation of Computer Integrated Manufacturing Technologies." Ph.D. dissertation, Carnegie Mellon University.

CHAPTER 5

Methodological Issues in Cross-sectional and Panel Estimates of the Link between Human Resource Strategies and Firm Performance

Mark A. Huselid and Brian E. Becker

In this chapter, we investigate several methodological challenges inherent in survey-based analyses of the impact of high-performance work systems on firm performance.[1] Drawing on a national panel survey of organizational human resource (HR) management systems, we compare the estimated relationship between HR strategy and firm performance in both cross-sectional and longitudinal data sets. Prior research relying on multifirm data sets has typically relied on cross-sectional estimates that are potentially subject to problems of unobserved firm-level characteristics, such as the quality of marketing or manufacturing strategies, that might bias the estimated HR strategy–firm performance relationship. While panel data can mitigate such heterogeneity bias, such data are even more sensitive to the attenuating effects of error in the measurement of HR management practices. Thus the main objective of this chapter is to provide direct estimates of the likely magnitude of both het-

This chapter is a slightly revised version of an article that originally appeared in *Industrial Relations* 35:3 (1996); reprinted by permission of Blackwell Publishers.

This study was partially funded by the Human Resource Planning Society, the Society for Human Resource Management (SHRM) Foundation, the School of Management and Labor Relations at Rutgers University, and the SUNY–Buffalo School of Management. The interpretations, conclusions, and recommendations, however, are ours and do not necessarily represent the positions of these organizations.

We are grateful to Randall Schuler and seminar participants at MIT for their helpful comments on an earlier version of this chapter.

[1] Here the term "high-performance work systems" refers to the full range of HR management practices that enhance both employee and firm performance (Huselid, 1995). High-performance work practices include, but are not limited to, policies that facilitate employee involvement.

111

erogeneity bias and measurement error in cross-sectional estimates of the HR strategy–firm performance relationship.

The potential strategic impact of high-performance work systems is consistent with a new focus in the literature on *behavioral* strategies that rely on core competencies and capabilities as sources of competitive advantage, not only because they provide the most effective response to market demands, but also because they are not easily copied by competitors (Prahalad & Hamel, 1990; Stalk, Evans, & Shulman, 1992). A key element in the implementation of such strategies is the extent to which a firm's HR strategy, as reflected in the adoption of a high-performance work system, supports these larger strategic objectives (Huselid, 1995). As a result, the potential economic significance of firm HR management practices has increased substantially in this new role. In fact, the central thesis of this chapter is that a firm's HR strategy has a *strategic* impact that is reflected in organizational performance.

Our measure of HR strategy is based on prior work by Delaney, Lewin, and Ichniowski (1989) and Huselid (1995). In both cases the measure of HR strategy focused on the adoption of progressive or high-performance work practices. While the literature emphasizing the importance of fit between HR and corporate strategies (Baird & Meshoulam, 1988; Milgrom & Roberts, 1995) might suggest that there is no true continuum of "best practices" in this area, since the choice of HR strategy would be contingent on the larger corporate strategy, Delaney (1996), Delaney et al. (1989), Ichniowski (1990), MacDuffie (1995), and Pfeffer (1994) have focused more attention on a "best practice" approach. Our feeling is that such a distinction is largely overdrawn, since one of the common themes in these "best practices" is the importance of a skilled, flexible, and motivated workforce, and it is precisely this type of workforce that will enable a firm to "fit" its HR strategy to changing firm strategies in an effective and timely fashion (Huselid, 1995; Huselid & Becker, 1995). Though our approach is more consistent with the "core" or "best practice" hypothesis, this study does not directly test these two competing conceptual frameworks.

Our results indicate that both heterogeneity bias and measurement error may have a strong, but largely offsetting effect on cross-sectional estimates of the HR management–firm performance relationship. The net effects, based on a very conservative estimation procedure, suggest that a one-standard-deviation "improvement" in a firm's HR strategy is associated with a present value gain in cash flow and firm market value of $15,000 to $17,000 per employee. Finally, we provide an indirect test of the potential for an implementation-to-benefit lag in the returns for investments in such systems, and present results consistent with the expectation that high-performance work systems begin to provide returns that are reflected in firm profitability and market value one to two years after implementation.

Estimation Problems

The three prior studies (Huselid, 1995; Huselid & Becker, 1995; Ichniowski, 1990) that have examined both a broad measure of HR strategy and corporate financial performance have relied on cross-sectional data, as, we believe, will much of the future work in this area. One objective of this chapter is to provide a validity check on such an approach by specifically attempting to measure the magnitude of two potential biases, heterogeneity bias and measurement error, in these estimates. Consider the two-variable case based on pooled cross-sectional data (Hsiao, 1988), where β_{OLS} is the estimated effect of x_{it} (HR strategy) on firm performance in the single-equation model

$$\text{Firm performance}_{it} = \beta_{OLS} x_{it} + u_{it}, \tag{1}$$

for i cross-sectional units over t time periods, where $u_{it} = \alpha_i + e_{it}$. While e_{it} is the conventional random error term, α_i is an unmeasured firm-specific constant that varies across firms. In addition, rather than being an entirely accurate measure of HR strategy (x_{it}^*), x_{it} is subject to random measurement error such that

$$x_{it} = x_{it}^* + v_{it}. \tag{2}$$

Therefore, OLS cross-sectional models are subject to two types of bias, where

$$\text{plim}\,\hat{\beta}_{OLS} = \beta + \frac{\text{Cov}(x_{it}, \alpha_i)}{\sigma_x^2 + \sigma_v^2} - \frac{\beta\sigma_v^2}{\sigma_x^2 + \sigma_v^2} \tag{3}$$

and β is the true estimate of the effects of HR strategy. The second term on the right-hand side of the equation represents the correlation between the unmeasured firm effects (α_i) and x_{it}, in this case HR strategy. The typical concern in this literature is that unmeasured firm effects are *positively* correlated with HR strategy because the adoption of such practices is either contingent upon firm success or simply a reflection of firms that are more effectively managed across all functions. The effect of this term is to bias β_{OLS} upwardly. A less commonly mentioned, though not implausible, scenario would have the least profitable and most desperate firms turning to these policies as a solution to their predicament. In this case, the effect of the second term is to bias β_{OLS} *downwardly*. The third term on the right-hand side reflects the effects of measurement error in x_{it}, which serves to bias the OLS estimates toward zero. The problem is that while panel data offer an opportunity to mitigate the heterogeneity bias in the OLS estimates, this approach may exacerbate the effects of measurement error.

Heterogeneity Bias

The heavy reliance on cross-sectional data in this line of research inevitably raises a concern that any HR strategy–firm performance relationship reflects heterogeneity bias rather than substantive effects. This is a particularly important issue when researchers are attempting to isolate the effects of a particular set of organizational practices, since there is considerable evidence in the business press that firm reputations for a wide range of management practices are highly correlated. Whether these intercorrelations are genuine or merely reflect halo error on the part of outside observers is difficult to determine (Brown & Perry, 1994). Nevertheless, it is certainly plausible that if the adoption of a high-performance work system is a sign of good management, then implementing such practices would not be the only stroke of wisdom. Unfortunately, access to measures of these other management practices is very limited, and they are therefore difficult to control for statistically.

The existence of unmeasured management practices that are both positively correlated with the presence of a high-performance work system and firm performance means that cross-sectional estimates of the HR strategy–firm performance relationship would be overstated. However, to the extent that the simultaneous occurrence of these practices is merely associational rather than causal, panel data offer an opportunity for a cleaner estimate of the true effects of HR strategies.

The "associational" explanation is particularly plausible for the wide range of functional strategies, such as those in marketing and finance, that are likely to be developed independently of an HR strategy. Consider the example of a company that does many things well and has achieved an equilibrium position of excellence, but does not necessarily change all of its management practices at the same time in some overarching strategy. In such a company we could expect to observe changes in HR strategies over time without corresponding changes in other functional strategies. The positive association of these strategies would then be much stronger across firms at a point in time than within firms across time. When this is the case, the effects of HR strategy on firm performance can be separated from the effects of other functional strategies using panel data. Specifically, we will rely on the familiar fixed-effects model with constant slopes and intercepts that vary across firms (Hsiao, 1988). This least squares dummy variable model estimates the effects of HR strategies on firm performance from within-firm variation compared with cross-sectional estimates that can reflect both within- and between-firm variation in HR strategies and firm performance.

Measurement Error

The benefits of panel data sets come at a price, however. The risk is that panel estimates may be subject to even *greater* attenuation from measurement error than are cross-sectional estimates and that one is actually worse off using the panel estimates (Hsiao, 1988: p. 63). For example, one can eliminate individual effects (α_i) when there are two periods of data by transforming the data into first differences. In this specification the probability limit of the first-difference estimator β_{fdif} is (Hsiao, 1988: p. 64)

$$\text{plim}\,\hat{\beta}_{fdif} = \beta - \frac{\beta\sigma_v^2}{[(1-\rho_x)/(1-\rho_v)]\sigma_x^2 + \sigma_v^2}, \qquad (4)$$

where ρ_x and ρ_v are the first-order serial correlations for the independent variable and measurement error, respectively. Compared with the measurement error bias in a single cross-sectional OLS estimate, all that is required for measurement error to have a relatively greater attenuating effect on the first–difference estimator is for the serial correlation of true values of x to exceed the serial correlation of the measurement error (e.g., $\rho_x > \rho_v$). Since we would normally expect v to be nearly random, ρ_v should be very close to zero. Even assuming $\rho_v = .1$ and $\rho_x = .7$, the relative impact of true variance in our HR systems measure is diminished by two-thirds. In effect, the noise-to-signal ratio may be increased substantially in the panel estimate. Alternatively, ρ_v might be expected to increase when the same respondent provided the ratings at two points in time.[2]

Measurement error in the independent variables of interest is ubiquitous in economic and organizational research. Typically, either it is ignored or the researcher is able to make a reasonable assumption that

---

[2] For 171 of the 218 panel respondents in our data set, the survey was mailed to (and, presumably, usually completed by) the same individual in both periods. The simple correlation of our HR strategy measure at two points in time is .50 for the "same" respondents and .45 for "different" respondents. While there are a variety of reasons why these two estimates might differ (most notably, greater changes in the HR management system associated with a change in leadership of this function), the difference is not so large as to suggest that ρ_v is overwhelmingly greater for the "same" respondents.

relative to the total variance of the measure, the impact of measurement error is modest. This would be particularly true in cross-sectional estimates that are otherwise economically and statistically significant. The tendency to ignore the problem is reinforced by the fact that even when measurement error is suspected to be a non-trivial presence, the researcher typically has few solutions available. Econometricians have developed methods for indirectly estimating the magnitude of measurement error (e.g., Griliches & Hausman, 1986; Hsiao, 1988; Hsiao & Taylor, 1991) that exploit the variety of data structures and error structures available in a panel data set. While several of these methods provide estimates of both β and σ_v^2, they require more than the two periods of data available in our sample.

Measures and Methods

Our analyses are designed to assess the validity of previously reported cross-sectional estimates of the HR strategy–firm performance relationship and focus specifically on the results reported in Huselid (1995). The original cross-sectional analysis from the 1991 survey reported in Huselid (1995) includes 826 observations. Our panel replication has only 218 respondents with complete data in both years (1991 and 1993). As a result, the difference in results might be partly attributable to sample differences, apart from any heterogeneity bias. Therefore, we provide four points of comparison:

- 1991 cross-sectional results ($n = 826$)
- 1991 cross-sectional results, panel subsample ($n = 218$)
- 1991–1993 panel results ($n = 218$ per year, or $n = 436$)
- 1993 cross-sectional results, panel subsample ($n = 218$).

Next we evaluate the extent of bias in the panel results attributable to measurement error in our measure of HR strategy. Drawing on well-developed correction formulas (Griliches & Hausman, 1986; Hsiao, 1988) and estimates of measurement error based on independent psychometric analysis of the HR strategy measures, we derive a range of corrected estimates for both the effects and statistical significance of those corrected coefficients.

The Estimation Model

There is a well-developed empirical literature focusing on the determinants of firm performance, using both capital-market- and accounting-based measures of profitability (Brainard, Shoven, & Weiss, 1980; Hirsch, 1991; Hirschey & Wichern, 1984; Weiss, 1974). We draw on conventional econometric specifications from this literature as the basis for our estimation model. Measures of firm performance typically focus on market-based measures, such as Tobin's q, or accounting-based measures, like return on equity. The former, which compares the capital market's valuation of the future cash flows associated with a firm's asset base with the replacement cost of those assets, is a forward-looking risk-adjusted measure of a firm's financial performance. Following Hirsch (1991), we specify a model of firm performance by focusing on the firm and industry variables that are likely to contribute to sustained competitive advantage. These include firm investments in physical (plant and equipment), intangible (R&D), and human assets (employment), as well as recent sales growth.[3]

The focus of this chapter is not a completely specified model of firm performance. Our goal is to develop a sufficiently specified model such that the estimated effects of HR strategy on firm performance are unbiased. The limited econometric studies that include both broad measures of HR strategy and firm performance for a large sample of firms in part reflect the challenges of data collection in this area of research. Our analyses draw on a unique panel data set on the subject. While these data are not without their limitations, they provide a unique opportunity to test the validity of prior cross-sectional work by drawing on the methodological advantages of panel data.

Following Huselid (1995), we estimate a model of firm performance such that

$$\text{Firm performance} = f(\text{HR strategy}_{it}, \text{firm employment}_{it},$$
$$\text{capital intensity}_{it}, \text{unionization}_{it},$$
$$\text{sales growth}_{it}, \text{R\&D intensity}_{it}), \qquad (5)$$

where the observations are described for the ith firm in period t. The exact definition, source, and descriptive statistics for each variable identified in Equation 5 are included in Table 5.1.

---

[3] Typically, these models might also include firm and industry characteristics, such as firm-specific risk, industry unionism, and industry market concentration. These variables were included in Huselid (1995) and had only minor effects on the HR strategy estimates. We have not included them in the panel, because they were not available for the latter years at the time of the analysis. However, the second and third columns of Table 5.5, which report the 1991 cross-sectional results with and without these additional controls, demonstrate that such an omission has no significant effects on the magnitude of our estimates.

Table 5.1. *Variable Definitions, Sources, and Descriptive Statistics* (N = 436)

Variable	Definition and Source	Mean (S.D.)
Employee Skills and Organizational Structures	Mean of standardized survey items	0.082 (0.480)
Employee Motivation	Mean of standardized survey items	−0.019 (0.731)
Tobin's q	Natural log of market value of common and preferred stock for ith firm divided by the book value of net property, plant, and equipment (see Hirsch, 1991); *Compact Disclosure*	0.578 (1.047)
Gross rate of return on assets (GRATE)	Cash flow divided by gross capital stock (see Hirsch, 1991); *Compact Disclosure*	0.078 (0.163)
Total employment	Log of total employment; survey item	11.988 (0.776)
Capital intensity	Log of property, plant, and equipment divided by total employment; *Compact Disclosure*	4.132 (1.309)
Union coverage	Proportion of non-exempt employees belonging to a union; survey item	12.970 (25.146)
R&D/sales	Log of research and development expenditures divided by annual sales; *Compact Disclosure*	0.020 (0.038)
Growth in sales	(Sales$_{t-1}$ − sales$_{t-5}$)/sales$_{t-5}$; *Compact Disclosure*	0.592 (1.143)

1991 and 1993 Values for Tobin's q, GRATE, and HR Variables ($n = 218$)

Employee Skills and Organizational Structures, 1991	Mean of standardized 1991 survey items	.0557 (.4643)
Employee Motivation, 1991	Mean of standardized 1991 survey items	−.0476 (.7395)
Employee Skills and Organizational Structures, 1993	Mean of standardized 1993 survey items	.1087 (.4951)
Employee Motivation, 1993	Mean of standardized 1993 survey items	.0099 (.7228)
Tobin's q, 1991	Natural log of market value of common and preferred stock for *i*th firm divided by the book value of net property, plant, and equipment	.591 (1.07)
Tobin's q, 1993	Natural log of market value of common and preferred stock for *i*th firm divided by the book value of net property, plant, and equipment	.566 (1.02)
GRATE, 1991	Cash flow divided by gross capital stock	.0859 (.177)
GRATE, 1993	Cash flow divided by gross capital stock	.0701 (.147)

Measures of HR Strategy and Firm Performance

Our measure of HR strategy is based on survey questionnaire data that focus on organizational HR management practices in 1991 and 1993. The items we adopt are broadly representative of the high-performance work practices described elsewhere (Levine, 1995; Pfeffer, 1994; U.S. Department of Labor, 1993). Huselid (1995) factor-analyzed 13 items in an effort to identify separate dimensions of HR strategies that might be consistent across firms. By means of principal-components extraction with varimax rotation, two factors consisting of eight and three items, respectively, were identified. Scales were constructed for each factor by averaging those questions loading unambiguously on each respective factor. All 13 questions and their respective factor loadings are reported in Table 5.2. The validation of this scale is described in Huselid (1995).

Following Huselid (1995), we refer to these factors as *Employee Skills and Organizational Structures* and *Employee Motivation*. An "employee skills and organizational structures" strategy focuses on the development of organizational capabilities both through employee skill development and the provision of organizational structures that allow skilled and motivated employees to contribute directly to the performance of the firm. An "employee motivation" strategy emphasizes the formalization of pay–performance links and a merit-based philosophy in the organization. Although Huselid (1995) shows these scales to have acceptable convergent validity, the modest levels of reliability associated with each suggest that the development of improved measures of HR strategy should be a high priority.

Two dependent variables, Tobin's q and gross rate of return on assets (GRATE), were constructed to reflect capital market evaluations of firm performance as well as current accounting profits, respectively. Following Hirsch (1991), Tobin's q is defined as the natural log of the ratio of a firm's market value to the replacement cost of its tangible assets. In principle, a firm's market value is the sum of the market value of both equity and debt. In practice, the market value of debt and replacement value of assets are typically proxied with their book values (Hirsch, 1991). We consider q a measurement of management "value added," since it represents the premium the capital market will pay for a given portfolio of assets. If two firms have the same asset base, ceteris paribus, a higher Tobin's q for one of the firms would represent higher future income prospects for that firm. Clearly, the strategic impact of HR is on the market value of equity rather than on the value of debt, and is therefore the focus of our analyses. Reflecting this focus, Huselid (1995) restricted the numerator in his measure of q to the market value of

Table 5.2. *Questionnaire Items and Factor Structure for HR Strategy Measures in 1991 (N = 826)*

Questionnaire Item	Factor 1	Factor 2
Employee Skills and Organizational Structures, α = .67 What proportion of the workforce is included in a formal information-sharing program (e.g., a newsletter)?	.54	.02
What proportion of the workforce holds jobs that have been included in a formal job analysis?	.53	.18
What proportion of the workforce is regularly administered attitude surveys?	.52	−.07
What proportion of the workforce participates in quality of work life (QWL), quality circles (QC), and/or labor–management participation programs?	.50	−.04
What proportion of the workforce is *eligible* for company incentive plans, profit-sharing plans, and/or gain-sharing plans?	.39	.17
How many hours of training per year are typically received by an experienced employee (i.e., someone employed more than one year)?	.37	−.07
Employee Motivation, α = .66 What proportion of the workforce has merit increases or other incentive pay determined by a performance appraisal?	.17	.83
What proportion of the workforce receives formal performance appraisals?	.29	.80
What proportion of the workforce is promoted *primarily* on the basis of merit (as opposed to seniority)?	−.07	.56
Items not loading unambiguously on either factor What proportion of non-entry-level jobs have been filled from within in recent (i.e., over the past five) years?	.52	−.36
What proportion of the workforce has access to a formal grievance procedure and/or complaint resolution system?	.36	.13
What proportion of the workforce is administered an aptitude, skill, or work-sample test before employment?	.32	−.04
Among the five positions for which your firm hires most frequently, how many qualified applicants do you have per position (on average)?	−.15	.27

Source: Huselid (1995), Table 1.

Table 5.3. *Replication of Results with* q_{debt} *as the Dependent Variable*

	Table 5.6		Table 5.7	Table 5.8	
Variable	1991	1993	Fixed Effects	β_{fdif} without Controls	β_{fdif} with Controls
HRTOTAL	.1441***	.1268***	.0436	.0266	.0519
	(.0714)	(.0500)	(.0552)	(.0554)	(.0551)

Note: In our analyses we report results using a measure of Tobin's q that does not include a measure of debt in the numerator. The purpose here is to report results from similar analyses that include the book value of long-term debt in the numerator of the q variable (q_{debt}). As we indicate in the text, the estimates for the HRTOTAL variable are equivalent in both specifications. Standard errors are in parentheses.
*** Significant at <.01 level (one-tailed test).

equity as well. We have used both measures in this analysis with equivalent results (Table 5.3).

GRATE divides *current* cash flows by gross capital stock and is superior to traditional return on assets or equity measures of accounting profits because it is less subject to influence by depreciation and other non-cash transactions (Brainard et al., 1980). We include this measure of accounting profits to be consistent with prior work but consider it of secondary importance. The theoretical rationale for a strategic impact by the HR management system derives from its potential creation of sustained competitive advantage. While higher accounting profits are consistent with such an effect, we believe the more direct measure is change in the firm's market value of equity.

Sample

The data for this study are taken from a survey questionnaire mailed to 3,477 firms in 1992 and 3,847 firms in 1994. In both surveys respondents were asked to describe organizational practices employed during the preceding calendar year (1991 and 1993, respectively). The initial survey in 1992 was based on a potential population of the nearly 12,000 publicly held firms listed on U.S. stock exchanges available in *Compact Disclosure*, a commercially available database containing annual 10-K reports. This larger set was reduced by excluding firms with less than 100 employees, foreign-controlled firms, holding companies, or publicly held divisions or business units of a larger firm. The result was a sampling frame of 3,477 firms representing a broad cross section of U.S. industries. Following extensive pre-testing and pilot mailings, the survey was mailed to individuals whose name, position, and address had been verified by telephone. The result was 968 usable responses, or an overall response rate of 28 percent. In 1994, using an identical sampling method and a similar questionnaire, we surveyed 3,847 firms. We received 740 responses in the 1994 survey, for an overall response rate of 20 percent. A total of 294 firms responded to *both* surveys. Missing financial performance data in one or both years, frequently market value, reduced the sample to the 218 firms that are the basis for this study.

One of the principal challenges inherent in this line of research is the problem of low survey response rates. Response rates in the 20 to 30 percent range raise genuine questions about response bias, particularly in the panel of joint respondents, which is less than 10 percent of the population in any one year. Industry distributions of the sampling frame and respondents are similar in both years, with respondents slightly over-represented in manufacturing. Similarly, a comparison of the panel sample means with the full sample in each respective year for q, GRATE, and the two HR measures indicates only two differences that are statistically significant. In 1991 the panel value for GRATE (.085) is higher than the full sample value (.055), and the 1993 panel value for *Employee Skills and Organizational Structures* (.108) is higher than the full sample value (–.002).

Even a comparison of population and sample means would not directly address the potential level of response or selectivity bias. The concern is not that the mean values of two variables may differ in the sample and population, but that the conditional means (i.e., those corrected for all relevant controls) are different. Our only estimate of response bias on this dimension is an evaluation of the 1991 survey data (Huselid, 1995) using the familiar Heckman (1979) approach, which generates an inverse Mills ratio that is included in subsequent regressions as a control. The estimates for the effects of HR strategy on firm performance were very similar with and without such controls. Later in the chapter we replicate the 1991 cross-sectional models from Huselid (1995) based on the 218 panel respondents from 1991. Only the coefficient on *Employee Motivation* in the q model, which falls by nearly 50 percent, is meaningfully different in the two samples. We have spoken with a number of potential respondents throughout the survey process and on occasion have discussed the study with members of the HR community. Our impression is that most firms that do not respond have a blanket policy of not responding to any surveys and/or have workload demands that preclude participation even when they would like to do so. It is anticipated that such policies will make survey research on this topic more difficult in the future.

Results and Discussion

Cross-sectional Comparisons

Comparing the 1991 and 1993 values for the two dimensions of HR strategy (Table 5.1) reveals slightly higher values on both measures in 1993, though the differences are not statistically significant. The sample means on the two dependent variables in the panel samples fall slightly over this period, though once again these differences are not statistically significant. The comparative cross-sectional regressions are reported in Table 5.4. The first and second columns report the effects of the two dimensions of HR strategy and controls (not shown) on both measures of firm performance in the full cross-sectional sample from the 1991 survey, based on Huselid (1995). Three of the four coefficients indicated positive effects on firm performance that were both economically and statistically significant at conventional levels. The third and fourth columns replicate the Huselid (1995) model for the 218 respondents in the panel and provide some sense of the potential response bias in our panel of firms. Only the magnitude of the coefficient on *Employee Motivation* in the q model is different in any meaningful respect, falling by one-half. As already noted, the last two sets of columns report the cross-sectional estimates for the 1991 and 1993 surveys without several of the control variables included in Huselid (1995).

In Huselid (1995), a factor analysis of the characteristics of the firm's HR management system identified two factors, *Employee Motivation* and *Employee Skills and Organizational Structures*. However, while various HR management system characteristics in the sample may load on two different dimensions, it does not necessarily follow that these two dimensions will have different effects on firm performance. There is no theoretical reason why a bundle of staffing-related practices should have a different effect than a bundle of practices that influence employee motivation. Therefore, we made no *a priori* assumptions about the appropriate specification and tested directly whether the HR management system should be specified multidimensionally or unidimensionally. Our results are consistent with a unidimensional approach. A joint F test of the null hypothesis that the coefficients on the two HR management system dimensions were equal could not be rejected. The results of those tests are reported in Table 5.4 along with the effects of a unidimensional measure (HRTOTAL) of the HR management system that is the sum of the two dimensions already described. Given these results, we use the HRTOTAL variable as our measure of the HR management system in the remainder of the analysis. Thus the interpretation is that the effect of a change in the HR system is the same whether it occurs through a unit change in *Employee Motivation* or a unit change in *Employee Skills and Organizational Structure.*

In three of the four cross-sectional models, HR strategy had an economically and statistically significant effect on our measures of firm performance. The *q* results indicate that firms with high-performance work systems have higher ratios of market value to book value. Since *q* is measured in natural logarithms, the effects in Table 5.4 suggest that increasing a firm's usage of high-performance work systems by one standard deviation is associated with an increase in *q* of about 14 percent. For GRATE, the same change in high-performance work systems resulted in a 13 to 28 percent increase in this ratio for the average firm.[4]

Panel Results

The results of the OLS pooled cross-sectional fixed-effects and random-effects models are reported in Table 5.5. HRTOTAL had an economically and statistically significant effect on both dependent variables in the OLS pooled cross-sectional model (first and second columns). However, the fixed-effects results (third and fourth columns) are statistically insignificant and are only 25 to 30 percent as large as the OLS estimates. For both models of firm performance, the Lagrange multiplier test rejects the OLS results in favor of the fixed-effects models. This is equivalent to rejecting the hypothesis that the firm-specific intercepts included in the error term, u_{it}, in Equation 1 are equal across all firms.

We also estimated the HR strategy–firm performance relationship within a random-effects model. A fixed-effects formulation is more appropriate when the inferences will apply only to the cross-sectional units in the sample, while a random-effects approach is more appropriate when the inferences will extend to observations outside the sample (Greene, 1990: p. 486; Hsiao, 1988: p. 43). On that basis, the appropriate model for our analysis is a random-effects model. The effects of HRTOTAL in the random-effects models are approximately 70 percent as large as the OLS results and are statistically significant by conventional standards. Nevertheless, while a random-effects model has the virtue of providing more efficient estimates, it also assumes that the firm-

---

[4] The sample means for GRATE were .085 and .07 in 1991 and 1993, respectively. The coefficients on HRTOTAL were .011 and .019 in those same years.

Table 5.4. Cross-sectional Results for HR Strategy from 1991 (Full Sample), 1991 (Panel Sample), and 1993 (Panel Sample) Surveys

HR Strategy Variable	1991 Cross-sectional Sample[a] (n = 826)		1991 Panel Cross-sectional Sample with AMJ Controls (n = 218)		1991 Panel Cross-sectional Sample (n = 218)		1993 Panel Cross-sectional Sample (n = 218)	
	q	GRATE	q	GRATE	q	GRATE	q	GRATE
Employee Skills and Organizational Structures	.165* (.113)	.043** (.016)	.162 (.154)	.034 (.029)	.152* (.144)	.033 (.028)	.074 (.143)	.032* (.023)
Employee Motivation	.277*** (.091)	−.008 (.013)	.141 (.115)	−.003 (.022)	.142 (.147)	−.002 (.022)	.184** (.109)	.011 (.018)
Adjusted R^2	110	.064	.275	−.003	.279	.022	.233	.043
F	6.483***	3.356**	2.92***	.98	3.27***	1.13	2.78***	1.26

	$F_{1,180} = .0023$ $p = .96$	$F_{1,180} = .904$ $p = .34$	$F_{1,180} = .275$ $p = .60$	$F_{1,180} = .400$ $p = .527$
Joint F test of whether coefficients on *Employee Skills and Organizational Structures* and *Employee Motivation* are equal in the *q* and GRATE models				
Reanalysis of models in the third and fourth sets of columns with *Employee Skills and Organizational Structures* and *Employee Motivation* summed together	.1479** (.0842)	.0113 (.0162)	.1398** (.0700)	.0194** (.0113)
Adjusted R^2	.283	.043	.2363	.0475
F	3.38***	1.27	2.86***	1.29

Note: Unless otherwise noted, model also includes all variables in Equation 1. Standard errors are in parentheses.

[a] From Huselid (1995), Table 5 (Column 9) and Table 6 (Column 13).

* Significant at <.10 level (one-tailed test); ** significant at <.05 level (one-tailed test); *** significant at <.01 level (one-tailed test).

Table 5.5.　*Panel Survey Results, 1991–1993*

HR Strategy Variable	Pooled Data (No Fixed-Effects Controls)		Pooled Data (with Fixed-Effects Controls)		Pooled Data (Random-Effects Model)	
	q	GRATE	q	GRATE	q	GRATE
HRTOTAL	.1826***	.024***	.0529	.0066	.1218***	.0194***
	(.0513)	(.008)	(.0642)	(.0126)	(.0486)	(.0083)
Sample size	436	436	436	436	436	436
Adjusted R^2	.155	.067	.622	.393	.160	.076
F values	14.25***	.079***	4.21***	2.26***	NA	NA
Lagrange multiplier test of fixed effects	—	—	58.07***	13.07***	—	—
Hausman test of fixed- vs. random-effects model	—	—	—	—	18.44***	37.66***

Note: Unless otherwise noted, these models include all control variables described in Equation 1. Unlike the OLS models in Table 5.3, the OLS pooled cross-sectional model does not include a set of industry controls, since this model was the comparison against which the fixed-effects model was tested. Standard errors are in parentheses.
*** Significant at <.01 level (one-tailed test).

specific intercepts are uncorrelated with the regressors (Greene, 1990: p. 495). In effect, there is a trade-off between efficiency and consistency in the random- and fixed-effects models, and this trade-off provides an empirical basis on which to make the decision between them. The Hausman test (1978) provides a method to test whether the bias from the random-effects model exceeds the gain in efficiency. On that basis, the results of the Hausman test reported in Table 5.5 clearly reject the random-effects model in favor of the fixed-effects model.[5]

---

[5] We also evaluated the potential for non-linearities in the panel estimates by transforming HRTOTAL into two spline functions. The first spline, HRLARGE, reflected positive changes in the HR management system in excess of one standard deviation. The second spline, HRSMALL, captured all changes smaller than those included in HRLARGE. For q the coefficients (standard errors) were .079 (.075) and –.159 (.320) for HRSMALL and HRLARGE, respectively. For GRATE the coefficients (standard errors) were .0122

The Role of Measurement Error

If we accept the results of the fixed-effects model in Table 5.4 as appropriately cleansed of heterogeneity bias, we next have to determine the extent to which those panel estimates are attenuated by measurement error in HRTOTAL. Since our data set includes only two periods of data, we must rely on independent estimates of error variance in HRTOTAL (σ_v^2) and solve for β in Equation 4.[6] Unlike the case with conventional economic data sets, we are able to calculate the psychometric characteristics of our measures, including their reliability. We used Cronbach's α as a measure of internal consistency reliability, and specifically as an estimate of the ratio of true variance to total variance in our HR strategy measures (Nunnally & Bernstein, 1994). The more appropriate measures would be test–retest intrarater reliability (e.g., between one manager at two points in time) or interrater reliability (e.g., multiple respondents at the same level). As a measure of intrarater reliability, Cronbach's α is generally an overstatement of interrater reliability because it "assigns specific error (unique to the individual rater) to true (construct) variance" (Schmidt & Hunter, 1995: p. 209).[7] There is little evidence regarding the interrater reliability of measures such as ours because the convention in this literature is to use a single managerial respondent (Arthur, 1992; Cooke, 1992). Other studies have shown that ratings of organizational policies differ by organizational level (Barron & Black, 1996; Eaton, 1994). While multiple respondents are the basis for inter-

---

(.0149) and −.0419 (.063) for HRSMALL and HRLARGE, respectively. While the pattern of results suggests sharply diminishing returns to large changes over this time period, the estimates were not statistically significant either individually or in joint F tests.

[6] Equation 4 is derived from

$$\text{plim}\hat{\beta}_{\text{fdif}} = \beta\left(1 - \frac{2\sigma_v^2}{\text{Var}X_{\text{fdif}}}\right)$$

which is the basis for the following calculations.

[7] We have other evidence on intrarater reliability for our sample, though it is for a very small subsample of our data set. It is the more conventional measure of intrarater reliability, because it takes the form of two measures given to the same individual at two points in time. Another researcher surveyed this same sample six months after our second survey on another subject and asked several questions that we also included, though only in a binary form. The one continuous measure collected in both studies was union coverage. The intrarater reliability for the presence of a union was 1.00 ($n = 15$) (i.e., when both measures were coded as dummies) and .70 for the percentage of the workforce unionized (when both measures were coded as continuous). Given the objective and generally stable nature of this question, these results probably represent an upper bound on intrarater reliability for this sample.

rater reliability, the fact that these respondents were drawn from different levels of the organization make these data less applicable to our analysis.[8]

Cronbach's α for *Employee Motivation* and *Employee Skills and Organizational Structures* is .66 and .67, respectively. Therefore, we evaluated our HRTOTAL results for the range of Cronbach's α from .6 to .7. For such α's, error variance in these measures (σ_v^2) would range from .38 to .28, implying a ratio of error variance to true variance of .42 : .67.[9] While measures containing 30 to 40 percent error variance may seem excessive, they are actually quite modest for panel data. For example, Duncan and Hill (1985: p. 521) report ratios of error to true variance for purportedly objective measures such as hours worked and earnings in the Panel Survey of Income Dynamics in the range of 1.4 to 2.8.

Calculating the corrected estimates in Equation 4 posed several problems. Bivariate regressions based on first-differences were used because the correction formulas for these simple models are much more accessible than the multivariate formulas. However, these simple models are more likely to yield biased estimates because the control variables have been omitted. For both q and GRATE, the HRTOTAL coefficient in this simple model was negatively biased compared with the fully specified model. The bias was so large in the first-difference GRATE model that the bivariate coefficient was slightly negative. Since the direction of the measurement error correction is always away from zero, beginning with a negative estimate that is biased would only further distort the results. Therefore, we report results only for the q models. Estimates of the corrected β's for HRTOTAL as well as corrected standard errors are calculated for two levels of Cronbach's α (Table 5.6).[10]

The results in Table 5.6 indicate that even modest corrections for mea-

---

[8] This is in part a distinction between a particular policy and its implementation. We believe the chief HR officer (CHRO) within each firm is in the best position to describe the combination of both policy and practice. While the CHRO may not be aware of all of the variations in policy implementation throughout the firm, neither is the first-line supervisor likely to be well informed of implementation outside his or her responsibility. The ideal solution, multiple respondents from multiple levels of each organization, was beyond the resources available for this study.

[9] If Cronbach's α is .6, then the variance of the measure is 40% error variance. Since the variance of HRTOTAL is .952, then .38 (.4 × .952) of that variance is due to measurement error. The ratios of error variance to true variance are, as an example, .4/.6 = .67.

[10] The correction for the standard error of a bivariate regression, S_b, is (Greene, 1990: p. 161) $S_b = s/\sqrt{S_{xx}}$, where s is the standard deviation of residuals and $S_{xx} = (N - 1) \times \text{Var} X$. The assumption is that the variance of X includes error variance (σ_v^2) as well as true variance. Our assumption that Cronbach's α is a measure of the percentage of true variance allows us to calculate a "corrected" value for S_{xx}. For example, in Table 5.6 when Cronbach's α is .6 the calculations are as follows:

Table 5.6. *Corrected Estimates of $\beta_{HRTOTAL}$ Based on Equation 4 and Estimates of σ_v^2 Derived from Cronbach's α*

Models and Estimates	Dependent Variable: q (Model estimated without controls)
β_{fdif}	.0252 (.0639)
Assume Cronbach's $\alpha = .6$	
Implied σ_v^2	.380
Estimate of corrected β	.1245*
Estimate of corrected standard error	(.0825)
Assume Cronbach's $\alpha = .7$	
Implied σ_v^2	.285
Estimate of corrected β	.063
Estimate of corrected standard error	(.076)

Note: Standard errors are in parentheses.
*Significant at <.10 level (one-tailed test).

surement error increase the first-difference estimates of HRTOTAL by two to five times their uncorrected magnitudes. If Cronbach α is .6, the corrected estimates are in a range similar to those observed in the cross-sectional estimates and statistically significant at conventional levels. Considering that these adjustments are based on a simple first-difference estimate that appears to be less than half its true value, our summary conclusion is that attenuating effects of measurement error in the panel data are approximately equal to the positive heterogeneity bias.

The Economic Impact

Given the wide range of these potential estimates, it is difficult to provide an accurate evaluation of the economic magnitude of these effects. Nevertheless, given that the discussion of the HR management system has been placed within a strategic perspective, the ultimate test of the strate-

---

Footnote 10 (cont.)

$$\text{Var HRTOTAL}_{fdiff} = .95228$$
$$s = .919$$
$$\sigma_v^2 = .4 \times .95228 = .38 \text{ (see Table 5.6)}$$

$$\text{Corrected Var HRTOTAL}_{fdiff} = .5722$$
$$S_{xx} = 217 \times .5722$$
$$S_{xx}^{1/2} = 11.13$$

$$\text{Corrected } S_b = .0825 \text{ (see Table 5.6)}$$

gic impact of a high-performance work system is the magnitude of its effect on the firm's financial performance. The cross-sectional results in Huselid (1995) implied combined effects of a one-standard-deviation change in *Employee Skills and Organizational Structures* and *Employee Motivation* of $3,814 greater annual cash flow per employee and $18,641 greater market value per employee for GRATE and q, respectively.

We believe that a conservative approach to the generation of such estimates is to base them on coefficient values that are approximately midway between the cross-sectional estimates and the fixed-effects results. This would imply a coefficient on HRTOTAL of .10 to .12 and .012 to .015 for q and GRATE, respectively. The estimates from the q models imply per employee changes in firm market value of $14,350 to $17,275. The predicted changes in net revenue per employee (GRATE) in the same firms was $1,468 to $1,834. Since these latter estimates are annual cash flows, they can be transformed into present values assuming a reasonable interest rate and time period. Assuming an 8 percent, 15-year period, the net present value of those cash flows would be equivalent ($14,570 and $16,953 per employee) to the market value estimates just presented.

The Implementation-to-Benefit Lag

Our analysis to this point has not explicitly considered the potential for a lag between the implementation of a high-performance work system and any subsequent change in firm performance. Specifically, our HR strategy measures in each year were matched with contemporaneous (1991 and 1993, respectively) measures of firm performance. This approach is justified by the assumption that we are observing an equilibrium relationship among firms and the effects of implementation have been fully realized. Cross-sectionally, we observe the results of the implementation process, and as long as the implementation process has largely run its course, the time between implementation and improved financial performance should have little effect on our results. Alternatively, the panel analysis examines contemporaneous changes in both the HR management system and firm performance. If in fact there is a lag before the effects of changes in the HR management system are reflected in firm performance, as might be expected given the nature of the changes in question, our two-period panel may not be sufficient to capture those effects. This implies that the effects reported in the fixed-effects and first-difference models were considerably smaller than the cross-sectional results, not because they reflect heterogeneity bias in the cross-sectional results, but because it was simply too early to observe the full magnitude of the benefits.

Table 5.7. *Effects of 1991 HRTOTAL on 1991, 1992, and 1993 Values of the Dependent Variables*

Variable	1991 q	1992 q	1993 q	1991 GRATE	1992 GRATE	1993 GRATE
HRTOTAL	.1479** (.0843)	.1899** (.0815)	.1694** (.0847)	.0113 (.0162)	.0266** (.0177)	.0197* (.0137)

Note: These models are identical to the OLS panel cross-sectional sample (n = 218) in Table 5.4. except that the year of the dependent variable changes as described in the text. Standard errors are in parentheses.
*Significant at <.10 level (one-tailed test); **significant at <.05 level (one-tailed test).

Unfortunately we have no way to estimate directly the magnitude of any implementation-to-benefit lag. We can, however, use our data to provide a very modest but indirect test of whether such a lag might indeed even exist. For example, our 1991 cross-sectional data reflect the *levels* of HRTOTAL in that year. What proportion of those levels is due to recent changes that have not yet affected the firm's financial performance is impossible to estimate. However, it is reasonable to assume that some part of those 1991 levels include recent changes. Moreover, to the extent that the benefits of these changes are not realized immediately, we would expect that the effects of the 1991 "levels" would have a larger impact on firm performance in 1992 and 1993 than on firm performance in 1991. We present the results of these analyses in Table 5.7.

The pattern of results we report in Table 5.7 is consistent with our expectation of a lag between the implementation of new HR strategies and their subsequent effects on firm performance. For both q and GRATE the benefits in the subsequent years are higher than in the contemporaneous years. The pattern is particularly dramatic for GRATE, where the effects in 1992 and 1993 average more than twice the magnitude of the 1991 contemporaneous effects. This result may in part reflect accounting convention, where investments in HR management systems are charged as expenses in the current period, while their benefits can be reasonably expected to be realized across multiple periods. This relatively greater lagged effect for GRATE is also consistent with the fact that q is a forward-looking measure that should incorporate these subsequent increases in profitability over a shorter time period. These estimates also bear directly on two earlier results. First, the relatively greater lagged effect on GRATE means that the time period over which these cash flows will equal the market value effects (q) is much shorter than noted earlier. Second, these results imply that two-period panel estimates that rely on two-year windows are likely to understate the true effects of HR management systems on firm performance.

Caveats and Implications for Future Research

These results bring into serious question whether the analysis of panel data will represent an improvement over the analysis of cross-sectional data in this line of research. At a minimum, our findings suggest that when measures of HR strategy require respondents to make broad judgments regarding both the nature and depth of implementation of organizational HR strategies, the potential bias in panel estimates due to measurement error can be substantial. In principle, the richness of panel data can be exploited to recover the true effects of HR strategy, though the panel lengths necessary to provide those corrections will be difficult to generate. Likewise, our analyses of the potential for an implementation-to-benefit lag suggest that panels of four to five years could be required to specify this relationship fully. In the absence of such data, researchers can rely on independent evidence of measurement error, but there is no equally accessible method for estimating the possible implementation-to-benefit lags.

The value of panel data sets in assessing the HR strategy–firm performance link can be legitimately questioned with respect to mitigating the heterogeneity bias discussed earlier. The argument in favor of panel analyses turns on the assumption that *other* firm characteristics that may be reflected in the cross-sectional estimates (e.g., the quality of financial or operating strategies) are fixed over time, while HR strategy is not. If in fact these other organizational practices are appropriately modified along with the HR strategy, the result may be an upward bias as much in the panel estimates as in the cross-sectional estimates. Rather than relying on such assumptions, future research should devote more attention to the identification and measurement of these *other* management practices so that they can be explicitly controlled for in the estimation models.

Future research should proceed at multiple levels of analysis. Multi-firm, multi-industry data collection efforts should continue as a source of generalizable results that focuses on the effects of high-performance work systems on firm performance. Ideally these efforts could begin to incorporate sufficient firm-level detail, via case study or intensive interviews, to provide a validity check on the HR system measures and the nature of their relationship to firm performance. In addition to the improvement of multi-industry samples such as the one described in this study, we believe that much progress can be made by well-executed industry studies that utilize both conventional measures of firm performance and new work on the economic contribution of business units to overall firm performance, most notably work on economic value added (Stewart, 1991). Improving our understanding of the links between business unit performance and firm performance would enable future research to incorporate the benefits of both levels of analysis.

REFERENCES

Arthur, Jeffrey B. 1992. "The Link Between Business Strategy and Industrial Relations Systems in American Steel Minimills." *Industrial and Labor Relations Review*, 45:488–506.

Baird, Lloyd, and Ilan Meshoulam. 1988. "Managing Two Fits of Strategic Human Resource Management." *Academy of Management Review*, 13:116–128.

Barron, John, Mark Berger, and Dan Black. 1996. "How Well Do We Measure Training?" Mimeo, Purdue University, Department of Economics.

Brainard, William C., John B. Shoven, and Leonard W. Weiss. 1980. "The Financial Valuation of the Return to Capital." *Brookings Papers on Economic Activity* (2). Washington, DC: Brookings Institution.

Brown, Brad, and Susan Perry. 1994. "Removing the Financial Performance Halo from *Fortune's* 'Most Admired' Companies." *Academy of Management Journal*, 37:1347–1359.

Cooke, William N. 1992. "Product Quality Improvement Through Employee Participation: The Effects of Unionization and Joint Union–Management Administration." *Industrial and Labor Relations Review*, 46:119–134.

Delaney, John T. 1996. "Unions, Human Resource Innovations, and Organizational Outcomes." *Advances in Industrial and Labor Relations*, vol. 7. Greenwich, CT: JAI Press, pp. 207–245.

Delaney, John T., David Lewin, and Casey Ichniowski. 1989. *Human Resource Policies and Practices in American Firms*. Washington, DC: U.S. Government Printing Office.

Duncan, Greg J., and Daniel H. Hill. 1985. "An Investigation of the Extent and Consequences of Measurement Error in Labor-Economic Survey Data." *Journal of Labor Economics*, 3:508–532.

Eaton, Adrienne. 1994. "Factors Contributing to the Survival of Employee Participation Programs in Unionized Settings." *Industrial and Labor Relations Review*, 48:371–389.

Greene, William H. 1990. *Econometric Analysis*. New York: Macmillan.

Griliches, Zvi, and Jerry A. Hausman. 1986. "Errors in Variables in Panel Data." *Journal of Econometrics*, 31:93–118.

Hausman, Jerry A. 1978. "Specification Tests in Econometrics." *Econometrica*, 46(6):1251–1271.

Heckman, James J. 1979. "Sample Selection Bias as a Specification Error." *Econometrica*, 47:153–161.

Hirsch, Barry T. 1991. *Labor Unions and the Economic Performance of Firms.* Kalamazoo, MI: W. E. Upjohn Institute for Employment Research.

Hirschey, Mark, and D. W. Wichern. 1984. "Accounting and Market-Value Measures of Profitability: Consistency, Determinants, and Uses." *Journal of Business and Economic Statistics*, 2(4):375–383.

Hsiao, Cheng. 1988. *Analysis of Panel Data.* Cambridge University Press.

Hsiao, Cheng, and G. Taylor. 1991. "Some Remarks on Measurement Errors and the Identification of Panel Data Models." *Statistica Neerlandica*, 45:187–194.

Huselid, Mark A. 1995. "The Impact of Human Resource Management Practices on Turnover, Productivity, and Corporate Financial Performance." *Academy of Management Journal*, 38:635–672.

Huselid, Mark A., and Brian E. Becker. 1995. "The Strategic Impact of High Performance Work Systems." Working paper, Rutgers University, School of Management and Labor Relations.

Ichniowski, Casey. 1990. "Human Resource Management Systems and the Performance of U.S. Manufacturing Businesses." NBER Working Paper No. 3449. Cambridge, MA: National Bureau of Economic Research.

Levine, David I. 1995. *Reinventing the Workplace: How Business and Employees Can Both Win.* Washington, DC: Brookings Institution.

MacDuffie, John Paul. 1995. "Human Resource Bundles and Manufacturing Performance: Organizational Logic and Flexible Production Systems in the World Auto Industry." *Industrial and Labor Relations Review*, 48:197–221.

Milgrom, Paul, and John Roberts. 1995. "Complementarities and Fit: Strategy, Structure, and Organizational Change in Manufacturing." *Journal of Accounting and Economics*, 19:179–208.

Nunnally, Jum C., and Ira H. Bernstein. 1994. *Psychometric Theory*, 3d ed. New York: McGraw-Hill.

Pfeffer, Jeffrey. 1994. *Competitive Advantage Through People.* Boston, MA: Harvard Business School Press.

Prahalad, C. K., and Gary Hamel. 1990. "The Core Competence of the Corporation." *Harvard Business Review* (May–June): 79–89.

Schmidt, Frank K., and John E. Hunter. 1995. "Measurement Error in Psychological Research: Lessons from 26 Research Scenarios." *Psychological Methods*, 1(2):199–223.

Stalk, George, Philip Evans, and Lawrence Shulman. 1992. "Competing on Capabilities: The New Rules of Corporate Strategy." *Harvard Business Review* (March–April): 57–69.

Stewart, G. Bennett III. 1991. *The Quest for Value.* New York: HarperBusiness.

Weiss, Leonard W. 1974. "The Concentration–Profits Relationship and Anti-Trust." In H. J. Goldschmidt et al. (Eds.), *Industrial Concentration: The New Learning.* Boston: Little, Brown, pp. 184–223.

U.S. Department of Labor. 1993. *High Performance Work Practices and Firm Performance.* Washington, DC: U.S. Government Printing Office.

CHAPTER 6

The Adoption of High-Involvement Work Practices

Frits K. Pil and John Paul MacDuffie

There is a striking paradox in research on high-involvement work practices.[1] A growing body of literature establishes strong empirical links between such practices and improved economic performance, and reveals that these practices are most effective as part of a larger "bundle," or system, that includes complementary human resource (HR) practices (Arthur, 1992; Batt, 1995; Huselid, 1995; Ichniowski & Kochan, 1995; Ichniowski et al., 1994; Kochan & Osterman, 1990; MacDuffie, 1995a). Thus, from the perspective of economic rationality, one should expect high-involvement work practices to be widely used. Yet many argue that the imitation, learning, and diffusion of these practices have been slow and sporadic (Ichniowski & Shaw, 1995; Kochan & Osterman, 1994; Osterman, 1994; Pfeffer, 1994). The goal of this chapter is to explain why individual work practices (as well as bundles of high-involvement

This chapter is a slightly revised version of an article that originally appeared in *Industrial Relations* 35:3 (1996); reprinted by permission of Blackwell Publishers.

We are grateful to the International Motor Vehicle Program at MIT and the Sloan Foundation for financial support and to J. D. Power and Associates for access to their quality data. We also thank the following for their comments and advice: Peter Cappelli, Lorna Doucet, Barry Gerhart, Chris Ittner, Bruce Kogut, Paul Rosenbaum, Louis Thomas, Michael Useem, and Sidney Winter, as well as participants in the national Industrial Relations Research Association conference (January 1996, San Francisco) and the conference entitled "Understanding the Structure of Human Resources" (October 1995, Wharton School, Center for Human Resources). We are further indebted to the editors and reviewers of *Industrial Relations* for helpful suggestions.

[1] In using the term "high-involvement" as a descriptor for new work practices, we depart from the convention of many recent writings on this topic that use the term "high-performance." We do so because we believe that to label new work practices "high-performance" can be misleading in the absence of clear empirical tests of their actual link to economic performance in a given situation.

work practices and complementary HR practices)[2] are adopted more rapidly by some establishments than by others.

We develop a theoretical framework that draws on evolutionary economics, innovation, and strategy literature to identify three factors driving adoption: (1) the presence of complementary HR practices and technology; (2) low levels of economic performance achieved with current work practices; and (3) organizational characteristics and behaviors that reduce the cost of introducing new work practices. Longitudinal data from the international auto industry enable us to test several hypotheses about these factors.

We examine the adoption of high-involvement work practices by analyzing data gathered in two rounds of surveys (1989 and 1993–1994) from 43 automobile assembly plants located around the world (MacDuffie & Pil, 1996). Although the use of such practices increased considerably over this five-year period, the rate of increase varied dramatically from plant to plant. Given the growing international competitive pressure in this industry and its impact on product markets and business strategies, the lack of more extensive adoption of high-involvement work practices warrants close investigation.

This chapter builds on past research that examined how high-involvement work practices, when combined with complementary HR practices and manufacturing policies, contribute to the achievement of productivity and quality outcomes, facilitate management of the complexity associated with large product variety, underpin shop-floor problem-solving processes, and affect workers and institutions of worker representation (MacDuffie, 1995a, 1995b, 1997; MacDuffie & Kochan, 1995; MacDuffie & Krafcik, 1992; MacDuffie, Sethuraman, & Fisher, 1996). The bundle of high-involvement work practices identified in this previous work as a strong predictor of economic performance here

[2] The precise definition of "high-involvement work practices" in this area of inquiry varies from researcher to researcher, as does the nomenclature for such practices. We emphasize structural aspects of the organization of work (e.g., the use of work teams and small group activities organized for production-related problem-solving) and associated practices (e.g., job rotation, the division of labor for quality responsibilities between team members and supervisors or quality control staff), consistent with MacDuffie (1995a) and Osterman (1994). We thereby exclude from our definition certain HR policies (e.g., training, hiring practices) that other researchers (e.g., Huselid, 1995; Ichniowski et al., 1994) have included in this category. However, we consider these policies complementary to "high-involvement work practices," as explained later in the text, and thus relevant to explaining variation in the diffusion of such work practices. This chapter's focus on the adoption of high-involvement work practices, thus defined, reflects our observation that changes in these work practices are more difficult to carry out than changes in the complementary set of HR policies because they are more intricately bound up with core business processes and coordination requirements of the organization.

becomes the dependent variable for a dynamic analysis of changes in the utilization of these practices over time. This is the first in a series of studies that use these unique longitudinal data to explore economic, technological, and institutional factors promoting both convergence and divergence in the diffusion of high-involvement work practices across country and company boundaries (MacDuffie & Pil, 1996, 1997a,b; Pil, 1996; Pil & MacDuffie, in press).

Facilitating and Constraining Factors for Change in Work Practices

A theoretical perspective on organizational change that can help explain the limited adoption of high-involvement work practices can be found in evolutionary economics (Aldrich, 1979; Nelson & Winter, 1982). The evolutionary perspective suggests that organizations develop a set of organizational routines over time. These established patterns of operation are generally tacit and become ingrained in the collective knowledge of the organization. Organizational routines change infrequently and are subject to selection pressures. Only changes that result in positive change for the organization are retained.

Routines can change through trial-and-error experimentation and/or an organizational search for superior ways of doing things. With a trial-and-error approach, organizations "grope" their way toward superior routines (Lippman & Rumelt, 1982). This is often "a chaotic or probabilistic process not easily amenable to conscious attempts to increase its occurrence" (Mezias & Glynn, 1993, p. 79). While a search for superior routines reflects a more intentional and directed effort to achieve change, managers typically look only to familiar technologies and organizational practices – those that are, in Cyert and March's (1963) terminology, "in the neighborhood" – as solutions to problems. Given the chaotic nature of trial-and-error change, the "local" nature of searches for superior routines, and the embeddedness of established routines in daily organizational activity, organizations are always subject to a certain level of inertia (Nelson & Winter, 1982).

The literature on innovation provides further insight into how organizational change takes place, distinguishing two kinds of change – variously described as "evolutionary" versus "revolutionary" (Mezias & Glynn, 1993); "incremental" versus "radical" (Dewar & Dutton, 1986); or "frame-bending" versus "frame-breaking" (Tushman et al., 1986). While the former terms describe minor modifications in existing technologies and organizational practices, the latter terms describe "fundamental changes in the activities of an organization and represent clear

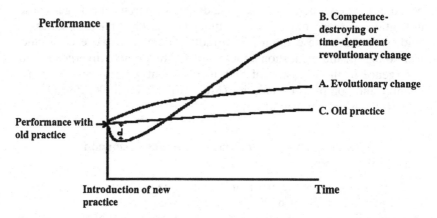

Figure 6.1. Learning curves under evolutionary versus competence-destroying change.

departures from existing practice" (Damanpour, 1991:561). Revolutionary, radical, or frame-breaking change is much harder to undertake and occurs much less frequently than evolutionary change (March, 1991; Mezias & Glynn, 1993; Tushman & Nelson, 1990). Furthermore, radical change – particularly change involving fundamental shifts in technology – can be "competence-destroying" (Tushman & Anderson, 1986), in the sense that the presence of an older technology both hampers the introduction of new technology and reduces the benefit associated with its introduction. We will argue in this chapter that a fundamental organizational change, such as the adoption of high-involvement work practices, can also be competence-destroying.

The notion of competence-destroying change has very significant implications for an organization's learning curve. Suppose that an organization has placed great emphasis on a strong Tayloristic approach to work organization, where supervisors are assigned the role of (and trained to be) autocratic disciplinarians and employees are viewed as little more than expendable labor. Switching to a system in which work is organized around employee teams would entail not just introducing a new system, but destroying the organization's experience with the old system. Whereas learning under incremental change would look like curve A in Figure 6.1, learning under competence-destroying change would have a slope that is much less steep. Furthermore, because of costs associated with unlearning old practices and introducing new ones, initially the organization's performance may be worse with the new practices (curve B) than with the old ones (curve C), even if over the long term the new practices are superior.

If new practices are time-dependent – that is, if returns to such practices are quite low in the short term and grow only over time – a learning pattern similar to that experienced with competence-destroying change is observed. For example, if an organization makes significant investments over a long time period in employee involvement activities and training, the impact on worker commitment and skills – and hence on economic performance – will be larger than when efforts are concentrated in a very short time period. Furthermore, because these changes are not costless, the organization's performance may be worse (or at least no better) immediately after introducing the new practices relative to its performance with the past practices.

Both competence-destroying and time-dependent change can lead to "competency traps." These arise when favorable experience with an inferior routine leads an organization to accumulate more experience with it (Levinthal & March, 1981; Levitt & March, 1988). Given a negative differential between the current performance of existing routines and the initial performance of a new, potentially superior routine (shown by area d in Figure 6.1), organizations may maintain the inferior routines with which they have had more favorable experience in the past. Thus superior practices that do not yield immediate results face a high risk of not being retained.

While these arguments can be applied to the adoption of specific practices or routines, they have more profound implications for the adoption of bundles of practices. Since organizations tend to approach change through trial-and-error attempts at problem-solving and localized searches for superior routines, they will rarely attempt the comprehensive and simultaneous replacement of an entire bundle of existing practices. Instead, an organization may decide to implement one or two new practices and assess their impact before proceeding any further. Such behavior poses a problem, since high-involvement HR practices and work systems are subject to complementarities (Ichniowski & Shaw, 1995; MacDuffie, 1995a; Milgrom & Roberts, 1995).

Practices are complementary when using them together results in greater performance than the sum of the performance resulting from using each practice separately. For example, when a high-involvement work practice is introduced in the presence of complementary HR practices and technologies, not only does the new work practice induce an incremental improvement in performance, but so do the complementary practices. However, if no complementary practices have been estab-

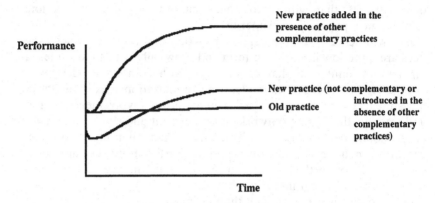

Figure 6.2. Performance implications of complementarities.

lished, the only improvement in performance is due to the new work practice itself. Without the performance boost of complementary practices, the new practice may not be adopted, particularly if it represents competence-destroying change or reveals its performance advantages only over the long term. This is shown in Figure 6.2. This figure demonstrates that in addition to the presence of complementarities, the adoption of new work practices will depend on the performance achieved with past practices, as well as factors that alter the initial cost of implementing the new practices.

Hypotheses

The first hypothesis, drawing on the foregoing discussion, concerns the impact of complementary HR practices and/or technologies on the adoption of high-involvement work practices.[3] Consider for a moment how HR practices might be complementary to new work practices. Careful hiring and selection procedures seek to identify new employees who are

---

[3] MacDuffie (1995a) also shows that low buffer levels are important and complementary to high-involvement work and HR practices. We do not consider policies on buffers here because of a pattern observed in the Round 2 data. As in previous work (MacDuffie & Krafcik, 1992) which found that companies often introduced technological change without making corresponding changes in work organization, we found that many plants reduced their use of buffers between 1989 and 1993–1994 without changing their work practices. This suggests that changes in buffers can be made independently of changes in work practices, at least in the short term. However, we did redo our analyses including "use of buffers" as an independent variable. In no equation was the 1989 level of buffers a significant predictor of change in work practices, and the coefficients in the remaining independent variables did not change appreciably.

able and willing to support the new work practices. Extensive training, both on and off the job, prepares production workers for new roles and responsibilities in shop-floor teams – for example, rotating jobs, revising work methods, taking over quality inspection, and performing equipment setup tasks. Similarly, supervisors and engineers need to be trained in their new roles as coaches and advisers to quality circles and teams. Breaking down the status barriers between managers and production workers (e.g., by establishing a common parking lot and cafeteria, dropping the necktie requirement for managers) can facilitate management's shift to new roles while improving communication and worker commitment (MacDuffie, 1995a).

Incentive systems may also have to change to support new work practices. As more and more activities are carried out by teams (both on-line and off-line), it becomes increasingly difficult and costly to monitor the efforts of individual workers. In a firm that makes compensation contingent on performance at the group or organizational level, workers will be more likely to engage in mutual monitoring and more highly motivated to participate in activities that improve the organization's overall performance (Blinder, 1990; Levine & Tyson, 1990).

Another complement to high-involvement work practices is the presence of flexible automation (MacDuffie & Krafcik, 1992; MacDuffie & Pil, 1997b; Parthasarthy & Sethi, 1993).[4] Flexibly deployed workers capable of effective problem-solving are critical for achieving many of the strategic goals associated with flexible automation. When flexible automation is used to generate more product variety, workers must master a larger variety of more complex tasks in order to avoid productivity or quality penalties. Flexible automation facilitates rapid changeovers from one model to another, but effective changeovers require flexible workers who are accustomed to rotating jobs and mod-

---

[4] It is certainly the case that flexible automation can also be part of a cost-minimization corporate strategy in which the primary goal of capital investment is the elimination of jobs and there are few incentives for management to invest in high-involvement work practices. Indeed, this was the case in the early to middle 1980s, particularly in certain U.S. and European companies (e.g., General Motors, Fiat) which sought to improve their competitiveness through investments in flexible automation that reduced their dependence on workforce skill and motivation. However, by the late 1980s and early 1990s, many of these "technology-only" strategies had proved ineffective – particularly efforts to boost substantially the amount of automation in the labor-intensive assembly area. Instead, companies appeared to be learning that flexible automation can be used in a very inflexible way *unless* implemented in the context of flexible work organization (e.g., teams) and flexible workers (e.g., highly trained and accustomed to cross-utilization and ongoing problem-solving). Thus, from the late 1980s forward, we believe that the characterization of flexible automation as strategically complementary to flexible work practices is accurate for most U.S., European, and Japanese companies.

ifying work methods (e.g., through their participation in work teams, problem-solving groups, and ongoing *kaizen*, or continuous improvement efforts). Finally, flexible automation lends itself more readily to worker involvement in making incremental process changes, since minor modifications in the software programs for robots may be carried out locally. Thus the first hypothesis is

H1. *Organizations will be more likely to adopt high-involvement work practices if they have already adopted complementary HR practices and/or flexible automation.*

This hypothesis leaves unspecified the way in which complementary HR practices and flexible automation influence the adoption of high-involvement work practices. It is possible that firms already using these complementary practices and technologies may discover through trial-and-error experimentation that high-involvement work practices are a good "fit" with these existing practices and yield performance gains in a relatively short period of time. However, firms may also examine what other firms are doing as they search for superior practices and discover the benefits that accrue from the complementarities among high-involvement work practices and the associated HR practices and flexible technologies.

From the perspective of the "new institutionalism" (DiMaggio & Powell, 1991), this latter approach – search through comparison with other firms – might lead to the adoption of high-involvement work practices even among firms that are *not* using complementary practices or technologies. In other words, firms often copy what other successful firms are doing (what DiMaggio & Powell call "mimetic isomorphism") whether or not they can implement new practices in the context of other complementary practices. Thus the relationship between prior usage of complementary HR practices and technologies and the adoption of high-involvement work practices will have to be quite strong for Hypothesis 1 to hold.

The second hypothesis considers whether the adoption of high-involvement work practices is more likely when organizations exhibit inferior performance. Cyert and March (1963) suggest that innovative change can be the result of either a search for the application of under-utilized resources or a reaction to adversity. There are conflicting perspectives on the impact of adversity, in terms of poor performance, on a firm's behavior. Some literature suggests that poorly performing organizations become increasingly committed to losing courses of action – that is, escalating commitment (e.g., Staw, 1976). Other literature suggests that poor performance is more likely to result in innovative change. Chandler (1962), for example, proposed that poor performance induced a search for new behaviors within organizations. More recently, Bolton (1993) showed empirically for a sample of high-tech firms that those exhibiting substandard performance were more likely to change the way they conduct research than were their better-performing counterparts.

The latter views are consistent with the evolutionary perspective on change outlined earlier. Under conditions of poor performance, an organization is already inclined to view current practices as suboptimal. Therefore, even though competence-destroying change may reduce the immediate benefit of new practices, the short-term differential between potential new practices and existing practices (area d in Figure 6.1) is not as great. As a result, the cost of change relative to maintaining the status quo is lower for poorly performing organizations, and change is more likely. The second hypothesis, therefore, is:

H2. *Organizations will be more likely to implement high-involvement work practices if they are exhibiting poor performance relative to competitors.*

The third hypothesis considers organizational behaviors and characteristics that can alter the cost of introducing new work practices. One such cost results from the difficulty of unlearning the old way of doing things. The current way of doing things is accepted as the norm by those who work in the organization, and patterns of interaction, communication, and trust develop around these routines (McNeil & Thompson, 1971). Over time, routines develop into customs backed by moral claims on how things are to be done (Doeringer & Piore, 1971). For example, in a Taylorist work environment, workers have a clear understanding of what is expected of them, and they learn to work in accordance with those expectations. There are seniority rules that are respected, clearly defined job roles, as well as an understanding among workers of what behavior management wishes to elicit and what will be given in return. When switching to a team-based environment, production workers and managers face great uncertainty. They have to learn new roles and new ways of interacting, and to develop a new degree of trust in the new system and each other. The less experience employees have had with the current system, the easier the change may be, because their expectations about the work environment will be less fixed and current routines less ingrained. This leads to the third hypothesis:

H3. *Organizations will be more likely to implement high-involvement work practices if their employees have less experience with existing practices.*

The fourth hypothesis considers how trust (or a lack of trust) between employees and managers can affect the likelihood of adopting high-involvement work practices. Many researchers have emphasized that the successful implementation of high-involvement work practices requires a mutual understanding not only that employees are committed to the organization they work for, but that the organization is committed to them in return (Aoki, 1990; Burack et al., 1994; Kochan & Osterman, 1994). According to Bailey (1992) and Levine and Tyson (1990), long-term employment relations and job security are the most important factors establishing such reciprocal obligation.

When long-term job security is brought into question through workforce reductions like layoffs, trust and commitment may disappear. Layoffs often break the implicit "psychological contract" between employees and the organization they work for – even among those employees who are not laid off (Brockner et al., 1987). The reduced trust accompanying such a break increases the difficulty of successfully implementing high-involvement work practices and reduces the likelihood of near-term benefits (Kochan, Katz & Mower, 1984). For example, it would be very difficult to implement a suggestion program focused on performance improvements if employees feared that such improvements might result in future job reductions. Thus the fourth hypothesis is:

H4. *Organizations will be less likely to introduce high-involvement work practices if they have recently undertaken layoffs or other actions that reduce trust on the part of the workforce.*

The fifth hypothesis considers organizational disruptions that can lower the cost of introducing high-involvement work practices. An organizational disruption can potentially "unfreeze" the existing way of doing things (Lewin, 1947; Schein, 1992) and thus represents a competence-destroying change in and of itself.[5] This reduces the penalty associated with trying a new way of doing things, relative to returning to the status quo. Such a disruption could take various forms that may vary by indus-

---

[5] The layoffs identified in Hypothesis 2 are, arguably, an "unfreezing" event as well. However, we choose to examine the effect of layoffs on adoption separately because they potentially affect the "psychological contract" in a way that the "unfreezing" events considered here (which offer opportunities to implement new practices because they force an interruption of ongoing activities) do not.

try context. In the airline industry or telecommunications industry, for example, deregulation might constitute such a disruption. In the automobile industry, product-market-related changes provide periodic disruptions. For example, opportunities are presented each time a new product (and the associated new process technology) is launched in a given factory to implement other changes in the organization and coordination of work as well. This leads to the fifth and final hypothesis:

H5. *Organizations will be more likely to introduce high-involvement work practices in the presence of changes that cause some "unfreezing" of the current way of doing things.*

Sample and Methods

To test the hypotheses put forth in the preceding section, we draw on data collected through the International Assembly Plant Study, carried out under the auspices of the International Motor Vehicle Program at MIT (MacDuffie & Krafcik, 1992; MacDuffie & Pil, 1995). These data were collected via plant-level surveys, first in 1989 (Round 1) and again in the fall of 1993 through the spring of 1994 (Round 2). In Round 1, 90 plants were contacted, and 70 completed and usable responses were received from plants representing 24 companies in 17 countries. In Round 2, 109 plants were contacted, and 86 completed surveys were returned. Of these, 83 were usable, reflecting data from 21 companies and 20 countries. The response rates of 77% in Round 1 and 79% in Round 2 are extremely high given the comprehensive nature of the survey. All the plants participating in Round 1 and 41 of the plants participating in Round 2 were visited by a member of the research team in order to verify data and provide feedback. Each participating plant also received a customized report showing its performance in relation to average values for plants by region.

The plants sampled in each round represent approximately one-half to two-thirds of the total assembly plant capacity worldwide. All told, this study represents the most comprehensive effort ever undertaken to gather longitudinal international data on new work practices and HR policies, the role of these practices in the overall production system, and their impact on economic performance.

Forty-three plants participated in both rounds of data collection. Of these, four are missing some data and were dropped for the purposes of the regression analyses, leaving a usable sample of 39 plants. About 60% of the Round 1 sample participated in the Round 2 data collection; 31 plants participating in Round 1 are not in the matched sample. This change in the sample from Round 1 to Round 2 is due in part to six plant closings and the opening of nine new plants. The remaining differences between the two rounds are the result of changes in the composition of auto company participation in the Assembly Plant Study – some Round 1 companies declined to participate in Round 2, and some companies that had not participated in Round 1 joined the study. Each change in a company-level decision to participate in the survey generally involves several assembly plants.

Operationalization of Variables

Dependent Variable

To investigate changes in the use of high-involvement work practices by our sample of assembly plants between 1989 and 1993–1994, we utilize a composite index, referred to as the "Work Practices" index, which reflects five specific work practices: (1) shop-floor "on-line" work teams, (2) "off-line" employee involvement or problem-solving groups, (3) job rotation, (4) suggestion programs (number of suggestions, as well as percent implemented), and (5) the decentralization of quality efforts (the degree to which production workers take direct responsibility for quality-related activities). Table 6.1 contains the details of how each of these work practices is measured.

The Work Practices index is calculated by pooling the data across the two time periods (1989 and 1993–1994), standardizing the data for each practice through a z-score transformation, and then additively combining the standardized scores[6] (see MacDuffie, 1995a, for more details). In order to have an index value that is easier to interpret, we apply a linear transformation to the sum of the z-scores, such that the plant with the lowest level of these high-involvement work practices has a score of 0 and the plant with the highest level has a score of 100. The distribution of the variable is unaffected by this transformation. Because we pool the data before these transformations, a specific bundle of practices will yield the same index score in either 1989 or 1993–1994.

Independent Variables

The first independent variable is an index of HR practices that are thought to be complementary to high-involvement work practices. The

---

[6] The Cronbach's standardized alpha score for this index was .69. Principal components analysis revealed that all variables in this index loaded on one factor.

Table 6.1. *Overview and Operationalization of Variables*

Variable	Description
High-involvement Work Practices index	Work structures and policies that govern shop-floor production activity and that foster worker involvement in decision-making and problem-solving. This is a composite index of the high-involvement work practices listed below. For each plant, scores on each practice were normalized across both time periods, summed, and then rescaled from 0 to 100. A low score indicates that a plant has few or no high-involvement work practices, and a high score indicates an extensive presence of work practices.
Elements in high-involvement Work Practices index	
% Employees in teams	Percentage of employees in on-line teams.
% Employees in involvement groups	Percentage of employees participating in some type of off-line problem-solving team (e.g., quality circles, employee involvement groups).
Job rotation	Level of rotation at production worker level: 1 = none, 2 = trained to do multiple skills but do not rotate, 3 = within teams, 4 = within teams and across teams in same department, 5 = within and across teams and across departments.
Suggestions by employees	Production-related suggestions per employee per year.
Suggestions implemented	Percentage of suggestions implemented.
Level at which quality control takes place	The level within the organization at which four key quality-control activities take place: 1 = production worker level, 4 = specialists; tasks considered: inspection of incoming parts, work in progress, finished goods, and gathering statistical process control data.
Complementary HR Practices index	Organization-wide HR policies that are complementary to high-involvement work practices. Like the Work Practices index, this is a composite index including several HR practices. For each plant, scores on each practice were normalized across both time periods, summed, and then rescaled from 0 to 100. A low score indicates a plant that has few or no complementary HR practices, and a high score indicates an extensive presence of complementary HR practices.

Table 6.1. *(cont.)*

Variable	Description
Practices included in complementary HR Practices index	
Hiring criteria	Criteria used to select production workers, first-line supervisors, and engineers. This is a sum of various criteria, with a lower number indicating a greater emphasis on using previous experience in a similar job, and a higher number indicating willingness to learn new skills and ability to work with others.
New training	Index of new training based on annual training hours of new production workers, supervisors, and engineers: 1 = 0–40 hours of training for category receiving least amount of training; 3 = 80+ hours.
Experienced training	Index of training for experienced employees based on annual training hours of experienced production workers, supervisors, and engineers: 1 = 0–20 hours of training for category receiving least amount of training; 2 = 20–40 hours; 3 = 40–60 hours; 4 = 60–80 hours; 5 = 80 hours +.
Contingent compensation	Index of the level and scope of pay for performance: 1 = no pay for performance; 6 = pay for performance at the individual or group level, and for production workers, supervisors, engineers, and managers. Intermediate values indicate some pay for performance for some of the employee groups.
Status differentials	This captures some of the surface indicators of status differences between managers and production workers. One is added for each of the following practices: no ties for managers, a common cafeteria, a common parking lot, and a common uniform for all employees.
Flexible automation	This measure captures the degree to which flexible automation in the form of robotics is used in the plant. It is the total sum of all robots in the body, paint, and assembly shops (programmable equipment capable of being reconfigured to alternate tasks – has at least three axes of motion). The number of robots is divided by the number of employees to yield the number of robots per employee, and is then rescaled from 0 to 100, where 100 represents the plant with the greatest number of robots per employee in 1989 and 1993–1994.

Table 6.1. *(cont.)*

Variable	Description
ln productivity	Natural logarithm of labor hours required to build a vehicle. This figure is adjusted for level of vertical integration of the plant, product characteristics, and labor time differences across plants. Higher labor hours per vehicle indicate lower productivity. For additional information on this measure, see Krafcik (1988) and MacDuffie and Pil (1995).
ln quality	Natural logarithm of consumer-perceived quality, defined as defects per 100 vehicles, from J. D. Power. J. D. Power quality data are adjusted to reflect only defects originating directly in the assembly plant. See MacDuffie and Pil (1995).
Production worker tenure	Average years all production workers have been working in the plant.
Managerial tenure	Average years five key top managers have been in the plant: plant manager, head of engineering, head of finance, head of human resources, and head of material services.
Layoffs of production workers and management, early retirement incentives	1 if the plant undertook the measure between 1989 and 1994, and 0 otherwise.
Major addition to the plant	1 if the plant added a new assembly line between 1989 and 1994.
New product introduction	The percentage of a plant's output that has been changed since 1988.

complementary HR practices included in this index are: criteria used for the selection and hiring of production workers; the extent of contingent compensation; training (both on and off the job) for new and experienced employees; and the extent of status differentiation between production workers and managers. The specific measurement of each HR practice can be found in Table 6.1, and specific arguments about why these practices are particularly complementary to the new work practices measured for this study can be found in MacDuffie (1995a). This "HR Policies" index was created in the same way as the Work Systems index – pooling data across both rounds, standardizing the data and summing across the practices, and then applying a linear transformation to get a 0–100 scale, where 0 indicates the plant with the fewest and 100 the plant with the most of these complementary HR practices.[7]

A second independent variable is flexible automation, operationalized as the number of robots in the plants, weighted by number of employees, where robots are defined as programmable equipment with three or more axes of motion.

A third set of independent variables includes two measures of plant-level performance: log productivity and log quality. The productivity measure follows a methodology developed by Krafcik (1988) to measure the number of labor hours required to produce a standardized vehicle. By adjusting for the type of vehicle produced, the level of vertical integration of the plant, and working time differences across plants, the resultant measure is comparable across all assembly plants. The quality measure is based on the number of defects per 100 vehicles. This figure is based on annual surveys of new car owners by J. D. Power and Associates. The J. D. Power data are adjusted to include only defects directly attributable to the assembly plant (Krafcik, 1988; MacDuffie & Pil, 1995). J. D. Power data are available only for vehicles sold in the United States and thus are missing for 7 of the plants in our matched sample. As a result, those regressions that include quality as an independent variable are limited to 32 plants. For both productivity and quality, higher values indicate poorer performance (i.e., more labor hours or more defects per vehicle).

Employee job tenure is the fourth independent variable. Since the more traditional "job control" work practices associated with mass production plants have been dominant for most of this century (Katz, 1985; Womack et al., 1990), the most direct proxy of how much experience employees (both workers and managers) have with those practices is their tenure level. We measure both production worker tenure and average tenure levels of the five top managers in the plant (plant manager, head of finance, head of engineering, head of human resources, and head of material services).

Company actions that reduce employee trust constitute the fifth set of independent variables. We asked plants about the layoff of production workers, the layoff of managerial employees, and the use of early retirement incentives as means to reduce the workforce between 1989 and 1993–1994 – actions frequently undertaken in the downsizing of many automotive companies in recent years. We believe that early retirement incentives would be less likely than actual layoffs to result in broken

---

[7] The Cronbach's standardized alpha score for this index was .59. Principal components analysis revealed that all variables in this index loaded on one factor.

trust, and thus unlike layoffs they might *not* reduce the likelihood that new high-involvement work systems will be implemented.

Finally, we identified two major types of disruptions in assembly plants that could result in the "unfreezing" of the current way of doing things: major product changeovers and significant new additions to the plants. When plants introduce a new product, assembly lines are reorganized, layouts are changed, jobs are redefined; there is a general upheaval in the way things are done. We measure the percentage of a plant's products (as a percentage of output volume) that were introduced between 1989 and 1993–1994. Significant new additions were measured as a dichotomous variable capturing whether or not a plant added a new assembly line between 1989 and 1993–1994.

Specifications

We use the 1993–1994 (Round 2) Work Practices index score as the dependent variable, including the 1989 (Round 1) Work Practices index score as an independent variable. Also included as independent variables are the level of complementary HR practices in 1989 and the level of flexible automation in 1989; log productivity and log quality; the variables on employee and managerial experience/tenure; the variables on layoffs and early retirements; and the variables on plant-level disruptions. Because of the extremely small sample size, we do not test any models including all of these variables. Instead, we first test an equation with only the 1989 level of work systems, HR policies, and flexible automation on the right-hand side, and add to these base variables each of the other blocks of variables (e.g., performance, experience/tenure, layoffs, disruptions) separately. For all the equations, the White (1980) test did not reject the null hypothesis that the error terms are homoskedastic.

Results

We begin by examining the change in the use of high-involvement work practices by the 39 matched plants in our sample. Table 6.2 reveals an overall increase in the use of high-involvement work practices by these plants from Round 1 to Round 2. With the exception of decentralized quality control, which remains at about the same level, there was a significant increase in the use of all high-involvement work practices between 1989 and 1993–1994. The most striking increases occur in the use of on-line work teams and off-line problem-solving groups (e.g., employee involvement groups, quality circles). This table suggests that

Table 6.2. *Change in High-Involvement Work Practices at Matched Plants, Mean (Standard Deviation)*

	Plants in 1989	Same Plants in 1993–1994	t-Test
High-involvement Work Practices index[a]	34.6 (24.9)	46.9 (23.2)	***
Individual practices in high-involvement Work Practices index			
Employees in work teams (%)	15.7 (29.1)	46.3 (39.3)	**
Employees in problem-solving groups (%)[b]	28.9 (37.6)	48.8 (38.7)	***
Job rotation[c]	3.0 (1.2)	3.2 (1.2)	*
Suggestions per employee	9.2 (28.3)	12.8 (33.2)	***
Suggestions implemented (%)	38.2 (36.6)	50.8 (32.3)	***
Responsibility for quality[d]	1.6 (1.2)	1.7 (1.3)	—
N	43	43	—

[a] 0 = low; 100 = extensive use of high-involvement work practices.
[b] E.g., quality circles, employee involvement groups.
[c] 1 = none; 5 = within and across work groups and departments.
[d] 1 = production workers; 4 = specialists.
*Significant at 10% level; **significant at 5% level; ***significant at 1% level.

plants can and do increase their use of high-involvement work practices and that this is the prevailing trend worldwide. However, there remains large variance in the degree to which plants change. Although the average change in the Work Systems index was 12.3 (on a 0–100 scale), the standard deviation for the change was 22.2. Some plants undertook only minor changes in their use of high-involvement work practices between 1989 and 1993–1994, while other plants showed dramatic increases and still others showed modest decreases.

We now turn to testing the hypotheses outlined earlier to explain why some plants change their use of high-involvement work practices more than others. Tables 6.3 and 6.4 provide descriptive statistics and Table 6.5 shows OLS regression analyses.[8]

[8] We also ran these in the form of rank regressions to test for the potential problems associated with small-sample regression. The results are substantively the same as those reported here.

Table 6.3. *Means and Standard Deviations for Regression Variables*

Variable	Mean	Standard Deviation
High-Involvement Work Practices index, 1989	34.6	24.9
High-Involvement Work Practices index, 1993–1994	47.6	22.8
Complementary Human Resources index, 1989	42.0	21.9
Flexible automation index, 1989	13.2	12.6
ln productivity	3.4	0.4
ln quality	4.2	0.4
Production worker tenure (years)	11.9	5.2
Managerial tenure (years)	10.0	6.1
Layoffs of production workers (%)	42	0.50
Layoffs of management (%)	47	0.47
Early retirement incentives (%)	58	0.58
Major addition to plant (%)	17	0.38
Plant's output that is new (%)	66	0.42

Hypothesis 1 suggested that organizations that utilize a greater number of complementary HR practices and/or technologies will be more likely to adopt high-involvement work practices than those that have fewer or no complements. This is the "bundling" or complementarity argument, but unlike MacDuffie (1995a), which examines bundles in a cross-sectional sample, the present study applies this argument to the dynamics of adoption of high-involvement work practices over time. Equation 1 (Table 6.5) assesses the impact of the 1989 level of complementary HR practices and flexible automation on the 1993–1994 level of high-involvement work practices, controlling also for the level of high-involvement work practices in 1989. This equation, with an adjusted R^2 value of .37, reveals that the Round 1 levels of work practices and complementary HR practices are statistically significant predictors of the Round 2 level of work practices – that is, plants are more likely to increase their use of high-involvement work practices when they have already implemented complementary HR practices, controlling for their initial level of work practices.

However, the 1989 level of flexible automation appears to have no significant impact on the use of high-involvement work practices in 1993–1994, when controlling for the Round 1 level of work practices and HR practices. It may be that the Round 1 sample contained a mix of some "high-tech" plants with complementary work practices but also plants in which a high level of flexible automation is coupled with tradi-

Table 6.4. *Correlation Matrix*

	Work '89	Work '93–94	HRM '89	Flex Auto '89	ln Prodvty	ln Quality	Prod wrkr	Mgr Ten	Layoffs	Mgmt Layoffs	Retire Incent.	% New Model
Work '89	1.0000											
Work '93–94	.5772**	1.0000										
HRM '89	.5496**	.5303**	1.0000									
Flex Auto '89	.5440**	.2769	.6096**	1.0000								
ln Prodvty '89	-.5551**	-.1721	-.3614*	-.6554**	1.0000							
ln Quality '89	-.5048**	-.2998	-.7098**	-.4799**	.2167	1.0000						
Prod Wrkr Ten	-.0596	-.1184	-.2515	.0184	-.2311	.3327	1.0000					
Mgr Ten	.1039	.3619*	.1137	-.0679	.1382	.0120	.0008	1.0000				
Layoffs	-.5824**	-.4393**	-.4538**	-.3127	.3014	.6371**	.1729	-.0983	1.0000			
Mgmt Layoffs	-.5409**	-.3785*	-.2814	-.3424*	.3176	.5690**	-.0557	.1865	.5549**	1.0000		
Retire Incent.	-.7091**	-.4633**	-.5364**	-.3950*	.3063	.6693**	.3402	.0202	.3714*	.5737**	1.0000	
% New Model	.3131	.5168**	.3857*	.3450*	-.2280	-.1190	-.2159	.3001	-.4727**	-.2051	-.1061	1.0000
Chg. in Plant	.2401	.2161	.1677	.0966	-.1301	-.1572	-.2449	-.1860	-.2268	-.2737	-.3780*	.1811

* Significant at .05 level; ** significant at .01 level (two-tailed).

Table 6.5. *Change in Use of High-Involvement Work Practices, 1989 to 1993–1994 (N = 39)*
(Dependent variable is high-involvement work practices in 1993–1994.)

Variable	Equation 1 B	Equation 1 SE	Equation 2[a] B	Equation 2[a] SE	Equation 3 B	Equation 3 SE	Equation 4 B	Equation 4 SE	Equation 5 B	Equation 5 SE
High-involvement Work Practices, index, 1989	0.44***	0.15	0.43**	0.19	0.34**	0.15	0.37*	0.21	0.40***	0.14
Complementary HR Practices index, 1989	0.41**	0.18	0.62**	0.23	0.31*	0.19	0.39*	0.23	0.32*	0.17
Flexible automation, 1989	−0.36	0.32	−0.13	0.39	−0.05	0.33	−0.36	0.34	−0.47	0.30
ln Productivity, 1989			4.42	11.1						
ln Quality, 1989			16.92	11.4						
Production worker tenure					−0.13	0.63				
Managerial tenure					1.50**	0.57				
Layoffs of production workers							−5.24	8.43		
Major addition to plant									2.1	7.45
Plant's output that is new (%)									19.17**	7.16
Constant	19.3***	6.59	−77.4	74.6	9.61	12.2	26.03**	10.97	12.84*	6.57
F-statistic	8.43***		4.8***		5.7***		4.91***		7.37***	
R^2 (adj.)	.37		.38		.45		.32		.46	

[a] Regressions including productivity and quality represent a reduced *n* of 32 because quality data are not available for any non-U.S. plants that do not export to the United States.
Significance levels: *10%, **5%, ***1%.

tional work practices. In these latter plants, capital investment may have been intended primarily as a means to reduce labor costs and thus as an alternative strategy to investing in high-involvement work practices. If these "high-tech" plants with traditional work practices experienced poor performance because they were not able to gain full benefit from their capital investment, we would expect them to have a strong incentive to move toward high-involvement work practices. But if their performance was adequate (but not stellar), these would be precisely those plants most likely to face the *disincentives* to investing in high-involvement work practices highlighted in this chapter, given the potential short-term costs of such a change.

In Equation 2, we test the hypothesis that the worst-performing plants will be those most likely to change their work systems. The positive coefficient for log quality suggests that plants with a greater number of defects per vehicle in 1989 are more likely to increase their use of high-involvement work practices by 1993–1994. However, the coefficient is not quite statistically significant ($p = .15$). Furthermore, productivity levels in 1989 appear to have no predictive power with respect to 1993–1994 usage of new work practices.[9]

A potential reason for the lack of strong support for the performance hypothesis is the fact that in the Round 1 data both performance measures are very highly correlated with the levels of complementary HR practices and work practices ($R = -.66$ and $-.50$, respectively, for quality [defects per 100 vehicles] and $R = -.36$ and $-.56$, respectively, for productivity [hours per vehicle]). Furthermore, we are faced with a reduced sample size because quality data are not available for all plants, limiting the power of the analyses and increasing the likelihood of a Type II error. Nevertheless, it should be noted that even controlling for 1989 performance, the overall predictive power of the model is still high (with an adjusted R^2 of .38) and the effect of complementary HR practices remains stable.

In Equation 3, we test the hypothesis about the impact of employee experience levels on the adoption of new work practices. Contrary to our expectations, higher tenure levels did not decrease the likelihood that high-involvement work practices would be adopted. Indeed, higher levels of managerial tenure had a positive and statistically significant association with greater increases in the use of high-involvement work

---

[9] We reran Equation 2 dropping the 1989 level of quality, but the impact of the 1989 productivity level remained insignificant. The same was true when only the impact of 1989 quality was considered.

practices, while the coefficient for production worker tenure is very close to zero.[10]

One possible explanation is that the introduction of high-involvement work practices requires significant cooperation, trust, and coordination between different functional groups in each plant, which will more likely be present if the managers of those groups have greater experience working together. While we had hypothesized that longer tenure for managers and production workers might be associated with more ingrained attitudes and less exposure to new points of view, it is possible that the intense competitive environment in the auto industry in recent years has provided a sufficient "shock" to motivate even longtime managers and employees to be open to changes in work practices.

The hypothesis about company actions that reduce employee trust is tested in Equation 4. While we report only the equation with production worker layoffs, we tested production worker layoffs, management layoffs, and early retirement programs, individually as well as in a group. None had an impact on the likelihood that high-involvement work practices would be adopted. This may reflect the dual nature of layoffs and other downsizing actions – what at General Motors are often called "significant emotional events." Such actions can certainly do damage to employee trust and loyalty and create strong resistance (or even paralysis) in response to efforts to undertake organizational change. But they may also have an "unfreezing" effect (similar to product-related disruptions) that facilitates change. Since both of these effects may be present in the sample, they may cancel each other out in the regression analyses.

The inclusion of these variables serves to reduce the coefficients and significance levels for other variables in the equation. We believe this is due to the extremely high correlation between levels of work practices in 1989 and downsizing activity (correlations range from .54 to .70). This suggests that plants that had few high-involvement work practices in

---

[10] We also investigated another characteristic of the workforce – wage levels – as a potential determinant of the implementation of new work practices using a dummy variable for plants in low-wage countries (Mexico, Brazil, Korea, and Taiwan). (All other plants were located in the United States, Canada, Western Europe, Australia, or Japan.) This variable had a positive coefficient but was not statistically significant ($t = 1.4$). Nevertheless, the positive coefficient contradicts the expectation that a "low-wage" strategy relying on traditional work practices might be dominant in these countries. This fits with our observation that plants in these countries often face constraints on capital investment and have, instead, sought to improve their performance by implementing the new work practices, HR policies, and manufacturing systems associated with "lean production."

1989 were also those most likely to undertake downsizing by 1993–1994. This is consistent with the "bundling" idea – that past support for high-involvement work practices would be linked to a visible commitment to avoiding layoffs – but it also fits with the observation that many plants with traditional work practices in 1989 suffered from inferior economic performance.[11]

The final hypothesis suggests that disruptions resulting in an "unfreezing" of the current way of doing things would make change easier and therefore the introduction of high-involvement work practices more likely. The results of Equation 5 support this claim. New model introductions and plant expansions are more likely to be viewed as "opportunities" for making other changes than are layoffs (assessed in the second hypothesis), which are more likely to be viewed as a "threat." But the analysis reveals that only new model introductions prompt more extensive adoption of new work practices. New plant additions do not appear to have a significant impact on whether firms change their work practices. Of note during this period, however, is that practically all of the plants that added new assembly lines were relatively new (e.g., Japanese transplants), and already had substantial levels of high-involvement work practices before their expansions.[12]

Change in Complementary Practices

While it is important to understand the impact of levels of complementary practices on the adoption of new work practices, *changes* in the

[11] There is the possibility that since layoffs often accompany poor performance, the effect of poor performance on the adoption of high-involvement work practices offsets the effects of layoffs. To control for this, we reran Equation 2 including layoffs. Poor quality became a significant predictor of change in work practices at the 10% level, while layoffs predicted a reduced likelihood of change ($p = .11$).

[12] In other analyses, we have examined subsamples of nine new plants ("births") that have started operations in the past 10 years and six closed plants ("deaths") that shut down between Round 1 and Round 2 (Pil, 1996, App. C). Almost none of these plants are in the matched sample that provides the basis for the analyses in this chapter, so these results are not featured prominently here. Other researchers (e.g., Ichniowski & Shaw, 1995) have found that "greenfield" plants are more likely to implement new work practices. Briefly, we find that the new plants in the Round 2 sample have higher levels of high-involvement work practices, on average, than the entire Round 2 sample but that these differences are not statistically significant. Furthermore, while the closure of older plants with poor performance and traditional work practices should, over time, boost the average level of new work practices in the overall population of plants, we found that the work practices at "closed" plants were more traditional than in the entire Round 1 sample but that again these differences were not statistically significant. These results bear further investigation, particularly since small sample sizes for the new and closed plants may affect the significance level of the t-tests.

Table 6.6. *Change in Correlations over Time*

	High-Involvement Work Practices, 1989	Complementary HR Practices, 1989
High-involvement work practices, 1989	1.0000	
Complementary HR practices, 1989	.5496**	1.0000
Flexible automation, 1989	.5440**	.6096**

	High-Involvement Work Practices, 1993–1994	Complementary HR practices, 1993–1994
High-involvement work practices, 1993–1994	1.0000	
Complementary HR practices, 1993–1994	.4627**	1.0000
Flexible automation, 1993–1994	.6152**	.2069

*Signif. < .05; **Signif. < .01 (two-tailed).

levels of complementary practices can also have an impact on adoption patterns for high-involvement work systems. However, choices about work, HR, and automation may, to some extent, be made simultaneously. If so, we would expect that the correlations between work practices, HR practices, and flexible automation would become stronger over time.

Looking at Table 6.6, we see that while the correlation between flexible automation and high-involvement work practices has grown larger and more statistically significant over time, the correlation between HR practices and automation is significantly reduced. On the basis of our fieldwork, we believe this is due in part to the decision by plants in newly industrialized countries to boost their investments in new HR practices significantly between 1989 and 1993–1994, but not their use of robotics. We suspect that the increase in training, performance-based pay, the elimination of status barriers, and more selective recruitment and hiring practices that we observe in these plants reflect the corporate parent's assessment that such investments will cost less than extensive capital investments, when the latter are difficult to justify in locations that have both low production volume and low wages.

To try to understand further the issue of simultaneity in the choices firms make, we jointly estimate the adoption of work practices, HR practices, and flexible automation (Table 6.7). We find that while levels of

Table 6.7. *Joint Estimation of the Adoption of High-Involvement Work Practices, Complementary HR Practices, and Flexible Automation*

	Dependent Variables (1993–1994 levels, $n = 37$)		
	High-Involvement Work Practices	Complementary HR Practices	Flexible Automation
Independent variables			
High-involvement work practices, 1989	0.417*** (0.152)	−0.042 (0.147)	0.452*** (0.134)
Complementary HR practices, 1989	0.410** (0.181)	0.430** (0.176)	0.034 (0.160)
Flexible automation, 1989	−0.288 (0.322)	−0.296 (0.313)	0.788*** (0.283)
Intercept	18.65*** (6.60)	39.23*** (6.42)	−0.217 (5.798)
F-statistic	8.40***	2.16	17.60***
R^2 (adj.)	.38	.08	.57

H_0: *Is the effect of the independent variable equal to 0 across all dependent variables?*

F-test (based on Wilks' lambda)

High-involvement work practices, 1989	4.83***
Complementary HR practices, 1989	2.8*
Flexible automation, 1989	4.74***

H_0: *Is the effect of the independent variable the same across all dependent variables?*

F-test (based on Wilks' lambda)

High-involvement work practices, 1989	0.00
Complementary HR practices, 1989	0.06
Flexible automation, 1989	4.21**

Note: Standard errors are in parentheses.
Significance levels: *10%, **5%, ***1%.

work practices in 1989 help predict the level of automation in 1993–1994, they do not predict levels of HR practices in 1993–1994. Similarly, while Round 1 HR practices help predict Round 2 work practices, they have no impact on the adoption of flexible automation. The Round 1 level of robotics appears to have no impact on the adoption of either HR or work practices. Furthermore, while a Wilks test cannot reject the null hypothesis that the impact of Round 1 levels of HR and work practices is the same for the adoption of work practices, HR practices, and flexible automation in Round 2, the effect of flexible automation in Round 1 is not the same across the three equations.

There may be some element of "regression to the mean" in these results. In the face of recessionary conditions that affected the entire automotive industry in the early 1990s (and lingered particularly long in Japan), many plants with high levels of high-involvement work practices in 1989 appear to have maintained the same or even slightly lower levels of these practices. This trend, combined with the boost in high-involvement work practices from plants with low levels of these practices in 1989, would weaken the statistical association between 1989 and 1993–1994 levels.

Overall, these results suggest that despite the "logic" of interdependence among high-involvement work practices, complementary HR practices, and flexible automation, the choices firms make about these practices do not necessarily happen simultaneously. While Round 1 levels of high-involvement work practices and complementary HR practices have very similar effects on Round 2 levels of work practices, Round 1 levels of work practices have almost no relationship to Round 2 levels of HR practices. So while some plants are changing their HR practices independent of changes in work practices, the adoption of high-involvement work practices tends to follow the adoption of complementary HR practices. This supports the idea that HR practices may be less difficult to adopt, since they have less impact on the way core tasks are organized. Yet, once adopted, HR practices appear to provide a strong incentive for firms to push further in the direction of high-involvement work practices. This analysis also suggests that the introduction of flexible automation does not necessarily exert a strong pull toward adopting flexible work practices but that flexible work practices do increase the likelihood that a plant will increase its reliance on flexible automation.

Discussion

In this chapter, we draw on theories of innovation and organizational change to explore various hypotheses related to the determinants of adoption for high-involvement work practices. While previous empirical studies suggest that such practices can contribute significantly to economic performance (e.g., MacDuffie, 1995a; Huselid, 1995; Ichniowski et al., 1994), there are strong theoretical reasons (and considerable empirical evidence) for believing that the diffusion of such practices is slower and more sporadic than would be expected from the perspective of economic rationality (e.g., Ichniowski & Shaw, 1995; Osterman, 1994; Pfeffer, 1994). High-involvement work practices may represent "competence-destroying" change, which is difficult to implement and may lead to poorer performance in the short term (and thus may *not* be an economically rational choice for individual managers held accountable for short-term results). These practices may also have a less favorable impact on performance if they are not given adequate time to develop. For both of these reasons, firms may be discouraged from making changes in work practices (particularly changes involving bundles of interdependent practices rather than individual practices) or from continuing with change efforts beyond an initial trial period.

Given these impediments to change, we argue that three key factors at the plant or establishment level drive the adoption of new work practices (and bundles of practices): (1) the level of complementary organizational practices and technologies that would increase the *benefit* of the new practices, (2) the performance levels the organization is achieving with its current practices, and (3) organizational characteristics or actions that alter the *cost* of introducing the new practices. We tested five hypotheses about the adoption of new work practices using two rounds of data (1989 and 1993–1994) from the International Assembly Plant Study, focusing on a matched sample of 43 automotive assembly plants.

Our empirical analyses indicated that there was an overall increase in the use of high-involvement work practices in automobile assembly plants around the world from Round 1 to Round 2, but with high variance in the degree to which existing plants changed their use of these practices. This variation results from the fact that some poor 1989 performers made major changes in work practices, while other plants made very few changes; similarly, among the better 1989 performers, some continued to increase their use of high-involvement work practices while others remained at the same level. In OLS regressions, we found that, as predicted, plants with HR practices that complement the use of high-involvement work practices were more likely to increase their use of those work practices. But the Round 1 level of flexible automation was *not* a significant predictor of the use of high-involvement work practices in the second round.

As noted earlier, this latter finding may be the result of different strategies for flexible automation that are reflected in the sample of Round 1 plants. Coupled with the joint estimation of effects from 1989 to 1993–1994 for the three key variables (work systems, HR policies, and flexible automation), it provides a sketch of the dynamics of the relationship between new work practices and new technology during this

period in the auto industry. Recall that the Round 1 level of work practices was a strong predictor of the Round 2 level of flexible automation
but not the converse. This suggests that either some "high-tech" plants
in Round 1 did *not* increase their use of high-involvement work practices or that some "low-tech" plants in Round 1 did increase their use of
such practices.

Our fieldwork suggests that both are the case. Round 1 plants that
turned to technology investments as a means to improve their competitive position in the mid-1980s were also the plants least likely to turn to
new work practices in the 1990s. In part, this was the result of some
underlying preconceptions regarding the role of labor in enhancing performance. On the other hand, many plants in newly industrialized countries are choosing to invest in high-involvement work practices rather
than to invest heavily in any type of new technology.

We found little support for the hypothesis that change in work practices is performance-driven. While the coefficient for quality was positive and relatively large, indicating that plants whose 1989 quality was
poor were more likely to implement new work practices, it was not quite
statistically significant. Furthermore, productivity in 1989 had a much
smaller coefficient (also positive) and was not a significant predictor of
change in work practices. This supports other analyses (MacDuffie & Pil,
1995) which find that a subset of assembly plants in the Round 2 sample
have been able to achieve impressive productivity results through top-
down reengineering, without fundamental changes in work practices;
however, the quality of the performance of these plants has not been
very strong.

Despite this finding, it is worth noting that the coefficients for the performance variables were not negative, challenging the view that poor-
performing plants would be *less* likely to make changes in work practices
(due to such factors as escalating commitment to past, ineffective policies; lack of financial resources for change; adversarial labor relations; or
incompetent management) than average performers. Furthermore, the
predictive power of complementary HR practices remained stable when
controlling for 1989 performance.

Finally, we investigated a series of factors that would alter the benefits and costs of introducing new practices. Our predictions concerning
the impact of employee tenure and layoffs, with respect to both production workers and managers, were not borne out by the data. We specu-
late that in the intensely competitive environment of the world auto
industry over the past decade, there has been a strong external impetus
for change that has overwhelmed differences between low-tenure and
high-tenure workers and managers in terms of receptivity to new work

practices. In this context, the benefits – particularly among members of the plant management team – of working together for longer periods of time, with respect to increased trust and cooperation, may come to the fore. We therefore do not find support for the popular perception that older, more experienced managers and workers are more resistant to change in work practices than are younger, newer employees.

With regard to layoffs, we note that downsizing actions can certainly damage the "psychological contract" between employees and a firm but that they may also provide additional impetus to efforts to change work practices. The story is complicated by the fact that plants which traditionally used few high-involvement work practices were also those most likely to undertake employee downsizing. (However, even when the implementation of new work practices is spurred on in a climate of layoffs and downsizing, it remains to be investigated whether its impact on economic performance is as great as it would be in a climate of trust and cooperation.) We did find strong evidence that plants which undergo a major disruption in their operations – creating a window of opportunity for various organizational changes – were more likely to adopt high-involvement work practices. What is particularly important about this finding is that some types of disruptions (e.g., model changes) occur naturally and periodically in an organization's life cycle, and as such provide perfect opportunities to undertake competence-destroying change in a way that minimizes the costs of the transition.

Other factors beyond those measured here, we believe, also help explain the patterns of adoption of high-involvement work practices. Our field work suggests, for example, that, while individual plant performance may not be a strong predictor of change in work practices, *companies* that moved most rapidly to adopt new work practices from 1989 to 1993–1994 typically shared many of the following: (1) they faced a serious competitiveness crisis in the late 1980s and early 1990s; (2) their senior managers (and, in some cases, senior union officials) perceived the source of the crisis as internal rather than external – the result of problems with organizing the production system according to traditional mass production principles – and validated this perception with benchmarking data evaluating competitors in various countries; (3) top managers (and union officials) reached the conclusion that lean production principles should be implemented; (4) the company had relatively little previous experience with work reform; (5) company and plant-level managers and union officials held neutral or positive views about the value of work reform as a means of improving performance; (6) the company found effective ways to cultivate organizational learning across internal functional or divisional boundaries; and (7) the company had access to some "learning model" – that is, established some kind of learning relationship (ranging from a joint venture to informal sharing of benchmarking data) with another company (not necessarily Japanese) already using these principles.[13]

Factors such as these help explain regional and company-level differences in the adoption of high-involvement work practices. (These are not highlighted in this chapter because the small sample size does not allow us to add regional or company dummies to the analysis.) These conditions were met by a number of European companies (as well as some new entrant plants), which proved to be the most aggressive adopters of high-involvement work practices. There is also some indication that plants in any region producing high levels of product complexity, either as a function of manufacturing strategy or because the plant serves many export markets, are more likely to adopt both flexible automation and high-involvement work practices. In contrast, many plants in the United States and Canada retained relatively traditional work practices, for the following reasons: (1) management and union were ambivalent about work reform that developed in response to earlier change efforts in the late 1970s and early 1980s; (2) competitive crises were not necessarily interpreted as having internal sources or as requiring a change in fundamental production principles; (3) organizational learning, with respect to innovations both inside and outside the plant, was not always carried out effectively; and (4) the fact that most of these plants remained highly focused on building a single model at relatively high volume provided less incentive to increase flexibility by changing work practices.

Taken as a whole, these analyses – the quantitative analyses described in this chapter, as well as the related qualitative analyses – suggest that both the decision to adopt high-involvement work practices and the actual implementation of practices are affected by a complex mix of factors. Each factor potentially shifts the perceived costs and benefits of making a change in work practices, in terms of how time-dependent or competence-destroying it is. Each factor also affects the expectations for change among all the critical players – top management, top union officials, plant-level managers and union officials, and plant-level employees. Some combinations of factors, therefore, not only provide more economic incentives for change, in terms of quantifiable costs and benefits,

---

[13] This list reflects our perception about the common characteristics of firms making the most changes in their use of high-involvement work practices and should not be interpreted either as a checklist of "must do's" or as a result of statistical analyses of the distribution of these characteristics.

but also provide a more persuasive and legitimate rationale for action than other combinations.

The study described in this chapter is one of the first to explore, both theoretically and empirically, the determinants of adoption of high-involvement work practices in organizations. It underscores the value of a "systems" perspective that examines complementarities among variables related to work organization, human resource policies, and flexible technologies. Finally, it highlights the need for future research to consider the adoption of high-involvement work systems from a dynamic rather than a static perspective.

REFERENCES

Aldrich, Howard. 1979. *Organizations and Environments*. Englewood Cliffs, NJ: Prentice-Hall.

Aoki, Masahiko. 1990. "Toward an economic model of the Japanese firm." *Journal of Economic Literature* 28(1):1–27.

Arthur, Jeffrey B. 1992. "The link between business strategy and industrial relations systems in American steel minimills." *Industrial and Labor Relations Review* 45(3):488–506.

Bailey, Thomas. 1992. "Discretionary effort and the organization of work: Employee participation and work reform since Hawthorne." Paper written for the Sloan Foundation, Columbia University.

Batt, Rosemary. 1995. "Performance and welfare effects of work restructuring: Evidence from telecommunications services." Ph.D. dissertation, MIT, Sloan School of Management.

Blinder, Alan S. 1990. "Pay, participation, and productivity." *Brookings Review* 8(1):33–38.

Bolton, Michele K. 1993. "Organizational innovation and substandard performance: When is necessity the mother of innovation?" *Organization Science* 4(1):57–75.

Brockner, Joel, Steven Grover, Thomas Reed, Rocki DeWitt, and Michael O'Malley. 1987. "Survivors' reactions to layoffs: We get by with a little help from our friends." *Administrative Science Quarterly* 32:526–541.

Burack, Elmer H., Marvin D. Burack, Diane M. Miller, and Kathleen Morgan. 1994. "New paradigm approaches in strategic human resource management." *Group and Organization Management* 19(2):141–159.

Chandler, Alfred D. 1962. *Strategy and Structure*. Cambridge, MA: MIT Press.

Cyert, Richard M., and James G. March. 1963. *A Behavioral Theory of the Firm*. Englewood Cliffs, NJ: Prentice-Hall.

Damanpour, Fariborg. 1991. "Organizational innovation: A meta analysis of effects of determinants and moderators." *Academy of Management Journal* 34:555–590.

Dewar, Robert D., and Jane E. Dutton. 1986. "The adoption of radical and incremental innovations: An empirical analysis." *Management Analysis* 32(1): 1422–1433.

DiMaggio, Paul J., and Walter W. Powell. 1991. *The New Institutionalism in Organizational Analysis*. Chicago: University of Chicago Press.

Doeringer, Peter B., and Michael J. Piore. 1971. *Internal Labor Markets and Manpower Analysis*. Lexington, MA: Heath.

Huselid, Mark A. 1995. "The impact of human resource management practices on turnover, productivity, and corporate financial performance." *Academy of Management Journal* 38(3):635–672.

Ichniowski, Casey, and Thomas A. Kochan. 1995. "What have we learned from workplace innovations?" Unpublished manuscript prepared for the U.S. Department of Labor.

Ichniowski, Casey, and Kathryn Shaw. 1995. "Old dogs and new tricks: Determinants of the adoption of productivity-enhancing work practices." In *Brookings Papers on Economic Activity: Microeconomics*. Washington, DC: Brookings Institution.

Ichniowski, Casey, Kathryn Shaw, and Giovanni Prennushi. 1994. "The effect of human resource management practices on productivity." Working paper, Columbia University.

Katz, Harry. 1985. *Shifting Gears: Changing Labor Relations in the U.S. Auto Industry*. Cambridge, MA: MIT Press.

Kochan, Thomas A., Harry C. Katz, and Nancy Mower. 1984. *Worker Participation and American Unions: Threat or Opportunity?* Kalamazoo, MI: W. E. Upjohn Institute for Employment Research.

Kochan, Thomas A., and Paul Osterman. 1990. "Employment security and employment policy: An assessment of the issues." In *New Developments in the Labor Market*, edited by K. Abraham and R. McKersie, pp. 155–183. Cambridge, MA: MIT Press.

—1994. *The Mutual Gains Enterprise*. Boston: Harvard Business School Press.

Krafcik, John F. 1988. "Comparative analysis of performance indicators at world auto assembly plants." M.S. thesis, MIT, Sloan School of Management.

Levine, David, and Laura D'Andrea Tyson. 1990. "Participation, productivity, and the firm's environment." In *Paying for Productivity*, edited by Alan Blinder, pp. 183–244. Washington, DC: Brookings Institution.

Levinthal, Daniel, and James G. March. 1981. "A model of adaptive organizational search." In *Decisions and Organizations*, edited by James March, pp. 187–218. New York: Basil Blackwell.

Levitt, Barbara, and James G. March. 1988. "Organizational learning." *Annual Review of Sociology* 14:319–340.

Lewin, Kurt. 1947. "Frontiers in group dynamics." *Human Relations* 1:2–38, 143–153.

Lippman, Steven, and Richard Rumelt. 1982. "Uncertain imitability: An analysis of interfirm differences in efficiency under competition." *Bell Journal of Economics* 13:418–438.

MacDuffie, John Paul. 1995a. "Human resource bundles and manufacturing performance: Organizational logic and flexible production systems in the world auto industry." *Industrial and Labor Relations Review* 48(2):199–221.

—1995b. "Workers' roles under lean production: The implications for worker representation." In *Lean Production and Labor: Critical and Comparative Perspectives*, edited by Steve Babson, pp. 54–69. Detroit, MI: Wayne State University Press.

—1997. "The road to 'root cause': Shop-floor problem-solving at three auto assembly plants." *Management Science* 43(4):479–502.

MacDuffie, John Paul, and Thomas A. Kochan. 1995. "Do U.S. firms invest less in human resources? Determinants of training in the world auto industry." *Industrial Relations* 34(2):145–165.

MacDuffie, John Paul, and John Krafcik. 1992. "Interacting technology and human resources for high performance manufacturing: Evidence from the international auto industry." In *Transforming Organizations*, edited by Thomas Kochan and Michael Useem. New York: Oxford University Press.

MacDuffie, John Paul, and Frits K. Pil. 1995. "The International Assembly Plant Study: Philosophical and methodological issues." In *Lean Production and Labor: Critical and Comparative Perspectives*, edited by Steve Babson, pp. 181–198. Detroit, MI: Wayne State University Press.

—1996. "High-involvement systems and manufacturing performance: The diffusion of lean production in the world auto industry." Working paper, University of Pennsylvania, Wharton School.

—1997a. "'High-involvement' work practices and human resource policies: An international perspective." In *Evolving Employment Practices in the World Auto Industry*, edited by Thomas Kochan, Russell Lansbury, and John Paul MacDuffie, pp. 9–44. Ithaca, NY: Cornell University Press.

—1997b. "Flexible technologies, flexible workers." In *Transforming Auto Assembly: International Experiences with Automation and Work Organization*, edited by Takahiro Fujimoto and Ulrich Jurgens, pp. 238–255. Frankfurt: Springer.

MacDuffie, John Paul, Kannan Sethuraman, and Marshall Fisher. 1996. "Product variety and manufacturing performance: Evidence from the International Assembly Plant Study." *Management Science* 42(3):1–20.

March, James G. 1991. "Exploration and exploitation in organizational learning." *Organization Science* 2:71–87.

McNeil, Kenneth, and James D. Thompson. 1971. "The regeneration of social organizations." *American Sociological Review* 36:624–637.

Mezias, Stephen J., and Mary Ann Glynn. 1993. "The three faces of corporate renewal: Institution, revolution, and evolution." *Strategic Management Journal* 14(2):77–101.

Milgrom, Paul, and John Roberts. 1995. "Complementarity and fit: Strategy, structure, and organizational change in manufacturing." *Journal of Accounting and Economics* 19(2):179–208.

Nelson, Richard R., and Sidney Winter. 1982. *An Evolution Theory of Economic Change.* Cambridge, MA: Harvard University Press.

Osterman, Paul. 1994. "How common is workplace transformation and who adopts it?" *Industrial and Labor Relations Review* 47(2):173–188.

Parthasarthy, Raghavan, and S. Prakash Sethi. 1993. "Relating strategy and structure to flexible automation: A test of fit and performance implications." *Strategic Management Journal* 14:529–549.

Pfeffer, Jeffrey. 1994. *Competitive Advantage Through People: Unleashing the Power of the Workforce.* Boston: Harvard Business School Press.

Pil, Frits K. 1996. "Understanding the international and temporal diffusion of high-involvement HR and work practices." Ph.D. dissertation, University of Philadelphia, Wharton School.

Pil, Frits K, and John Paul MacDuffie. In press. "What makes transplants thrive: Managing the transfer of 'Best Practices' at Japanese auto plants in North America." *Journal of World Business*; reprinted in extended form as "Transferring competitive advantage across borders: A study of Japanese transplants in North America" in Jeffrey Liker, Mark Fruin, and Paul Adler, *Remade in America: Transplanting and Transforming Japanese Production Systems.* Oxford University Press.

Schein, Edgar H. 1992. *Organizational Culture and Leadership.* San Francisco: Jossey-Bass.

Staw, Barry. 1976. "Knee-deep in the big muddy: A study of escalating commitment to a chosen course of action." *Organizational Behavior and Human Performance* 16:27–44.

Tushman, Michael L., and Philip Anderson. 1986. "Technological discontinuities and organizational environments." *Administrative Science Quarterly* 35:1–8.

Tushman, Michael L., and Richard Nelson. 1990. "Introduction: Technology, organizations, and innovation." *Administrative Science Quarterly* 35:1–8.

Tushman, Michael, L., William H. Newman, and Elaine Romanelli. 1986. "Convergence and up-heaval: Managing the unsteady pace of organizational evolution." *California Management Review* 29(1):29–44.

White, Halbert. 1980. "A heteroskedasticity-consistent covariance matrix estimator and a direct test for heteroskedasticity." *Econometrica* 48(4):817–838.

Womack, James, Daniel Jones, and Daniel Roos. 1990. *The Machine That Changed the World.* New York: Rawson-Macmillan.

CHAPTER 7

The Effects of Total Quality Management on Corporate Performance: An Empirical Investigation

George S. Easton and Sherry L. Jarrell

Introduction

The emergence of total quality management (TQM) has been one of the most significant recent developments in U.S. management practice. The focus on the development of TQM systems in the United States appears to have begun around 1980 in response to global competition, primarily in U.S. manufacturing companies facing competition from Japan. By the middle to late 1980s, the U.S. TQM movement had developed significant momentum, in part due to the creation of the Malcolm Baldrige National Quality Award by Congress in 1987 and participation in the award by leading companies such as AT&T, Motorola, Texas Instruments, Westinghouse, and Xerox.

Exactly what constitutes TQM is a subject of debate. In this chapter, we define TQM to be a management system that substantially addresses the criteria of the Malcolm Baldrige National Quality Award (NIST, 1994). Although a complete definition of TQM is beyond the scope of the chapter, we can list some of the key characteristics:[1]

This is a slightly revised version of an article that originally appeared in *Journal of Business*, vol. 71, no. 2 (1998): © by the University of Chicago; reprinted by permission. The authors thank the companies that participated in the interviews. We also thank the editor of the *Journal of Business* and two anonymous referees for comments that substantially improved the manuscript. In addition, we thank the following for comments and suggestions: George Benson, George Benston, William Golomski, Mark Holder, Tom Hustad, Phillip Lederer, Albert Madansky, Harry Roberts, Vinod Singhal, and Marc Zenner. Finally, we thank Melissa J. Smith and Karin Sparf Chill for excellent research assistance. This research was partially supported by NSF grants SBR-9523962 (Easton) and SBR-9523003 (Jarrell), a grant from the "Field Studies in Quality Management" conference at the Simon School of Business, University of Rochester, March 1993, and summer research grants from the Graduate School of Business, University of Chicago, and the School of Business, Indiana University.

[1] See Easton (1995) for a discussion of the characteristics of TQM in the United States.

172

- *Process focus.* Process focus means an emphasis on the concept of process as a fundamental building block of the organization. This results in a widespread emphasis on process definition, process management, and process improvement.
- *Systematic improvement.* Systematic improvement means a widespread systematic organizational focus on quality improvement, cycle-time reduction, and waste (cost) reduction and the adoption of a prevention-based orientation.
- *Company-wide emphasis.* The process concept and the emphasis on improvement are applied throughout the company, including product development and business support processes.
- *Customer focus.* Customer focus includes (1) emphasis on customer requirements and customer satisfaction to define product and service quality ("customer-defined quality"); (2) emphasis on customer service (lead-time reduction, on-time delivery, field support, technical support, etc.); (3) integration of customer information into the management and improvement systems – particularly into the new-product development process and the production and service quality control and improvement processes; and (4) efforts to become integrated with customers as appropriate (often called "partnering"), such as joint improvement teams, participation in the customer's new-product development processes, or involving customers in the company's own internal processes, such as planning, new-product development, R&D, or technology forecasting.
- *Management-by-fact.* Management-by-fact means an emphasis on the deployment of systematic analysis and fact-based decision making driven by objective data and information. This includes a focus on the deployment and tracking of metrics.
- *Employee involvement and development.* Employee involvement in improvement (quality, cycle time, and waste), usually through teams, is widespread, and there is a strong emphasis on employee development through training. This emphasis is generally associated with a tendency to drive decision making close to the actual processes and thus to a corresponding increase in employee empowerment.
- *Cross-functional management.* There is explicit emphasis on cross-functional management that includes cross-functional improvement as well as cross-functional involvement in key processes, such as new-product development. Part of the cross-functional emphasis stems from the focus on processes (which typically cross multiple functions), although the emphasis is

much stronger, recognizing cross-functional issues and involvement as requiring specific focus in order to achieve highly effective management systems.

- *Supplier performance and supplier relationships.* Supplier management includes emphasis on supplier quality and service performance, supplier capabilities, supplier improvement, and supplier involvement and integration (supplier partnerships), such as joint quality improvement, and participation in new-product development, technology development and planning, and even strategic planning.

- *Recognition of TQM as a critical competitive strategy.* There is widespread recognition that implementation and aggressive refinement of the above management model is a critical competitive strategy and thus a primary concern of all levels of management, including senior management. The role of senior management in providing leadership for the development and deployment of quality management is a natural consequence of the recognition of quality management as a critical competitive strategy.

There is considerable controversy concerning the effectiveness of TQM, and research examining its impact is only beginning to emerge. Most of this research is based on cross-sectional surveys that examine the association between manager perceptions of the impact of TQM and model constructs based on questionnaire items that are intended to capture various aspects of the deployment of TQM. Little empirical research has attempted to determine the impact of TQM on corporate performance by directly examining publicly available financial data. Most of these studies focus not on TQM directly, but rather on related events such as winning a quality award (e.g., Hendricks and Singhal, 1996) or achieving ISO-9000 registration (e.g., Anderson et al., 1995). For a critical review of existing research on TQM that measures performance using publicly available financial data, see Easton and Jarrell (1999).

This study examines the impact of TQM on financial performance for a sample of 108 firms. The study is based on a comprehensive research methodology that combines (1) interview-based research to identify a sample of firms that have, in fact, made serious efforts to implement TQM systems in a majority of their business and (2) an empirical analysis of publicly available financial data using an improved benchmark and control methodology (Jarrell, 1991) for isolating the impact of the adoption of TQM. We believe that the methodology developed in this study for examining the impact of a complex management phenomenon is an improvement over approaches generally taken in the literature and represents one of the contributions of this chapter.

Overview of the Research Methodology

The basic approach used in this study adapts the event study methodology, commonly used in empirical corporate finance, to examine the impact of TQM on firm financial performance. In this study, the "event" corresponds to the beginning of serious efforts to deploy a comprehensive TQM system. The impact of TQM is assessed by examining the unexpected changes in financial performance for a five-year period following the beginning of deployment of the TQM system.

In most event studies in empirical finance, both the event and when it occurred can be unambiguously defined without much difficulty (e.g., the announcement of a merger). In this study, however, determining both whether and when an event has occurred is more difficult. First, whether or not a firm has seriously pursued TQM cannot be determined by relying on the firm's public pronouncements. Many firms claim to be implementing TQM when, in fact, they have made essentially no changes (other than in their public rhetoric). In other cases, TQM has been implemented in only a small fraction of their business. Second, firms seldom publicly announce the beginning of the deployment of their TQM systems. In fact, there is often no completely unambiguous start date. Rather, there is a period during which the firm's activities focus and efforts begin in earnest.

The lack of publicly available information about firms' implementations of TQM, the unreliability of their public statements, and the ambiguity of the start date of their TQM implementations are addressed in this study by interviews of a senior quality executive at each of the potential sample firms. Potential sample firms were first identified through public information sources as described in the next section. Interviews were then used to determine (1) whether a firm has, in fact, seriously pursued the development of a TQM system; (2) the approximate extent of development and deployment of the firm's approaches; and (3) the approximate date that serious efforts began. The interviews were conducted by a former senior examiner for the Malcolm Baldrige National Quality Award. The interview methodology is discussed in detail in the section entitled "Interview Methods."

The use of in-depth semi-structured interviews to select the sample firms is an important difference between this study and typical studies based on questionnaires. The key reasons are that the interviews are interactive, flexible, and allow in-depth discussion and focused probing.

This permits considerable verification of the information obtained and allows for clarification of terminology and adjustment for the specific knowledge and experience base of the interview subject. In addition, interviews conducted by an interviewer trained in evaluation against a TQM "standard" (the Baldrige Award criteria) allow external rather than respondent self-assessment of the company's TQM system against a well-developed operational definition.

In contrast, questionnaire-based approaches generally allow self-selection into the sample and rely on the managers' perceptions without critical evaluation. It is also very difficult in survey-based research to address the large variation in interpretation of terminology in different companies, and it is frequently unclear how respondents actually operationalize the questions. As a result, most questionnaire-based research is fairly superficial. These research issues are discussed further in Easton and Jarrell (1999). Interview-based approaches, of course, also have disadvantages. These include dependence on the skill and knowledge of the interviewers, the difficulty of precise replication of the methodology, and the inability to examine the data collection instrument used.

In this study, interviews are also used to divide the sample firms into two groups based on the development of their TQM systems. The performance of these two groups is then compared. This provides an intra-sample validation of the overall research method since, if TQM has a positive impact on performance, the more advanced firms should perform better than the less advanced firms.[2]

The event study approach is another important difference between this study and cross-sectional studies that examine the association between performance and the reported use of various practices (e.g., employee participation). Such cross-sectional studies generally do not attempt to determine when the practices were initiated or to examine performance changes associated with actual implementation. The failure to focus specifically on performance changes associated with the actual changes in management practices greatly increases the possibility of confounding factors. Further, such studies provide weak evidence concerning causality, even when statistically significant associations are observed, because the direction of causality is often unclear. In many cases, it is at

[2] The validity of this comparison as an intra-sample validation is discussed further in the subsection entitled "Intra-sample validation." Because the decision to continue TQM implementation is endogenous, early financial success during the post-event period could influence the subsequent development of the firm's TQM system. The empirical analysis in the subsection just cited indicates that this phenomenon does not drive the results of the comparison between the more advanced and less advanced firms.

least as plausible that, because of the availability of additional resources, improved performance drives the more extensive use of the "progressive" practices typically examined in these studies as it is that the progressive practices caused the improved performance. While it is impossible to *prove* causality through observational studies (including this one), studies that focus as tightly as possible on the period of the management changes and that use a carefully developed control methodology clearly provide far more compelling evidence than those that do not.

The control methodology used to develop the performance measures is another critical research issue. To assess the impact of TQM, the company's actual performance would ideally be compared with what the performance would have been had the company not implemented TQM (i.e., a perfect "clone" but with no TQM). Since this is not possible, a benchmark performance measure must be constructed that, on average, captures what the performance would have been without TQM. In this study, performance is assessed using both accounting-based variables and daily stock returns over a five-year period following the event. The performance measures are constructed somewhat differently for the accounting and stock return variables. For the accounting variables, the primary approach consists of two components. First, a firm's *unexpected performance* is measured by the difference between the firm's actual performance and an analyst's forecast made just before the event. Second, the event firm's unexpected performance is compared with the unexpected performance of a carefully matched control portfolio of three firms that do not appear to have implemented TQM. The control firms are matched to the event firm based on industry, on time period, on analysts' projections of future performance, and, to the extent possible, on market size, debt-to-equity ratios, and a market risk factor. The impact on performance is then measured by the *excess unexpected performance*, the difference between the unexpected performance of the event firm and the unexpected performance of its control portfolio.

The use of analysts' forecasts in the accounting performance variables is important because such forecasts incorporate an expert's evaluation of the future impact of the firm's particular circumstances. It is these forecasts that allow the performance measure to adjust for firm-specific exogenous factors that are likely to affect future performance, including factors influencing the endogenous decision to implement TQM. The failure to control for such factors can introduce potentially significant bias into the results. Such factors may not be apparent in the firm's historical financial data (e.g., emerging foreign competition, the expiration of a patent, developing labor issues, or pending regulatory or tax changes).[3]

The use of the control portfolios is also critical to correct for subsequent exogenous events during the post-event period (e.g., a recession). Since the control portfolio is also matched on the analyst's projection of future performance, the research design provides an additional control against systematic differences between the event and control firms in terms of the bias in the analysts' forecasts.[4]

The idea of assessing performance relative to a prediction of future performance (i.e., the unexpected performance) is a fundamental idea in financial theory. It is intrinsic to any analysis based on stock returns, because stock prices are derived from the market's consensus forecast of expected future performance. Ideally, market consensus forecasts would have been used here. However, these are not directly available.[5] Analysts' forecasts, which represent an expert assessment, are used instead to proxy for market expectations.[6]

---

[3] Adjusting for endogeneity of the decision to implement TQM (or any similar management decision) requires predicting what performance would have been had the same firms not implemented the changes. Thus, the performance measures used in this study must account for variables associated with the decision to implement TQM that would affect future performance even if TQM were not implemented. There are a variety of approaches that might be taken other than the use of analysts' forecasts. For example, one might try to build econometric models that include exogenous variables thought to be associated with the choice to implement TQM. The actual performance of the event company could then be compared with the model's prediction. Forecasts based on such statistical models, however, have several disadvantages relative to analysts' forecasts (see note 5). They are generally not developed on a firm-by-firm basis, do not incorporate information from sources other than the time series of accounting data, and are subject to errors caused by model building, outliers in the data, etc.

[4] What is required is that the difference between the analysts' forecasts for the event firm and for the control portfolio be an unbiased estimate of the market consensus forecast of the expected difference. This means that the control portfolio methodology must correct for any systematic bias in the analysts' forecasts, provided that such biases apply, on average, equally to the event and control firms (under the null hypothesis of no effect due to TQM).

[5] The IBES market consensus forecasts are not used because they are limited to short-term earnings per share forecasts and are not time-stamped in a way that allows reliable determination of when the forecasts were made relative to the event times. This study requires long-term forecasts and examines variables other than earnings per share.

[6] In addition to the theoretical basis discussed here, there is also considerable empirical evidence that analysts' forecasts are effective proxies for market expectations (e.g., see Schipper, 1991; Brown, 1993). There is also evidence that analysts' forecasts are superior to time-series forecasts, at least for simple time-series models. Brown et al. (1987) find that the forecasting ability of Value Line analysts is superior to that of univariate time-series models. Brown and Rozeff (1978) compare the earnings predictions of Value Line analysts and forecasts in Standard and Poor's Earnings Forecaster with those from three

In contrast to the methodology used here, traditional approaches in the empirical finance literature use pre-event firm performance or post-event industry average performance as the control benchmark. Both of these approaches are unsatisfactory. The pre-event performance benchmark fails to control for subsequent exogenous macroeconomic events. The post-event industry benchmark assumes that the firm, had it not adopted TQM, would have performed like the typical firm in the industry. This fails to address the endogeneity of the decision to implement TQM. Some more recent approaches are based on fitting structural models and comparing actual performance with the model's prediction (see, e.g., Healy et al., 1992). While superior to the pre-event performance or post-event industry benchmark methods, such approaches generally assume that the structural equation is the same across event firms and is unaffected by subsequent exogenous events. They further assume that all of the factors likely to affect future performance, including those associated with the decision to implement TQM, are evident in the pre-event financial performance data used to estimate the structural equation. Thus, they do not adequately control for bias due to endogeneity of the decision to implement TQM.[7]

The method developed in this chapter is used to assess the performance of the TQM firms with regard to appropriately scaled variables based on net income, operating income, and sales. Unfortunately, analysts' forecasts are not available for some other variables of interest (e.g., variables based on inventory levels or number of employees). For these variables, performance is measured by *excess actual performance*, the difference between the actual performances of the event firm and the control portfolio. While the evidence provided by these variables is much less compelling than when analysts' forecasts are available, we believe the results do contain some useful indications, particularly in the context of the overall analysis.

different time-series models, including random walk and Box–Jenkins models, and find that Value Line analysts produce more small annual forecast errors and fewer large annual forecast errors. Finally, Brown et al. (1987), who examine Value Line forecasts, and Fried and Givoly (1982), who examine forecasts from Standard and Poor's Earnings Forecaster, find that one-year-ahead analyst forecasts have a greater association with excess stock returns over the next year than do one-year-ahead earnings forecasts made by time-series models. These studies support the view that analyst expectations are a better proxy for market expectations than are forecasts from time-series models. The subsection entitled "Analysts' Forecasts" also provides empirical evidence validating the Value Line forecasts for the sample of event and control firms used in this study.

[7] This remark also applies to the approach suggested by Barber and Lyon (1995). Their article examines several methods from event studies using accounting-based measures, and concludes that test statistics are well specified only when sample firms are matched with control firms of similar pre-event performance.

The impact of TQM is also evaluated using with-dividend continuously compounded daily stock returns. Because the stock price incorporates the market's forecast of a firm's future performance, it is not appropriate to use analysts' forecasts when examining stock returns. It is important, however, to control for the impact of post-event exogenous events. Thus, the performance measure for stock returns is based on the *excess actual returns*, the difference between the returns of the event firm and its control portfolio. For this measure to be valid, it is important that the event firms and control portfolios are well matched in terms of non-diversifiable risk. This is achieved by means of the method of matching control firms discussed earlier, which includes consideration of expected future performance, market size, debt-to-equity ratios, and a market risk factor. Thus, the matched control portfolios control for both post-event exogenous events and non-diversifiable risk.

Despite the similarity in methodology, this study differs from typical empirical finance event studies in some important ways. First, this study does not focus on the impact of information events ("announcements") on the capital market. While we examine stock returns, we use them for a different purpose – as a comparatively "clean" overall performance measure. Second, the event dates are determined not from public information, but rather from private information obtained through interviews. Third, the phenomenon of interest (the deployment of TQM) does not occur at a discrete point in time like a typical "announcement," but rather occurs over a period of at least several years. Thus, we do not expect stock price reactions around event time zero. Instead, we examine a five-year period following the beginning of the implementation of TQM. While some of the benefits of TQM, such as certain types of cost reductions, can be obtained relatively quickly, many others, such as improvements in new product development or increased market share due to increased customer satisfaction, require at least several years to become evident in the firm's accounting data. Many benefits of TQM may even occur after the five-year post-event period that we examine. Further, during the period in which the firms in this sample began implementing TQM, the capital markets had little basis for assessing TQM's impact; the evidence is only now beginning to emerge. Thus, it is not unreasonable to expect that the impact on stock return performance will occur throughout the five-year post-event period as the results (positive and negative) of TQM implementation accrue and become evident in the firms' accounting data.

In interpreting this study, it is important to understand that we are attempting to examine transient performance effects due to the introduction of a new management "technology." In a theoretical setting where managers always instantaneously select the optimal strategy for maximizing firm performance based on the available information set, a firm's decision to implement TQM or not would always be deterministically driven as the optimal response to exogenous variables. After controlling for all of these exogenous variables, there would be no observable effect due to TQM. This theoretical argument is not unique to TQM; it also applies to other management decisions, including restructuring decisions (e.g., mergers), which are frequently the focus of similar research examining their performance impact.

These assumptions, of course, are unrealistically strong. Managers do not always make optimal decisions and certainly do not always do so instantaneously. What managers seek are strategies for moving their companies toward a dynamically changing optimum. Potential strategies include the implementation of TQM (among many others – including restructuring). It is of interest to examine whether such strategies generate value for the companies that implement them. The performance impact can be examined only because of deviations from the theoretical setting just described. These deviations should be transient as competitive pressure drives the economic system toward optimality.

Data Sources and Sample Design

Candidate event firms were initially identified through publicly available information sources. The search was intended to be comprehensive, but not exhaustive. The primary sources were the ARS full-text data base of on-line annual reports from Nexus/Lexus (since 1987), the Businesswire full-text data base of press releases (since 1986), Standard and Poor's Corporate Register of Directors (1993), and the list of Baldrige Award site-visited companies in the report by the U.S. General Accounting Office (1991) on quality practices.

The study was conducted in two phases. The pilot phase was based on annual report searches for the key words "total quality management," "just-in-time" or "JIT," "Baldrige," "Deming," "Juran," and "Crosby." These searches identified 274 firms. Relevant excerpts were then reviewed to select only the firms whose annual reports clearly indicated implementation of at least one specific quality management approach (e.g., statistical process control [SPC], JIT, quality training, or improvement teams).

Review of the annual report searches resulted in a list of 78 firms. These firms were contacted to set up an interview with a senior manager familiar with the development of the firm's quality management systems. Of the 78 firms, 59 were interviewed. In 11 cases, firms were not interviewed because it became clear in trying to set up the interview that the firm was not actually implementing TQM. In the remaining 8 cases, the request was refused. Of the 59 firms interviewed, 15 were eliminated because the interviews did not indicate serious efforts to implement TQM in a majority of their business. An additional 5 firms were eliminated because the required performance data were not available. The remaining 39 firms formed the pilot sample. Interviews for the pilot sample were conducted between January and March 1993.

In the second phase of the study, additional candidate firms were sought from a variety of sources. First, an additional 54 firms were selected after a second review of the original 274 firms identified through the annual report searches. Second, new firms were sought through additional searches and sources. The Businesswire data base was searched for references to quality awards. Searches were also made for quality-related executive titles. The annual report data base was searched for "quality" within five words of "vice president" or "director," and the Businesswire data base was searched for "total" or "continuous" within three words, and "focus" and "satisfaction" within five words, of "vice president" or "director." These searches identified 89 firms. The 1993 Standard and Poor's Register of Directors and Executives was searched for "quality" within five words of "vice president" or "director," identifying 71 firms. Finally, lists of site-visited firms from the General Accounting Office study and lists of the institutional affiliations of Baldrige Award examiners for the years 1989 to 1993 (available from the Baldrige Award Office) were reviewed, identifying 67 additional firms. Thus, 281 new candidate firms were identified in the second phase of the study.

As in the pilot phase of the study, the information on these firms was reviewed for evidence of specific quality management approaches. This resulted in a list of 129 firms, which were then contacted for interviews. Of these, 117 agreed to be interviewed. Of the 12 firms that were not interviewed, 6 declined to participate and 6 obviously did not have TQM programs. Of the firms that were interviewed, 38 were eliminated because the interviews did not confirm serious efforts to implement TQM in a majority of the business and 10 were eliminated because the required performance data were not available. This resulted in 69 additional event firms. These interviews were conducted between August 1993 and January 1994.

In summary, information on more than 500 firms was reviewed to identify potential sample firms. Of these, a total of 207 were approached for interviews. Fourteen firms declined to participate, giving an overall response rate of 93%. In attempts to set up the interviews, 17 firms were determined not to have a TQM system. A total of 176 firms were actually interviewed, and 53 firms (30% of those interviewed) were eliminated because their efforts to implement TQM did not appear to be adequate. An additional 15 firms were eliminated because the required performance data were unavailable. This process resulted in 108 event firms in the final sample (see Appendix A).

The Value Line Investment Survey was used as the source of analysts' forecasts, as the primary source of the accounting data, and to select the control firms (see the section entitled "Analysis Methods"). For the measures based on the Value Line analysts' forecasts, performance is examined for years 1, 2, and the average of years 3 to 5 following the event. Long-term data were available for 100 of the 108 events. The COMPUSTAT data base compiled by Standard and Poor's was used for data that Value Line does not report (inventory levels and the number of employees). Daily stock returns were obtained from the data base compiled by the Center for Research in Security Prices at the University of Chicago.

Interview Methods

Each candidate sample firm was contacted, first by a letter describing the project and then by telephone, to set up an interview with a senior manager familiar with the development of the company's quality management systems (generally a vice president or director of quality). The interviews generally lasted about 45 minutes and were conducted by George S. Easton, a former senior examiner for the Malcolm Baldrige National Quality Award. The objective of the interview was to develop a time line of the development of the company's TQM systems, to determine what key approaches were used, and to assess the actual extent of deployment through in-depth probing in a few areas. The interviews were semi-structured and allowed flexibility in the topics discussed. The managers were promised complete confidentiality concerning the interview content.

The interview occurred in two phases. The objective of the first phase was to elicit from the manager, with minimal prompting, the major milestones in the development of the company's TQM approaches. Questions were asked as necessary to establish the level of detail desired and to determine as specifically as possible the dates of the events surrounding the beginning of the TQM approaches. Questions about approaches or methods not mentioned by the manager were avoided in order not to influence the manager's description. These impromptu descriptions are very revealing about what aspects of the development of the TQM system the manager believes are important and what the key drivers of the company's system actually are – that is, how the company "thinks" about its TQM systems.

The second phase of the interview was intended to fill in any important gaps and to probe some key areas in order to assess actual levels of deployment. The list of interview topics given in Appendix B was used to prompt the interviewer. The objective was not to discuss every topic, but rather to discuss in detail a few areas as appropriate for the company's approaches and the expertise and experience of the manager being interviewed. If not adequately addressed by the initial description of the time line, four areas were always covered: production, customer satisfaction measurement, supplier management, and new product development and design. In general, the extent of deployment of approaches mentioned was assessed by asking specific questions concerning the number of employees involved, their training, and the dates of the various events mentioned. Other questions used to determine the actual extent of deployment included: What were the most important barriers to implementation? What would you do differently if you were to begin implementing this approach again? What lessons were learned, and what changes or improvements have been made since the initial approach? When the approaches described have actually been deployed, there is generally a rich "story" surrounding them and it is fairly easy for a knowledgeable interviewer to determine whether significant deployment has actually occurred.

Companies were included in the sample if, based on the interviews, they appeared to have made serious efforts to implement TQM approaches in the majority of their business. Deployment must have been in a majority of the company (as measured by sales) in order for there to be any reasonable expectation that the results could be observed in the company's overall financial data. The standard of "serious efforts" for inclusion in the sample is quite low; it is not a requirement that the company's efforts resulted in a comprehensive and well-integrated approach.

Companies were eliminated from the sample for a variety of reasons. In many cases, the reason was that the TQM efforts were deployed in only a small fraction of the company. Other reasons ranged from a lack of evidence of any significant deployment efforts to confusion of TQM with other approaches (such as quality improvements due solely to automation).

The start dates for the sample companies were chosen, based on the time line developed from the interview notes, to be about six months after the beginning of the first major initiative. This initiative was usually the deployment of widespread quality training. In some companies, however, other initiatives marked the beginning of their TQM systems, such as major changes in customer satisfaction measurement or new product development, widespread deployment of SPC, or deployment of a quality management systems assessment process (e.g., Baldrige-based assessment). The start date was chosen to be six months after the beginning of the first major initiative because most such initiatives take a substantial time to roll out. For example, it is not uncommon for widespread training initiatives to take more than a year to complete in a large company, and there is usually an additional lag before substantive organizational or operational changes occur.

The start date determines when the analysts' forecasts were made that are used in the performance measures. In order for the difference between the actual post-event performance and the analyst's forecast to capture the unexpected performance due to TQM, the forecasts should be made before the analyst incorporates knowledge about the firm's TQM initiatives. This suggests selecting an early event time 0 to ensure that the analyst is not aware of the TQM initiative. However, too early an event time 0 truncates the post-event period, which is limited to five years, and may result in a failure to capture the main performance improvement due to TQM. The selection of event time 0 to be six months after the initial deployment of the first major initiative constitutes a compromise between these conflicting objectives.

Despite the fact that event time 0 was selected to be six months after the beginning of the first major initiative, there are several reasons that it is unlikely that the analysts' forecasts are affected: (1) there is almost never any public information available about the initiatives until later than this period; (2) any claims made by management about their intentions contain little substantive information about whether serious efforts to implement TQM will actually be made; (3) during the period we are studying, TQM was new and thus there would be little or no basis for updating the forecasts; and (4) the texts accompanying the Value Line analysts' forecasts were also reviewed and in no case was there any mention of the firm beginning a quality-related initiative. More important, however, any such leakage into the analysts' forecasts biases against finding an effect due to TQM, and thus makes the results of this study conservative.

The companies that were retained for the sample were divided into a group of 44 firms with more advanced TQM systems and a group of 64 firms with less advanced TQM systems by making a rough estimate, based solely on the interviews, of what each firm's score would be in terms of the approach and deployment (not results) areas of the Baldrige criteria. It should be noted that the interviews focused only on the approaches taken and the extent of their deployment and not on operational or financial results. The firms selected as more advanced had estimated scores above 450 out of 1,000 possible points. This represents considerable success in developing and deploying a TQM system. The median score of companies that apply for the Baldrige Award is generally below 500.

The key differences between the more advanced and less advanced firms were in the scope of the issues addressed by their TQM systems and the extent of deployment of their approaches. Some of the firms in the less advanced group had successfully deployed basic approaches such as quality training and improvement teams, but had not further developed their quality management systems. Others had developed approaches that address a broader scope of the Baldrige criteria but had only limited deployment. In contrast, firms in the more advanced group demonstrated better deployment of the basic approaches together with the deployment of a broader scope of systems. These companies typically have had multiple major phases in the development of their TQM systems, whereas less advanced firms typically have completed only one major phase. For example, a typical advanced firm might start with an initial phase focused internally on SPC and quality improvement teams, followed by a second phase, which might focus on design quality, internal self-assessment, or customer satisfaction measurement (and feedback of such information into the company's internal processes). Subsequent phases would then focus on approaches and issues not already addressed.

Analysis Methods

This study examines statistical evidence against the null hypothesis that implementation of TQM does not improve corporate performance. Performance is measured by accounting variables, primarily focusing on net income, operating income, sales, and inventory, and by with-dividend continuously compounded stock returns. As discussed in the section entitled "Overview of the Research Methodology," in order to be convincing, the performance measures must (1) take into account firm-specific factors, including those associated with the (endogenous) decision to implement TQM; and (2) compensate for post-event macroeconomic or industry-specific developments that are likely to affect firm performance. The approach used here was developed by Jarrell (1991) to address these issues.

Control Portfolio Selection

All of the performance measures examined rely on matched control portfolios. For each event firm, a control portfolio of three firms that do not appear to have implemented TQM is formed by matching them to the TQM firm on the basis of industry, calendar time, projected performance, and, to the extent possible, market size, debt-to-equity ratios, and a market risk factor (the Value Line "safety" ranking).[8] Matching on industry and calendar time is designed to control for various economic and regulatory influences. The industry classifications are defined by the Value Line Investment Survey and verified with the Standard Industrial Classification (SIC) code. The matching included a detailed review of product lines as described by Value Line, so the matching realized is substantially better than that obtained by using the Value Line industry classifications or SIC codes alone.

The "projected performance" matching of the control firms to the event firms is based on the Value Line "timeliness" rank. The timeliness rank summarizes the analyst's assessment of the firm's expected stock price performance over the next 12 months relative to the other firms covered by Value Line.[9] Whenever possible, firms were selected whose timeliness rank at the time of the event differed by no more than 1 from the event firm rank. These firms were then narrowed to three control firms per event, first by choosing those closest in size to the TQM firm and then (if more than three remained) those whose debt-to-equity ratio and Value Line safety rank are closest to the TQM firm. Size is measured by the market value of debt plus the market value of equity and preferred stock as reported by the Value Line during event year 0.

Matching on the basis of the timeliness rank incorporates into the

---

[8] Eighteen control firms were interviewed to provide some verification that the control firms had not made significant efforts to implement TQM. All were determined to be appropriate controls. It would be impractical to interview the entire control sample. In addition, especially for larger firms, failure to detect TQM-related efforts through the searches performed provides considerable evidence that these firms had not made significant TQM efforts. More important, however, contamination of the control portfolio by firms that implemented TQM should bias the results against finding an effect associated with TQM.

[9] The timeliness rank is scaled from 1 to 5 (1 corresponds to the highest projected performance) and is updated approximately every quarter. Value Line indicates that the rank is based on three criteria: (1) the firm's industry-adjusted price–earnings ratio from the preceding 12 months relative to the past 10 years; (2) the year-to-year change in the quarterly earnings of the stock compared with that of all Value Line stocks; and (3) an earnings "surprise" factor.

control portfolios as much information as possible about the expected performance of the TQM firms. Because the control firms are selected to have an outlook similar to that of the event firm, such matching has the potential to control for effects such as systematic differences in forecast accuracy between firms forecast to perform very well and those forecast to perform poorly. The existence of this type of bias is plausible. For example, due to the phenomenon of regression toward the mean, analysts' forecasts may be systematically too high for firms that are expected to perform very well and systematically too low for firms that are expected to perform poorly. In such a case, failure to control for projected performance could introduce bias into the results, especially if the sample has a high concentration of firms that are expected to perform either very well or very poorly.[10] Similarly, matching that considers the timeliness rank also minimizes the effects of any systematic differences in responses to subsequent economic events between firms with very positive and very negative outlooks.[11]

[10] Analysis of the forecasts for the control firms (which, with respect to this issue, are not contaminated by the effects of implementing TQM) does show a very slight, but not statistically significant pattern of overestimation for firms with low timeliness ranks (strong expected performance) and underestimation of performance for firms with high timeliness ranks (poor expected performance). This, however, should not be interpreted as a justification for not using the analysts' forecasts, since the bias associated with the high and low timeliness ranks is very small and is not statistically significant. Further, it is much smaller than would occur when matching to firms with very different timeliness ranks and is corrected by the matching strategy used here. Finally, the average timeliness rank of the event firms is 3.08, so there is no concentration of firms in the sample with very high or very low timeliness ranks.

[11] A specific example illustrates these issues. The event firm United Technologies (UT), a diversified company, has a TQM starting year of 1984. At that time, UT's timeliness rank was 1, the highest rank. According to the analyst, "The key here is technological integration. Unlike the typical conglomerate, UT isn't simply equal to the sum of various unrelated parts." The analyst goes on to say, "Whatever it may have once been, UT is now a large and diverse company with a clear business strategy." If the timeliness rank is ignored in matching the controls, ITT Corp. (timeliness rank 4) would replace Kaman Corp. (timeliness rank 2). While ITT is a better match than Kaman in terms of size, it is far worse in terms of the analyst's assessment of future prospects. Specifically, ITT's "top priority is to become a major force in telecommunications, through its new digital telephone switch, the System 12." While the "System 12 is succeeding overseas," it is "incompatible with the current generation of equipment used here." The analyst concludes that "success in this country will not come overnight," "the telecommunications thrust is expensive," and ITT "will probably step up its divestiture activity." In contrast, for Kaman "1984 is shaping up as a record year" as a result of "record gains from both the diversified and industrial distribution divisions." For example, examining the operating margin, UT and all three of the original control firms (including Kaman) ended up performing worse than their year 3 to 5 forecasts. UT's performance was about 2% worse than the average of the control portfolio. ITT's performance, however, was substantially

*Accounting Variables: The Primary Performance
Benchmark Method*

The primary performance benchmark compares each event firm's and corresponding control firms' performance with Value Line analysts' forecasts made before the event. Specifically, for event firm i in post-event year t, the *unexpected performance* $U_i^E(t)$ is

$$U_i^E(t) = P_i^E(t) - F_i^E(t),$$

where $P_i^E(t)$ is the actual performance of TQM firm i in post-event year t, and $F_i^E(t)$ is the Value Line analyst's forecast of that performance made before the event. The unexpected performance $U_i^{C_j}(t)$ for the firms in the control portfolio is similarly defined:

$$U_i^{C_j}(t) = P_i^{C_j}(t) - F_i^{C_j}(t),$$

where $P_i^{C_j}(t)$ is the actual performance and $F_i^{C_j}(t)$ is the forecast performance in period t for control firm j corresponding to event i. The unexpected performance $\overline{U}_i^C(t)$ for the control portfolio is the average of the unexpected performance for the three control firms: $\overline{U}_i^C(t) = \frac{1}{3}\Sigma_{j=1}^3 U_i^{C_j}(t)$.

For the accounting variables, the primary measure examined for evidence of the impact of TQM on firm performance is the *excess unexpected performance* $XU_i(t)$, the difference between the unexpected performance of the event firm and the unexpected performance of the corresponding control portfolio. Thus,

$$XU_i(t) = U_i^E(t) - \overline{U}_i^C(t).$$

Value Line analysts' forecasts are given for one year ahead, two years ahead, and the average of three to five years ahead. Thus, the excess unexpected performance cannot be calculated separately for post-event years 3, 4, and 5. Instead, following the analysts' forecasts, the long-term performance measure is based on unexpected average performance for years 3 to 5. Specifically, for event firm i, the unexpected average annual performance $\overline{U}_i^E(3-5)$ for post-event years 3 to 5 is

$$\overline{U}_i^E(3-5) = \overline{P}_i^E(3-5) - \overline{F}_i^E(3-5),$$

better than forecast (unlike any of the three original control firms), so the substitution of ITT for Kaman would make the performance of UT appear worse (2.5% worse than the control portfolio instead of 2% worse). While this result is anecdotal and thus may be due merely to random variation, it is also possible that the conditions that resulted in ITT's poor timeliness rank make it a poor control for the forecast error of a firm expected to perform very well.

where $\overline{P}_i^E(3\text{--}5) = (P_i^E(3) + P_i^E(4) + P_i^E(5))/3$ and $\overline{F}_i^E(3\text{--}5)$ is the analyst's forecast of the average annual performance over years 3 to 5. Unexpected average performance for years 3 to 5 is calculated for each control firm in the same manner. Paralleling the foregoing development, the excess unexpected average performance for years 3 to 5 is then calculated.

Accounting Variables: When Forecasts Are Unavailable

Value Line analysts' forecasts are not available for variables based on inventory levels and the number of employees. For these variables, *excess actual performance* is examined.[12] The excess actual performance $X_i(t)$ for event i in post-event time t is

$$X_i(t) = P_i^E(t) = \overline{P}_i^C(t),$$

where $\overline{P}_i^C(t) = \frac{1}{3}\Sigma_{j=1}^3 P_i^{C_j}(t)$. Note that $P_i^E(t)$ and $P_i^{C_j}(t)$ are the actual performances for the event and control firms as defined in the preceding subsection. In addition, excess average performance for both a five-year pre-event and a five-year post-event period is examined; that is,

$$\overline{X}_i^{\text{pre}} = \frac{1}{5}\sum_{t=-5}^{-1} P_i^E(t) - \frac{1}{5}\sum_{t=-5}^{-1} \overline{P}_i^C(t),$$

and

$$\overline{X}_i^{\text{post}} = \frac{1}{5}\sum_{t=1}^{5} P_i^E(t) - \frac{1}{5}\sum_{t=1}^{5} \overline{P}_i^C(t).$$

Finally, the difference between the post- and pre-event excess average performance is also examined:

$$D_i = \overline{X}_i^{\text{post}} - \overline{X}_i^{\text{pre}}.$$

Stock Returns

The impact of TQM is also examined using with-dividend continuously compounded daily stock returns. As discussed in the earlier section on research methodology, it is not appropriate to use analysts' forecasts in conjunction with stock returns. Thus, the stock return performance

---

[12] As discussed in the section on research methodology, we believe the validity of analysis based on excess actual performance is considerably weaker than that based on excess unexpected performance. We nevertheless examine these variables because of their close link to the methods of TQM. In the context of the other analysis presented, we believe these variables do provide some useful indications.

measure is the *excess cumulative daily return*. The excess cumulative daily return $XCR_i(t)$ for event i at post-event day t is

$$XCR_i(t) = CR_i^E(t) - \overline{CR}_i^C(t),$$

where $CR_i^E(t)$ is the post-event cumulative daily return at day t for event firm i and $\overline{CR}_i^C(t)$ is the average of the cumulative returns at day t for firms in the corresponding control portfolio. Thus, $\overline{CR}_i^C(t) = \frac{1}{3}\Sigma_{j=1}^{3} CR_i^{Cj}(t)$, where $CR_i^{Cj}(t)$ is the post-event cumulative return at day t for firm j of the control portfolio C for event i. The cumulative returns $CR(t)$ are defined similarly for the event and control firms: $CR(t) = \Sigma_{t'=1}^{t} r(t')$, where $r(t')$ is the with-dividend continuously compounded daily stock return for day t' following event time 0. The excess average monthly stock returns for the pre- and post-event period and the difference of the differences are also examined, where the monthly returns are calculated by cumulating the with-dividend continuously compounded daily returns for the month.

As already described, the control portfolio methodology matches control and event firms as closely as possible, with the result that the event and control firms are closely matched on systematic risk. However, the stock returns analysis was also repeated using beta excess returns. The results, which are not presented here, are similar, indicating that differences in systematic risk between the events and controls are not driving the stock return results.

Results

This section describes the results for both the accounting measures and stock returns. All results are for either excess unexpected or excess actual performance (depending on the availability of analysts' forecasts) of the TQM firm in comparison with the matched non-TQM control portfolio. The analysis of the accounting variables focuses on net income, operating income, and inventory scaled by measures of firm size based on sales, assets, or number of employees. Results for sales-to-assets are also presented. Results are given for the full sample of 108 TQM events and for the subsamples of event firms with more advanced and less advanced TQM systems. The analysis is repeated using only the 93 manufacturing firms. We examine manufacturing firms separately because the early development of U.S. TQM took place primarily in manufacturing companies and, as a result, the methods of TQM are better developed in this context.

Summary statistics for the full sample of 108 TQM event firms are given in Tables 7.1 to 7.3. Event year 0, the beginning of the firm's TQM

Table 7.1. *Distribution of the Year of Implementation of TQM*

Year of Implementation	No. of TQM Firms
1981	1
1982	3
1983	9
1984	11
1985	7
1986	15
1987	17
1988	10
1989	17
1990	15
1991	3
Total	108

Table 7.2. *Distribution of TQM Firms by Industry*

Industry	No. of Firms	Industry	No. of Firms
Aerospace	4	Machinery	5
Air transport	1	Medical supplies	2
Auto parts	3	Metals and mining	1
Auto and truck	3	Office equipment and	
Banking	2	supplies	4
Building materials	1	Oilfield services	1
Chemicals	12	Packaging and containers	2
Computers and peripherals	10	Paper and forest products	5
Diversified	3	Petroleum	1
Electric utilities	2	Precision instruments	3
Electronics/electrical		Publishing	1
equipment	12	Semiconductors	11
Financial services	1	Steel	1
Food processing	1	Telecommunications	4
Furniture and home		Tire and rubber	2
furnishings	1	Trucking and transport	
Home appliances	2	leasing	5
Household products	1		
Machine tools	1	Total	108

Table 7.3. *TQM Firm and Control Firm Market Size*

Market Size[a]	TQM Firms	Non-TQM Control Firms
Mean size	$5.4 billion	$2.4 billion
Median size	$1.5 billion	$0.9 billion
Minimum	$75.9 million	$47.6 million
Maximum	$73.3 billion	$35.0 billion

[a] Market size is the market value of equity (including preferred stock) plus the market value of total debt. Both the debt and equity variables are taken from the Value Line Investment Survey published during event year 0.

implementation, spans the years 1981 to 1991 (Table 7.1). The sample firms represent 32 different industries (Table 7.2) and range in market size from $76 million to $73 billion with a mean of $5.4 billion (Table 7.3).

Statistical Analysis Methods

All tables, except for Tables 7.10 and 7.19, report the medians of the performance measures. The medians are used because, especially for the accounting variables, the data are not normally distributed. Deviations from the normal distribution include the presence of outliers, wide tails, and, for some variables, skewness. Medians are extremely robust for these types of problems. The tables for the accounting variables also present sign-test p-values testing the one-sided null hypothesis that TQM does not improve performance against the alternative that performance is improved. Sign tests were used because they are non-parametric and thus robust to the kinds of deviations from the normal distribution just described. The Wilcoxon signed-rank test was not used, because it assumes that the distribution of the data is symmetric, an assumption violated by the accounting data. When there is skewness, the test is not valid and can be inconsistent with the actual medians (e.g., the sample median can be negative, while the Wilcoxon test indicates that the center of symmetry of the distribution is positive).

The tables also compare the results for the less advanced and more advanced TQM firms. Wilcoxon rank-sum tests were used to test the null hypothesis that the distribution of the performance measure for the more advanced firms is not stochastically larger than that of the less advanced firms (against the alternative that it is stochastically larger). A distribution $F(x)$ is stochastically larger than a distribution $G(x)$ if $F(x)$

$\geq G(x)$ for all x, but $F(x) \neq G(x)$. Unlike the Wilcoxon signed-rank test, the Wilcoxon rank-sum test does not assume that the distributions are symmetric or that, under the null hypothesis, the two distributions are identical. Wilcoxon rank-sum tests are also used for several other comparisons between subsamples. The specific hypotheses are described in the table notes.

For the cumulative daily stock return data in Tables 7.9, 7.12, 7.18, and 7.21, Wilcoxon signed-rank tests are used rather than sign tests. The reasons are that (1) normal probability plots do not indicate departure from symmetry; (2) there is much empirical evidence indicating that daily stock returns are reasonably close to normally distributed; and (3) Wilcoxon signed-rank tests are more powerful than sign tests when the underlying distribution is symmetric.

Tables 7.10 and 7.19 present analyses of the cumulative daily stock return data based on the assumption that the stock returns are multivariate normal. Thus, sample means are reported. The p-values in these tables use test statistics that are based on estimates of the variances and covariances between firms whose event year 0 is the same calendar year. Thus, comparison of these tables with Tables 7.9 and 7.18 allows an assessment of the impact of any correlation due to industry and event-year clustering.

Accounting Variables: Excess Unexpected Performance

Table 7.4 shows the results for excess unexpected performance for net income/sales (NI/S), net income/assets (NI/A), operating income/sales (OI/S), operating income/assets (OI/A), and sales/assets (S/A). For the full sample of firms, the table shows that the median excess performance for the average of years 3 to 5 is positive for all of the variables. Thus, more than half of the event firms performed better in comparison with the analysts' forecasts than did the matched control portfolios for all of the variables examined. This improvement for years 3 to 5 is significant at the 1% level for OI/A, at the 5% levels for NI/S and NI/A, and at the 10% level for S/A. Performance is also improved for all the variables in years 1 and 2 except for OI/S and OI/A, where there is a decline in performance in year 2. While the results for years 1 and 2 are generally not statistically significant, this provides some evidence against the idea that implementing TQM hurts short-term performance. Note that the improvement is much larger in years 3 to 5 than in years 1 and 2 for all of the variables except OI/S, consistent with the hypothesis that the most important impact of implementing TQM is on longer-term performance.

Table 7.4. *Excess Unexpected Performance for the Accounting Variables*

Variable	Year	Full Sample Median (%)	p-sgn	n	Less Advanced TQM Firms Median (%)	p-sgn	n	More Advanced TQM Firms Median (%)	p-sgn	n	p-wrs
NI/S	1	0.26	.11	108	-0.03	.55	64	0.54	.03	44	.04
	2	0.25	.19	108	-0.03	.55	64	0.54	.09	44	.09
	3–5	0.60	.03	100	0.47	.11	56	1.12	.09	44	.12
NI/A	1	0.39	.11	108	-0.04	.65	64	0.83	.01	44	.02
	2	0.49	.07	108	0.40	.13	64	0.52	.23	44	.22
	3–5	0.91	.03	100	0.37	.17	56	1.86	.05	44	.06
OI/S	1	0.03	.50	108	-0.43	.92	64	0.58	.06	44	.11
	2	-0.12	.78	108	-0.47	.92	64	0.10	.38	44	.10
	3–5	0.04	.46	100	0.16	.45	56	-0.01	.56	44	.30
OI/A	1	0.46	.11	108	-0.17	.73	64	1.27	.01	44	.04
	2	-0.12	.61	108	0.02	.55	64	-0.12	.67	44	.54
	3–5	1.52	.01	100	0.37	.17	56	2.98	.01	44	.04
S/A	1	1.72	.05	108	0.46	.35	64	3.86	.03	44	.10
	2	1.17	.25	108	0.05	.55	64	2.82	.15	44	.36
	3–5	4.89	.07	100	0.03	.55	56	8.40	.01	44	.01

Note: Medians and p-values for the excess unexpected performance for net income/sales (NI/S), net income/assets (NI/A), operating income/sales (OI/S), operating income/assets (OI/A), and sales/assets (S/A). The medians are expressed as percentages. Results are reported both for the full sample of 108 events and for the subsamples of 64 event firms with less advanced TQM systems and 44 event firms with more advanced TQM systems. The data and forecasts were obtained from Value Line. The columns labeled "p-sgn" contain p-values for the one-sided sign test of the null hypothesis H_0 – true median ≤ 0 – against the alternative H_A – true median > 0. The sample sizes are given in the columns labeled "n." The column labeled "p-wrs" contains p-values for the one-sided Wilcoxon rank-sum test of the null hypothesis that the underlying distribution of the more advanced firms is not stochastically larger than that of the less advanced firms.

For the firms with more advanced TQM systems, except for OI/S, the results for years 3 to 5 are uniformly better than for the firms with less well developed systems. For the more advanced firms, in spite of the much smaller sample size ($n = 44$), year 3 to 5 performance improvement is significant at the 1% level for OI/A and S/A, at the 5% level for NI/A, and at the 10% level for NI/S. The results are also better for year 3 to 5 performance than for year 1 and 2 performance for all variables except OI/S. For the more advanced firms, the improvement in year 1 is significant for all of the variables and significant in year 2 at the 10% level for NI/S. For the less advanced firms, while all of the medians for years 3 to 5 are positive, none of the variables is significant. There is no indication that short-term performance is improved for the less advanced firms and, in fact, there may be some evidence that OI/S declines.

The p-values for the Wilcoxon rank-sum test indicate that the improvement in year 3 to 5 performance of the more advanced firms in comparison with that of the less advanced firms is significant at the 1% level for S/A, the 5% level for OI/A, and the 10% level for NI/A. The difference in year 1 performance is significant at the 5% level for NI/S, NI/A, and OI/A and at the 10% level for S/A. The difference in year 2 performance is significant at the 10% level for NI/S and OI/S.

In summary, Table 7.4 provides strong evidence of overall improvement in longer-term performance with regard to these accounting variables for the full sample of TQM events. This improvement is stronger for the more advanced firms and weaker for the less advanced firms, with the performance of the less advanced firms, for the most part, not statistically different from that of the controls. The longer-term performance is stronger than the short-term performance. For the full sample, there is no evidence that short-term performance is hurt by the implementation of TQM. There is, in fact, evidence that even the short-term performance of the more advanced TQM firms is improved.

Accounting Variables: Excess Actual Performance

Table 7.5 shows excess actual net income/employee (NI/E) and operating income/employee (OI/E) for a period from five years before the event to five years after the event. For the full sample, there appears to be an overall declining trend in NI/E preceding the event and a generally improving trend following the event, resulting in positive (but not significant) median performance for year 5. At the bottom of each panel, the table shows the excess average year −5 to −1 performance, the excess average year 1 to 5 performance, and the difference between the pre-event and post-event period excess average performance. The median average performance is negative for both the pre- and post-event periods. The median difference between the pre- and post-event period averages is positive but not statistically significant.

For OI/E, the performance varies around zero through year 1 following the event. For years 2 to 5, there is an improving trend with significant positive performance at the 5% level in years 3 and 5. Note that, due to the availability of the data, the sample size decreases over years 2 to 5, making it more difficult to obtain statistical significance for the longer-term data. In year 5, the median improvement in operating income for the event firms in comparison with the control firms is approximately $3,000 per employee. The median post-event period average is positive and statistically significant at the 10% level. The median difference in the pre–post averages is positive but not significant.

For the more advanced TQM firms, a similar but stronger pattern occurs. The median excess NI/E turns positive in year 2 and, with a p-value of .11, is almost significant at the 10% level in year 5. The median excess NI/E in year 5 is approximately $840. The median post-event period average is positive but not significant. The median difference in the pre–post averages, however, is positive and significant at the 10% level, providing some evidence of improvement between the pre- and post-event periods. For OI/E, the performance is significantly positive at the 5% or 10% level during years 2 to 5 following the event, with a median excess OI/E of $4,830 in year 5. The median post-event period average is about $3,680 and is significant at the 1% level. The median difference in the pre–post averages is about $2,630 and is significant at the 10% level. In contrast, for the less advanced firms, excess NI/E is negative, although improving, throughout the post-event period. The excess OI/E fluctuates around zero and is not statistically significant. For both of these variables, the median pre–post averages and their median difference are not significant. The post-event average excess performance and the difference in the pre–post averages are greater for the more advanced than for the less advanced firms, with significance at the 3% level or better for both variables.

Table 7.6 shows the excess actual sales per employee (S/E). For the full sample, the median excess S/E during years 3 to 5 is negative, ranging from –$1,890 to –$5,900. The results for years 3 to 5 among the more advanced firms are positive, although not statistically significant. For the less advanced firms during years 3 to 5, S/E is clearly negative. S/E is significantly better for the more advanced firms than for the less advanced firms during years 1 to 5, with significance at the 10% level for years 1 and 5 and at the 5% level for years 2 to 4. For both the full sample and the more advanced firms, there appears to be an overall improving trend

Table 7.5. *Excess Actual Net Income per Employee and Operating Income per Employee*

Variable	Year	Full Sample			Less Advanced TQM Firms			More Advanced TQM Firms			
		Median ($1,000/ Employee)	p-sgn	n	Median ($1,000/ Employee)	p-sgn	n	Median ($1,000/ Employee)	p-sgn	n	p-wrs
NI/E	-5	-0.48	.82	98	-0.50	.79	57	-0.47	.73	41	.50
	-4	-0.41	.86	100	-0.35	.70	57	-0.72	.89	43	.73
	-3	-0.77	.95	102	-0.50	.70	59	-0.92	.98	43	.68
	-2	-0.02	.58	105	0.02	.45	62	-0.15	.73	43	.63
	-1	-1.16	.99	108	-0.53	.92	64	-1.54	.97	44	.64
	0	-1.20	.95	108	-1.56	.97	64	-1.16	.67	44	.13
	1	-0.83	.93	108	-1.02	.95	64	-0.47	.67	44	.04
	2	-0.46	.78	105	-1.88	.85	61	0.16	.56	44	.04
	3	-0.17	.54	90	-1.39	.72	47	0.13	.38	43	.33
	4	-0.27	.59	71	-1.28	.76	33	0.29	.44	38	.34
	5	0.70	.22	61	-0.70	.65	27	0.84	.11	34	.35
	-5 to -1	-0.72	.86	108	-0.68	.73	64	-0.78	.85	44	.66
	1 to 5	-0.30	.68	108	-1.43	.87	64	0.47	.33	44	.03
	Difference	0.29	.19	108	-0.04	.55	64	0.88	.09	44	.03

OI/E										
-5	0.44	.22	84	0.24	.39	51	0.83	.24	33	.28
-4	-0.23	.67	85	-0.16	.61	51	-0.78	.70	34	.43
-3	-0.07	.58	87	0.31	.50	53	-0.70	.70	34	.64
-2	-0.44	.62	90	-1.14	.66	56	-0.07	.57	34	.38
-1	0.22	.42	93	0.26	.55	58	0.22	.37	35	.31
0	-0.26	.62	94	-0.67	.74	58	0.74	.43	36	.19
1	-0.18	.17	94	-1.33	.82	58	2.68	.31	36	.08
2	1.39	.02	92	-0.24	.55	56	2.68	.07	36	.06
3	2.78	.22	78	2.03	.18	43	3.63	.02	35	.18
4	2.04	.22	61	-2.86	.77	29	2.52	.06	32	.09
5	3.03	.05	51	1.27	.27	24	4.83	.06	27	.25
-5 to -1	0.07	.34	93	0.16	.45	58	0.06	.37	35	.27
1 to 5	1.19	.09	94	-1.28	.74	58	3.68	.00	36	.01
Difference	0.46	.34	93	-0.22	.74	58	2.63	.09	35	.03

Note: Medians and *p*-values for the excess actual performance for net income/employee (NI/E) and operating income/employee (OI/E) for event years -5 to 5. The rows labeled "-5 to -1," "1 to 5," and "Difference" give the results for the average pre-event period performance, the average post-event period performance, and the difference between the pre-event period and post-event period averages, respectively. The units for the medians are $1,000s per employee. Results are reported both for the full sample of 108 events and for the subsamples of 64 event firms with less advanced TQM systems and 44 event firms with more advanced TQM systems. The data were obtained from COMPUSTAT. The columns labeled "*p*-sgn" contain *p*-values for the one-sided sign test of the null hypothesis H_0 – true median ≤ 0 – against the alternative H_A – true median > 0. The sample sizes are given in the columns labeled "*n*." The column labeled "*p*-wrs" contains *p*-values for the one-sided Wilcoxon rank-sum test of the null hypothesis that the underlying distribution of the more advanced firms is not stochastically larger than that of the less advanced firms.

199

Table 7.6. *Excess Actual Sales per Employee*

Variable	Year	Full Sample			Less Advanced TQM Firms			More Advanced TQM Firms			
		Median ($1,000/ Employee)	p-sgn	n	Median ($1,000/ Employee)	p-sgn	n	Median ($1,000/ Employee)	p-sgn	n	p-wrs
S/E	−5	−4.36	.96	98	−4.63	.97	57	−4.09	.73	41	.14
	−4	−7.37	.97	100	−8.71	.99	57	−3.50	.62	43	.09
	−3	−7.38	.99	102	−8.38	.99	59	−7.02	.89	43	.16
	−2	−5.03	.99	105	−5.64	.99	62	−1.50	.82	43	.26
	−1	−8.07	1.00	108	−8.07	1.00	64	−6.59	.85	44	.17
	0	−6.80	.99	108	−9.56	.99	64	−3.30	.85	44	.10
	1	−11.01	.98	108	−16.96	.99	64	−1.63	.67	44	.07
	2	−5.74	.91	105	−8.70	.98	61	3.84	.44	44	.04
	3	−5.90	.77	90	−15.68	.93	47	2.15	.38	43	.03
	4	−1.89	.68	71	−15.45	.98	33	4.06	.13	38	.03
	5	−3.33	.70	61	−12.18	.88	27	2.63	.43	34	.07
	−5 to −1	−6.23	.99	108	−7.43	.99	64	−3.04	.85	44	.14
	1 to 5	−5.60	.95	108	−8.59	.98	64	−0.37	.56	44	.04
	Difference	−2.43	.81	108	−4.84	.92	64	1.10	.44	44	.12

Note: Medians and p-values for the excess actual performance for sales/employee (S/E) for event years −5 to 5. The rows labeled "−5 to −1," "1 to 5," and "Difference" give the results for the average pre-event period performance, the average post-event period performance, and the difference between the pre-event period and post-event period averages, respectively. The units for the medians are $1,000s per employee. Results are reported both for the full sample of 108 events and for the subsamples of 64 event firms with less advanced TQM systems and 44 event firms with more advanced TQM systems. The data were obtained from COMPUSTAT. The columns labeled "p-sgn" contain p-values for the one-sided sign test of the null hypothesis H_0 − true median ≤ 0 − against the alternative H_A − true median > 0. The sample sizes are given in the columns labeled "n." The column labeled "p-wrs" contains p-values for the one-sided Wilcoxon rank-sum test of the null hypothesis that the underlying distribution of the more advanced firms is not stochastically larger than that of the less advanced firms.

Table 7.7. *Excess Percent Year 0 to 4 Change in Sales, Assets, and Employees*

Variable	Full Sample			Less Advanced TQM Firms			More Advanced TQM Firms			
	Median (%)	p-sgn	n	Median (%)	p-sgn	n	Median (%)	p-sgn	n	p-wrs
%ΔS	10.39	.00	72	5.54	.08	33	13.92	.01	39	.04
%ΔA	13.25	.00	72	12.98	.04	33	15.61	.00	39	.35
%ΔE	8.61	.00	71	9.23	.02	33	6.12	.07	38	.84

Note: Medians and p-values for the excess percent change in sales (%ΔS), assets (%ΔA), and number of employees (%ΔE). Results are reported both for the full sample of 108 events and for the subsamples of 64 event firms with less advanced TQM systems and 44 event firms with more advanced TQM systems. The data were obtained from COMPUSTAT. The columns labeled "p-sgn" contain the p-values for the one-sided sign test of the null hypothesis H_0 – true median ≤ 0 – against the alternative H_A – true median > 0. The sample sizes are given in the columns labeled "n." The column labeled "p-wrs" contains p-values for the one-sided Wilcoxon rank-sum test of the null hypothesis that the underlying distribution of the more advanced firms is not stochastically larger than that of the less advanced firms.

during the post-event period. The median pre- and post-event averages are negative for both the less and more advanced firms, and thus for the full sample. For the more advanced firms, the median difference in the pre- and post-event averages is positive but not significant. The median post-event excess average performance is greater for the more advanced firms than for the less advanced firms ($p = .04$).

Table 7.7 shows the excess percent change in sales, assets, and employees between years 0 and 4. The table shows that, in comparison with the control firms, the event firms grew according to all three measures. This was also the case for both the less advanced and more advanced firms. All of the results are significant, with strong significance ($p = .00$) for the full sample. For the more advanced firms, the percent growth in sales was significantly better than for the less advanced firms at the 5% level. It is interesting that the percent growth in the number of employees was smaller for the more advanced firms than for the less advanced firms.

Table 7.8 gives the results of excess actual performance for total inventory to sales (I/S) and total inventory to cost of goods sold (I/CGS).[13]

---

[13] COMPUSTAT's cost of goods sold (CGS) often includes selling, general, and administrative expenses (SGA). When this is the case, the corresponding COMPUSTAT SGA

Table 7.8. Excess Actual Total Inventory/Sales and Total Inventory/Cost of Goods Sold

Variable	Year	Full Sample			Less Advanced TQM Firms			More Advanced TQM Firms			
		Median (%)	p-sgn	n	Median (%)	p-sgn	n	Median (%)	p-sgn	n	p-wrs
I/S	−5	−1.02	.11	95	0.47	.66	54	−1.77	.01	41	.07
	−4	−0.94	.03	95	−0.38	.34	54	−2.86	.01	41	.10
	−3	−0.95	.06	98	0.22	.60	57	−2.36	.01	41	.02
	−2	−0.76	.12	101	−0.38	.45	60	−1.79	.06	41	.11
	−1	−0.81	.08	103	0.71	.22	61	−1.19	.14	42	.06
	0	−0.64	.04	103	−0.11	.30	61	−1.43	.02	42	.03
	1	−0.52	.22	103	0.86	.70	61	−1.95	.04	42	.01
	2	−0.88	.04	100	−0.06	.45	58	−1.51	.01	42	.05
	3	−1.58	.04	85	−0.11	.56	44	−1.84	.01	41	.04
	4	−1.18	.20	68	1.29	.86	31	−2.13	.02	37	.07
	5	−0.06	.45	58	0.33	.79	25	−0.60	.24	33	.13
	−5 to −1	−1.04	.08	103	−0.03	.50	61	−2.90	.02	42	.02
	1 to 5	−0.93	.06	103	0.29	.60	61	−1.59	.00	42	.02
	Difference	0.03	.58	103	−0.12	.40	61	0.27	.78	42	.56

I/CGS										
-5	-1.29	.04	85	-0.66	.39	51	-3.66	.01	34	.07
-4	-1.33	.04	85	-0.27	.50	51	-3.65	.01	34	.05
-3	-0.90	.05	88	-0.06	.55	54	-6.07	.01	34	.00
-2	-0.43	.34	91	0.95	.70	57	-3.20	.11	34	.03
-1	-1.43	.03	93	-1.05	.18	58	-4.74	.05	35	.01
0	-1.19	.04	94	-0.22	0.35	58	-4.13	.02	36	.01
1	-0.94	.13	94	0.69	.65	58	-3.72	.02	36	.01
2	-1.03	.17	92	0.02	.55	56	-1.70	.07	36	.06
3	-1.23	.21	78	0.83	.73	43	-2.77	.05	35	.04
4	-0.12	.50	61	1.29	.93	29	-1.92	.11	32	.10
5	0.01	.71	51	0.38	.73	24	0.01	.65	27	.23
-5 to -1	-1.43	.11	93	0.24	.65	58	-4.74	.01	35	.01
1 to 5	-0.87	.13	94	-0.48	.45	58	-2.28	.07	36	.03
Difference	0.19	.66	93	-0.09	.45	58	0.43	.84	35	.68

Note: Medians and *p*-values for the excess actual performance for total inventory/sales (I/S) and total inventory/cost of goods sold (I/CGS) for event years –5 to 5. The rows labeled "–5 to –1," "1 to 5," and "Difference" give the results for the average pre-event period performance, the average post-event period performance, and the difference between the pre-event period and post-event period averages, respectively. The medians are expressed as percentages. Results are reported both for the full sample of 108 events and for the subsamples of 64 event firms with less advanced TQM systems and 44 event firms with more advanced TQM systems. The data were obtained from COMPUSTAT. The cost of goods sold used here is the sum of the COMPUSTAT "cost of goods sold" and "selling, general, and administrative expense" data items. Note that in the COMPUSTAT data base, "cost of goods sold" is often not reported separately from "selling, general, and administrative expense." The columns labeled "*p*-sgn" contain *p*-values for the one-sided sign test of the null hypothesis H_0 – true median ≥ 0 – against the alternative H_A – true median < 0. The sample sizes are given in the columns labeled "*n*." The column labeled "*p*-wrs" contains *p*-values for the one-sided Wilcoxon rank-sum test of the null hypothesis that the underlying distribution of the more advanced firms is not stochastically smaller than that of the less advanced firms.

For the I/S variable, the median excess actual performance of the full sample is negative during the post-event period, indicating lower inventory levels for the sample firms than for the controls (an improvement). The results are significant at the 5% level for years 0, 2, and 3. The more advanced firms show a similar but stronger pattern, with significantly reduced I/S levels for years 0 to 4. For the less advanced firms, there is no clear pattern. The excess I/S levels for the more advanced firms are significantly lower than for the less advanced firms in all post-event years except year 5. The median excess post-event average I/S levels are also significantly negative for the full sample ($p = .06$) and are strongly significantly negative for the more advanced firms ($p = .00$). The excess post-event average inventory levels are also significantly lower for the more advanced firms than for the less advanced firms ($p = .02$). The excess I/S for both the full sample and the more advanced firms is negative during the pre-event period, and there is some suggestion that excess I/S levels increase during the pre-event period and subsequently decrease during the post-event period. The median differences in the pre–post averages, however, are positive, although not significant. I/CGS for the full sample shows a similar pattern.

In summary, the results for net income, operating income, and sales per employee indicate improved performance in comparison with the controls for the more advanced firms in the post-event period. The median performance throughout the post-event period for all of these variables is greater for the more advanced firms than for the less advanced firms with a significant difference for excess S/E. Excess inventory is lower for the event firms than for the controls during the post-event period for both of the inventory variables examined. The inventory results are stronger for the more advanced firms.

Excess Cumulative Daily Stock Returns

Table 7.9 shows the results for the excess cumulative with-dividend continuously compounded daily stock returns. The cumulative returns begin in July of event year 0. For the full sample, the median excess cumulative return is 21.02% in year 5. The improvement is strongly significant

---

Footnote 13 (cont.)

  variable is missing. To correct for this inconsistency, the variable used here (which we refer to as CGS) is actually the sum of COMPUSTAT's CGS and SGA variables. Also note that, for the I/S variable, the five firms with missing data in all years are service firms. For the I/CGS variable, the 14 firms with missing data in all years are service firms – only one service firm remains. Thus, the results in Table 7.8 are very similar to the results for the manufacturing firms alone (Table 7.17).

Table 7.9. *Excess Cumulative Percent Daily Stock Returns*

Variable	Year	Full Sample			Less Advanced TQM Firms			More Advanced TQM Firms			
		Median (%)	p-sr	n	Median	p-sr	n	Median	p-sr	n	p-wrs
Excess cumulative returns	1	3.19	.05	107	1.55%	.28	63	4.72	.02	44	.10
	2	3.82	.18	106	−2.80%	.66	63	9.41	.02	43	.05
	3	3.91	.10	103	−1.72%	.78	60	17.28	.00	43	.00
	4	6.04	.02	87	−1.43%	.67	46	18.48	.00	41	.00
	5	21.02	.00	69	14.20%	.10	32	22.11	.00	37	.20
Excess average monthly returns	−5 to −1	−0.24	.98	106	−0.30%	.83	63	−0.22	.98	43	.59
	1 to 5	0.25	.00	108	0.13%	.16	64	0.36	.00	44	.06
	Difference	0.50	.00	106	0.36%	.07	63	0.66	.00	43	.09

Note: Medians and p-values for the excess cumulative percent with-dividend continuously compounded daily stock returns for event years 1 to 5. The rows labeled "−5 to −1," "1 to 5," and "Difference" give the results for the average monthly returns for the pre-event period, the post-event period, and the difference between the pre-event period and post-event period average monthly returns, respectively. The monthly returns are calculated by cumulating the daily returns in the month. Results are reported both for the full sample of 108 events and for the subsamples of 64 event firms with less advanced TQM systems and 44 event firms with more advanced TQM systems. The cumulative returns data were calculated from the daily returns database compiled by the Center for Research in Securities Prices at the University of Chicago. The columns labeled "p-sr" contain p-values for the one-sided Wilcoxon signed-rank test of the null hypothesis H_0 − true median ≤ 0 – against the alternative H_A − true median > 0. The sample sizes are given in the columns labeled "n." The column labeled "p-wrs" contains p-values for the one-sided Wilcoxon rank-sum test of the null hypothesis that the underlying distribution of the more advanced firms is not stochastically larger than that of the less advanced firms.

(p = .00). For the more advanced firms, the median excess cumulative returns are 17.28%, 18.48%, and 22.11% for years 3, 4, and 5, respectively, with p = .00 for all three years. The excess cumulative returns for the more advanced firms are also positive and significant at the 5% level in years 1 and 2. The excess cumulative returns are not statistically significant for the less advanced firms in years 1 through 4. Year 5 performance, however, is positive and significant (p = .10). The differences between the excess cumulative returns for more and less advanced firms are significant at the 5% level in years 2 to 4, and at the 10% level in year 1. Thus, consistent with the accounting variables, the cumulative stock returns indicate improved long-term performance for the TQM firms, with stronger results for the more advanced TQM firms.

Table 7.9 also shows the median pre- and post-event period excess average monthly returns and the median difference of the pre–post averages. For both the full sample and subsamples of less and more advanced firms, the excess average pre-event monthly returns are negative. For both the full sample and the more advanced firms, the post-event excess average return is strongly positive (p = .00). The median difference in the pre–post averages is strongly significantly positive for both the full sample and the more advanced firms (p = .00). For the less advanced firms, the pre–post difference is positive and significant at the 10% level. The post-event excess average monthly returns and the pre–post difference averages are significantly larger for the more advanced firms (p = .06 and .09, respectively).

Table 7.10 shows an analysis of the excess cumulative returns based on the assumption that the distribution of the stock returns is multivariate normal. This analysis corrects for any correlation between the excess returns of firms with the same event year 0. There is very little industry and event-year clustering in the sample, and thus it would appear unlikely that such correlation would have any impact on the results. Comparison of Tables 7.10 and 7.9, however, allows a direct assessment of any such impact. The two tables show that the results are essentially the same, with similar patterns in the levels of significance, verifying that correlation due to event-year clustering does not have a consequential impact on the results.

Downsizing

This section examines whether the observed positive performance of the TQM firms might be explained by downsizing that took place in conjunction with or during the same period as the deployment of TQM. There appears to be little consensus concerning a uniform definition

Table 7.10. *Excess Cumulative Percent Daily Stock Returns: Covariance-Based Analysis*

Variable	Year	Full Sample			Less Advanced TQM Firms			More Advanced TQM Firms			
		Mean (%)	p-cv	n	Mean (%)	p-cv	n	Mean (%)	p-cv	n	p-2
Excess	1	3.37	.17	97	1.17	.40	56	6.36	.11	41	.23
cumulative	2	4.48	.17	97	-0.71	.55	57	11.88	.04	40	.09
returns	3	7.26	.11	99	-3.79	.67	57	22.26	.00	42	.01
	4	12.91	.04	86	-1.83	.57	46	29.87	.00	40	.01
	5	24.21	.01	69	15.71	.15	32	31.55	.00	37	.20

Note: Averages and p-values for the excess cumulative percent with-dividend continuously compounded daily stock returns. Results are reported both for the full sample of 108 events and for the subsamples of 64 event firms with less advanced TQM systems and 44 event firms with more advanced TQM systems. The cumulative returns data were calculated from the daily returns database compiled by the Center for Research in Securities Prices at the University of Chicago. The columns labeled "p-cv" contain p-values for the one-sided test of the null hypothesis $H_0 - \mu \leq 0$ – against the alternative $H_A - \mu > 0$. The estimates of the standard deviations of the means used in the test statistics are based on estimates of the variance–covariance matrices for events in the same year. The variance–covariance estimates are calculated from five years of monthly returns, where the monthly returns are calculated by cumulating the daily returns in the month. The sample sizes are given in the columns labeled "n." The column labeled "p-2" contains p-values for the one-sided two-sample test of the null hypothesis $H_0 - \mu_{more} \leq \mu_{less}$ – against the alternative $H_A - \mu_{more} > \mu_{less}$ – where μ_{less} and μ_{more} are the true means of the less advanced and more advanced firms, respectively.

of the term "downsizing." The extent to which some downsizing-like activity is a natural consequence of the development of quality management systems is also debatable. The empowerment of employees, one of the principles of TQM, is likely to lead to the elimination of some levels of management and supervision over time. We examine the effects of downsizing here by evaluating the relationship between performance and percent changes in the number of employees. We believe that this captures what is commonly meant by downsizing – major reductions in the number of employees.

In order for the data to support the hypothesis that downsizing drives the results, (1) a large number of the event firms should be downsizing in comparison with the controls; (2) the firms that do not downsize should not show significant positive performance; and (3) the firms that do downsize in comparison with the controls should show significant positive performance consistent with downsizing driving the results, especially when compared with the firms that do not downsize.

Requirement (1) is not supported by the data. Overall, both the event firms and the control firms grow in terms of the number of employees during the post-event period. The median percent change in employees between years 0 and 4 is 5.4% for the event firms and 1.0% for the controls. For the more advanced events only, the four-year percent growth in employees is 2.1% for the event firms and 1.0% for the controls. For the less advanced events, the percent growth in employees is 9.2%, while the growth in the control portfolios is again 1.0%. Thus, the number of employees grows for most firms in the sample and most event firms grow faster than their control portfolios. This is consistent with the results for excess percent change in employees given in Table 7.7.

Requirements (2) and (3) are examined by comparing the performance of events showing negative excess percent change in employees with those showing positive excess percent change in employees. Tables 7.11 and 7.12 give the results for the accounting variables and stock returns, respectively. Examination of these tables shows that the required patterns are not evident. Specifically, requirement (2) is not supported by the data. The vast majority of the performance measures for the events that do not downsize are positive and frequently significant. In particular, the results for the excess cumulative stock returns in Table 7.12 show significant (at the 5% level) positive excess returns in years 4 and 5 for both the full sample of firms that did not downsize and the more advanced firms that did not downsize. Thus, there is evidence of a positive association between the implementation of TQM and performance of firms that do not downsize.

Finally, requirement (3) is also not supported by the data. There is no clear pattern of improved performance for the firms with negative excess percent change in employees over those with positive excess percent change in employees, and none of the corresponding p-values comparing the "negative" and "positive" firms is significant. For the accounting variables for the full sample shown in Table 7.11, a positive difference is observed in only two of the eight performance variables. It is interesting that for both the accounting measures and the stock returns, for the less advanced subsample, the performance for events with a negative excess percent change in employees is worse (except for S/E) than for those with a positive excess percent change in employees. For the more advanced events, the opposite tends to be the case.

Results for the Manufacturing Firms Only

The analysis just described was repeated omitting the 15 events (indicated in Appendix A) corresponding to predominantly service companies. Tables 7.13 to 7.21 present the results. These results are not specifically discussed here. Overall, however, the results for the manufacturing firms alone are stronger and have increased statistical significance.

Other Variables and Research Issues Examined

Analysts' Forecasts. In order to provide some empirical validation of the use of Value Line analysts' forecasts, the mean-squared errors (MSEs) of the analysts' forecasts were compared with the MSEs of forecasts made by simple AR 1 models. The AR 1 models were estimated for each firm using the time series of annual values obtained from COMPUSTAT for the 11 years before and ending with event year 0 (i.e., $t = -10$ to $t = 0$). Forecasts were then made for post-event years 1 to 5. For years 1 and 2, the MSE of the forecast is the average squared difference between the forecast and the realized value. In order to parallel the long-term forecasts provided by the Value Line analysts, the AR 1 forecasts for years 3 to 5 are averaged and compared with the average value of the realized values for years 3 to 5 by computing the average of the squared differences. The MSEs for the Value Line analysts' forecasts were computed in a similar manner using data and forecasts obtained from Value Line. Missing values in the COMPUSTAT pre-event data resulted in the loss of a number of firms in the calculation of the AR 1 MSEs. For comparability, such missing firms were also deleted from the calculation of the Value Line MSEs.

Table 7.22 shows the efficiencies of the AR 1 forecasts relative to the

Table 7.11. *Long-Term Performance of the Accounting Variables for TQM Firms with Positive and Negative Excess Percent Change in Employees*

Variable	Excess %ΔE	Full Sample			Less Advanced TQM Firms			More Advanced TQM Firms			p-wrs
		Median (%)	p	n	Median (%)	p	n	Median (%)	p	n	
NI/S	−	0.76	.29	30	−0.26%	.60	14	1.75%	.23	16	.16
	+	0.57	.03	41	0.71%	.01	19	0.40%	.42	22	.68
			.59†			.85†			.33†		
NI/A	−	0.63	.43	30	−0.98%	.79	14	2.51%	.23	16	.02
	+	1.65	.01	41	0.53%	.08	19	1.86%	.07	22	.31
			.79†			.96†			.36†		
OI/S	−	0.95	.29	30	−1.01%	.60	14	1.86%	.23	16	.21
	+	−0.02	.62	41	0.08%	.50	19	−0.15%	.74	22	.40
			.54†			.74†			.42†		
OI/A	−	2.28%	.29	30	−2.03%	.79	14	3.18%	.11	16	.03
	+	2.50%	.01	41	0.23%	.32	19	3.12%	.01	22	.10
			.88†			.93†			.70†		
S/A	−	−2.21%	.71	30	−22.49%	.91	14	6.33%	.40	16	.01
	+	4.57%	.06	41	−0.04%	.68	19	9.95%	.01	22	.03
			.95†			.93†			.80†		

		median	p	n	median	p	n	median	p	n	p
NI/E	−	-0.28	.71	30	-1.53	.91	14	0.29	.40	16	.15
	+	0.79	.50	41	0.87	.50	19	-0.07	.58	22	.54
			.71†			.87†			.37†		
OI/E	−	1.51	.42	26	-5.73	.97	11	5.05	.06	15	.09
	+	2.04	.25	35	1.99	.41	18	2.04	.31	17	.21
			.76†			.81†			.48†		
S/E	−	-2.58	.71	30	-11.27	.91	14	0.13	.40	16	.29
	+	-1.78	.62	41	-17.62	.97	19	6.26	.14	22	.04
			.45†			.34†			.70†		

Note: Medians and *p*-values for the accounting performance variables. For net income/sales (NI/S), net income/assets (NI/A), operating income/sales (OI/S), operating income/assets (OI/A), and sales/assets (S/A), the median excess unexpected performance for post-event years 3 to 5 is reported (expressed as percentages). For net income/employee (NI/E), operating income/employee (OI/E), and sales/employee (S/E), the median excess actual performance for post-event year 4 is reported expressed in units of $1,000s per employee. The rows labeled "−" and "+" correspond to events with negative and positive year 0 to 4 excess percent change in employees, respectively. Results are reported both for the full sample of 108 events and for the subsamples of 64 event firms with less advanced TQM systems and 44 event firms with more advanced TQM systems. The data were obtained as described in Tables 7.4 and 7.5 for the corresponding variables. Except as indicated by †, the columns labeled "*p*" contain *p*-values for the one-sided sign test of the null hypothesis H_0 – true median ≤ 0 – against the alternative H_A – true median > 0. The sample sizes are given in the columns labeled "*n*." The *p*-values labeled "†" are for Wilcoxon rank-sum tests of the null hypothesis that the underlying distribution for the events with negative excess percent change in employees is not stochastically larger than that for the events with positive excess percent change in employees. The column labeled "*p*-wrs" contains *p*-values for the one-sided Wilcoxon rank-sum test of the null hypothesis that the underlying distribution of the more advanced firms is not stochastically larger than that of the less advanced firms.

211

Table 7.12. *Excess Cumulative Percent Daily Stock Returns for TQM Firms with Positive and Negative Excess Percent Change in Employees*

Year	Excess %ΔE	Full Sample			Less Advanced TQM Firms			More Advanced TQM Firms			
		Median (%)	p	n	Median (%)	p	n	Median (%)	p	n	p-wrs
1	−	−0.68	.33	30	−3.03	.72	14	9.75	.10	16	.13
	+	1.90	.12	40	−0.34	.32	18	4.12	.13	22	.31
			.69†			.86†			.36†		
2	−	−2.49	.75	29	−12.89	.96	14	4.01	.18	15	.03
	+	2.41	.37	40	−5.93	.72	18	7.73	.16	22	.20
			.84†			.87†			.56†		
3	−	4.83	.52	29	−15.02	.98	14	17.28	.04	15	.01
	+	3.78	.06	40	−2.92	.41	18	17.71	.07	22	.09
			.84†			.98†			.36†		
4	−	4.55	.18	29	−9.27	.92	14	34.86	.01	15	.00
	+	8.00	.02	40	0.88	.24	18	12.07	.03	22	.21
			.68†			.95†			.21†		
5	−	21.27	.05	29	7.74	.51	14	34.29	.01	15	.10
	+	20.78	.01	40	24.03	.04	18	17.95	.04	22	.59
			.56†			.86†			.17†		

Note: Medians and *p*-values for the excess cumulative percent with-dividend continuously compounded daily stock returns. The rows labeled "−" and "+" correspond to events with negative and positive year 0 to 4 excess percent change in employees, respectively. Results are reported both for the full sample of 108 events and for the subsamples of 64 event firms with less advanced TQM systems and 44 event firms with more advanced TQM systems. The cumulative returns data were calculated from the daily returns data base compiled by the Center for Research in Securities Prices at the University of Chicago. Except as indicated by †, the columns labeled "*p*" contain *p*-values for the one-sided Wilcoxon signed-rank test of the null hypothesis H_0 – true median ≤ 0 – against the alternative H_A – true median > 0. The sample sizes are given in the columns labeled "*n*." The *p*-values labeled "†" are for Wilcoxon rank-sum tests of the null hypothesis that the underlying distribution for the events with negative excess percent change in employees is not stochastically larger than that for the events with positive excess percent change in employees. The column labeled "*p*-wrs" contains *p*-values for the one-sided Wilcoxon rank-sum test of the null hypothesis that the underlying distribution of the more advanced firms is not stochastically larger than that of the less advanced firms.

212

Table 7.13. *Excess Unexpected Performance for the Accounting Variables – Manufacturing Firms Only*

Variable	Year	Full Sample			Less Advanced TQM Firms			More Advanced TQM Firms			
		Median (%)	n	p-sgn	Median (%)	n	p-sgn	Median (%)	p-sgn	n	p-wrs
NI/S	1	0.14	93	.27	−0.07	93	.65	0.53	.09	35	.08
	2	0.29	93	.15	0.08	93	.45	0.97	.09	35	.06
	3–5	0.72	87	.01	0.64	87	.06	1.23	.05	35	.10
NI/A	1	0.35	93	.20	0.03	93	.55	0.94	.09	35	.05
	2	0.51	93	.01	0.40	93	.12	0.59	.02	35	.09
	3–5	1.65	87	.01	0.52	87	.11	2.26	.01	35	.02
OI/S	1	−0.13	93	.58	−0.50	93	.96	0.70	.05	35	.14
	2	−0.27	93	.89	−0.48	93	.96	0.07	.50	35	.12
	3–5	0.33	87	.26	0.16	87	.44	1.66	.25	35	.11
OI/A	1	0.91	93	.11	−0.34	93	.65	1.29	.01	35	.08
	2	0.03	93	.50	−0.01	93	.55	0.03	.50	35	.49
	3–5	2.22	87	.00	0.62	87	.11	3.28	.00	35	.01
S/A	1	1.15	93	.15	.46	93	.45	6.35	.09	35	.13
	2	1.80	93	.15	0.05	93	.55	5.35	.05	35	.19
	3–5	4.57	87	.10	−0.62	87	.66	8.54	.01	35	.01

Note: Medians and *p*-values for the excess unexpected performance for net income/sales (NI/S), net income/assets (NI/A), operating income/sales (OI/S), operating income/assets (OI/A), and sales/assets (S/A) for the manufacturing events only. The medians are expressed as percentages. Results are reported both for the entire sample of manufacturing events and for the subsamples of manufacturing firms with less advanced and more advanced TQM systems. The data and forecasts used to construct the performance measures were obtained from Value Line. The columns labeled "*p*-sgn" contain the *p*-values for the one-sided sign test of the null hypothesis H_0 – true median ≤ 0 – against the alternative H_A – true median > 0. The sample sizes are given in the columns labeled "*n*." The column labeled "*p*-wrs" contains *p*-values for the one-sided Wilcoxon rank-sum test of the null hypothesis that the underlying distribution of the more advanced firms is not stochastically larger than that of the less mature firms.

Table 7.14. *Excess Actual Net Income per Employee and Operating Income per Employee – Manufacturing Firms Only*

		Full Sample			Less Advanced TQM Firms			More Advanced TQM Firms			
Variable	Year	Median ($1,000/ Employee)	p-sgn	n	Median ($1,000/ Employee)	p-sgn	n	Median ($1,000/ Employee)	p-sgn	n	p-wrs
NI/E	−5	0.28	.37	84	0.13	.50	51	0.36	.36	33	.42
	−4	−0.25	.59	85	0.42	.50	51	−0.41	.70	34	.65
	−3	−0.44	.80	87	0.05	.50	53	−0.58	.94	34	.65
	−2	0.19	.23	90	0.03	.34	56	0.29	.30	34	.47
	−1	−0.49	.89	93	−0.14	.74	58	−1.35	.91	35	.55
	0	−1.20	.89	93	−1.24	.88	58	−1.19	.75	35	.11
	1	−0.82	.85	93	−0.95	.88	58	−0.40	.63	35	.06
	2	0.07	.50	91	−1.66	.66	56	0.41	.37	35	.06
	3	0.29	.37	78	−0.23	.56	44	0.40	.30	34	.36
	4	0.79	.40	63	−1.28	.64	31	1.44	.30	32	.26
	5	1.85	.11	54	0.70	.50	25	2.74	.07	29	.41
	−5 to −1	0.03	.50	93	0.17	.45	58	−0.19	.63	35	.57
	1 to 5	0.50	.34	93	−1.26	.74	58	1.31	.09	35	.03
	Difference	0.27	.27	93	0.07	.45	58	0.71	.25	35	.06

OI/E

−5	0.44	.22	84	0.24	.39	51	0.83	.24	33	.28
−4	−0.23	.67	85	−0.16	.61	51	−0.78	.70	34	.43
−3	−0.07	.58	87	0.31	.50	53	−0.70	.70	34	.64
−2	−0.44	.62	90	−1.14	.66	56	−0.07	.57	34	.38
−1	0.22	.42	93	0.26	.55	58	0.22	.37	35	.31
0	−0.13	.58	93	−0.67	.74	58	0.89	.37	35	.14
1	−0.05	.58	93	−1.33	.82	58	3.38	.25	35	.05
2	1.41	.15	91	−0.24	.55	56	3.02	.05	35	.04
3	2.80	.01	77	2.03	.18	43	3.94	.01	34	.13
4	2.19	.18	60	−2.86	.77	29	2.65	.04	31	.05
5	3.03	.05	51	1.27	.27	24	4.83	.06	27	.25
−5 to −1	0.07	.34	93	0.16	.45	58	0.06	.37	35	.27
1 to 5	1.25	.07	93	−1.28	.74	58	3.79	.00	35	.00
Difference	0.46	.34	93	−0.22	.74	58	2.63	.09	35	.03

Note: Medians and *p*-values for the excess actual performance for net income/employee (NI/E) and operating income/employee (OI/E) for event years −5 to 5 for the manufacturing events only. The rows labeled "−5 to −1," "1 to 5," and "Difference" give the results for the average pre-event period performance, the average post-event period performance, and the difference between the pre-event period and post-event period averages, respectively. The units for the medians are $1,000s per employee. Results are reported both for the entire sample of manufacturing events and for the subsamples of manufacturing firms with less advanced and more advanced TQM systems. The data were obtained from COMPUSTAT. The columns labeled "*p*-sgn" contain *p*-values for the one-sided sign test of the null hypothesis H_0 – true median ≤ 0 – against the alternative H_A – true median > 0. The sample sizes are given in the columns labeled "*n*." The column labeled "*p*-wrs" contains *p*-values for the one-sided Wilcoxon rank-sum test of the null hypothesis that the underlying distribution of the more advanced firms is not stochastically larger than that of the less advanced firms.

Table 7.15. *Excess Actual Sales per Employee – Manufacturing Firms Only*

Variable	Year	Full Sample			TQM Firms			TQM Firms			
		Median ($1,000/ Employee)	p-sgn	n	Median ($1,000/ Employee)	p-sgn	n	Median ($1,000/ Employee)	p-sgn	n	p-wrs
S/E	-5	-4.07	.88	84	-4.06	.92	51	-4.09	.64	33	.17
	-4	-6.76	.96	85	-8.71	.98	51	-3.53	.70	34	.08
	-3	-7.36	.99	87	-8.38	.99	53	-7.10	.89	34	.15
	-2	-6.69	.00	90	-6.69	.99	56	-5.04	.89	34	.21
	-1	-8.18	.00	93	-10.13	1.00	58	-4.86	.84	35	.11
	0	-6.38	.98	93	-10.82	.98	58	-2.29	.84	35	.05
	1	-10.35	.95	93	-16.01	.98	58	-0.87	.63	35	.04
	2	-5.82	.90	91	-9.58	.96	56	1.71	.50	35	.03
	3	-4.38	.63	78	-14.60	.85	44	2.63	.30	34	.03
	4	-1.78	.60	63	-10.71	.96	31	4.06	.11	32	.03
	5	-0.44	.55	54	-8.75	.79	25	2.96	.36	29	.07
	-5 to -1	-6.83	.99	93	-7.43	.99	58	-4.38	.91	35	.11
	1 to 5	-2.70	.93	93	-6.61	.96	58	-0.76	.63	35	.03
	Difference	-0.45	.73	93	-7.38	.93	58	2.73	.25	35	.03

Note: Medians and *p*-values for the excess actual performance for sales/employee (S/E) for event years –5 to 5 for the manufacturing firms only. The rows labeled "–5 to –1," "1 to 5," and "Difference" give the results for the average pre-event period performance, the average post-event period performance, and the difference between the pre-event period and post-event period averages, respectively. The units for the medians are $1,000s per employee. Results are reported both for the entire sample of manufacturing events and for the subsamples of manufacturing firms with less advanced and more advanced TQM systems. The data were obtained from COMPUSTAT. The columns labeled "*p*-sgn" contain *p*-values for the one-sided sign test of the null hypothesis H_0 – true median ≤ 0 – against the alternative H_A – true median > 0. The sample sizes are given in the columns labeled "*n*." The column labeled "*p*-wrs" contains *p*-values for the one-sided Wilcoxon rank-sum test of the null hypothesis that the underlying distribution of the more advanced firms is not stochastically larger than that of the less advanced firms.

216

Table 7.16. *Excess Percent Year 0 to 4 Change in Sales, Assets, and Employee – Manufacturing Firms Only*

Variable	Full Sample			Less Advanced TQM Firms			More Advanced TQM Firms			
	Median (%)	p-sgn	n	Median (%)	p-sgn	n	Median (%)	p-sgn	n	p-wrs
%Δ S	7.40	.02	69	5.25	.24	31	11.37	.02	38	.10
%Δ A	7.53	.01	69	8.33	.08	31	7.22	.04	38	.53
%Δ E	7.44	.03	69	13.68	.04	31	1.53	.21	38	.80

Note: Medians and p-values for the excess percent change in sales (%ΔS), assets (%ΔA), and number of employees (%ΔE) for the manufacturing events only. Results are reported both for the entire sample of manufacturing events and for the subsamples of manufacturing firms with less advanced and more advanced TQM systems. The data were obtained from COMPUSTAT. The columns labeled "p-sgn" contain p-values for the one-sided sign test of the null hypothesis H_0 – true median ≤ 0 – against the alternative H_A – true median > 0. The sample sizes are given in the columns labeled "n." The column labeled "p-wrs" contains p-values for the one-sided Wilcoxon rank-sum test of the null hypothesis that the underlying distribution of the more advanced firms is not stochastically larger than that of the less advanced firms.

217

Table 7.17. *Excess Actual Total Inventory/Sales and Total Inventory/Cost of Goods Sold – Manufacturing Firms Only*

Variable	Year	Full Sample			Less Advanced TQM Firms			More Advanced TQM Firms			
		Median (%)	p-sgn	n	Median (%)	p-sgn	n	Median (%)	p-sgn	n	p-wrs
I/S	-5	-1.02	.14	85	0.57	.71	51	-3.66	.01	34	.04
	-4	-1.25	.04	85	-0.29	.39	51	-3.59	.01	34	.04
	-3	-1.11	.05	88	0.34	.66	54	-4.84	.00	34	.00
	-2	-1.09	.10	91	-0.30	.50	57	-3.10	.03	34	.04
	-1	-1.11	.07	93	-0.71	.26	58	-3.65	.09	35	.02
	0	-0.76	.05	93	-0.07	.35	58	-3.76	.02	35	.01
	1	-0.52	.27	93	1.03	.74	58	-4.66	.05	35	.00
	2	-0.94	.07	91	-0.06	.45	56	-2.93	.02	35	.02
	3	-2.06	.07	78	-0.11	.56	44	-2.85	.01	34	.02
	4	-1.89	.22	63	1.29	.86	31	-2.80	.03	32	.04
	5	-0.03	.55	54	0.33	.79	25	-0.87	.36	29	.11
	-5 to -1	-1.19	.07	93	0.08	.55	58	-3.69	.01	35	.00
	1 to 5	-0.93	.11	93	0.42	.65	58	-2.72	.01	35	.01
	Difference	0.24	.66	93	-0.09	.45	58	1.40	.84	35	.63

218

I/CGS										
-5	-1.29	.04	85	-0.66	.39	51	-3.66	.01	34	.07
-4	-1.33	.04	85	-0.27	.50	51	-3.65	.01	34	.05
-3	-0.90	.05	88	-0.06	.55	54	-6.07	.01	34	.00
-2	-0.43	.34	91	0.95	.70	57	-3.20	.11	34	.03
-1	-1.43	.03	93	-1.05	.18	58	-4.74	.05	35	.01
0	-1.27	.03	93	-0.22	.35	58	-5.18	.01	35	.01
1	-0.95	.11	93	0.69	.65	58	-4.11	.01	35	.00
2	-1.03	.15	91	0.02	.55	56	-1.91	.05	35	.05
3	-1.52	.18	77	0.83	.73	43	-2.78	.03	34	.04
4	-0.15	.45	60	1.29	.93	29	-1.96	.08	31	.08
5	0.01	.71	51	0.38	.73	24	0.01	.65	27	.23
-5 to -1	-1.43	.11	93	0.24	.65	58	-4.74	.01	35	.01
1 to 5	-0.92	.11	93	-0.48	.45	58	-2.50	.05	35	.02
Difference	0.19	.66	93	-0.09	.45	58	0.43	.84	35	.68

Note: Medians and *p*-values for the excess actual performance for total inventory/sales (I/S) and total inventory/cost of goods sold (I/CGS) for event years –5 to 5 for the manufacturing events only. The rows labeled "–5 to –1," "1 to 5," and "Difference" give the results for the average pre-event period performance, the average post-event period performance, and the difference between the pre-event period and post-event period averages, respectively. The medians are expressed as percentages. Results are reported both for the entire sample of manufacturing events and for the subsamples of manufacturing firms with less advanced and more advanced TQM systems. The data were obtained from COMPUSTAT. The cost of goods sold used here is the sum of the COMPUSTAT "cost of goods sold" and "selling, general, and administrative expense" data items. Note that in the COMPUSTAT database, "cost of goods sold" is often not reported separately from "selling, general, and administrative expense." The columns labeled "*p*-sgn" contain *p*-values for the one-sided sign test of the null hypothesis H_0 – true median ≥ 0 against the alternative H_A – true median < 0. The sample sizes are given in the columns labeled "*n*." The column labeled "*p*-wrs" contains *p*-values for the one-sided Wilcoxon rank-sum test of the null hypothesis that the underlying distribution of the more advanced firms is not stochastically smaller than that of the less advanced firms.

Table 7.18. *Excess Cumulative Percent Daily Stock Returns – Manufacturing Firms Only*

Variable	Year	Full Sample			Less Advanced TQM Firms			More Advanced TQM Firms			
		Median (%)	p-sr	n	Median (%)	p-sr	n	Median (%)	p-sr	n	p-wrs
Excess cumulative returns	1	2.17	.11	92	1.55	.33	57	2.72	.06	35	.16
	2	5.40	.17	91	-0.17	.55	57	9.74	.04	34	.09
	3	5.79	.05	89	-0.70	.60	55	17.44	.00	34	.00
	4	7.14	.01	75	-1.07	.59	43	33.31	.00	32	.00
	5	23.51	.00	61	19.07	.11	30	31.21	.00	31	.10
Excess average monthly returns	-5 to -1	-0.33	.98	91	-0.30	.83	57	-0.47	.99	34	.70
	1 to 5	0.34	.00	93	0.17	.11	58	0.52	.00	35	.05
	Difference	0.55	.00	91	0.41	.04	57	0.94	.00	34	.04

Note: Medians and *p*-values for the excess cumulative percent with-dividend continuously compounded daily stock returns for event years 1 to 5 for the manufacturing events only. The rows labeled "–5 to –1," "1 to 5," and "Difference" give the results for the average monthly returns for the pre-event period, the post-event period, and the difference between the pre-event period and post-event period average monthly returns, respectively. The monthly returns are calculated by cumulating the daily returns in the month. Results are reported both for the entire sample of manufacturing events and for the subsamples of manufacturing firms with less advanced and more advanced TQM systems. The cumulative returns data were calculated from the daily returns database compiled by the Center for Research in Securities Prices at the University of Chicago. The columns labeled "*p*-sr" contain the *p*-values for the one-sided Wilcoxon signed-rank test of the null hypothesis H_0 – true median ≤ 0 – against the alternative H_A – true median >0. The sample sizes are given in the columns labeled "*n*". The column labeled "*p*-wrs" contains *p*-values for the one-sided Wilcoxon rank-sum test of the null hypothesis that the underlying distribution of the more advanced firms is not stochastically larger than that of the less advanced firms.

Table 7.19. *Excess Cumulative Percent Daily Stock Returns: Covariance-Based Analysis – Manufacturing Firms Only*

Variable	Year	Full Sample			Less Advanced TQM Firms			More Advanced TQM Firms			
		Mean (%)	p-cv	n	Mean (%)	p-cv	n	Mean (%)	p-cv	n	p-2
Excess	1	2.87	.23	82	0.76	.44	50	6.15	.16	32	.25
cumulative	2	4.83	.18	82	0.71	.46	51	11.59	.09	31	.16
returns	3	9.90	.07	85	-0.99	.54	52	27.04	.00	33	.02
	4	15.67	.03	74	-0.42	.52	43	37.99	.00	31	.01
	5	28.64	.00	61	16.16	.15	30	40.72	.00	31	.12

Note: Averages and *p*-values for the excess cumulative percent with-dividend continuously compounded daily stock returns for the manufacturing events only. Results are reported both for the entire sample of manufacturing events and for the subsamples of manufacturing firms with less advanced and more advanced TQM systems. The cumulative returns data were calculated from the daily returns database compiled by the Center for Research in Securities Prices at the University of Chicago. The columns labeled *p*-cv contain *p*-values for the one-sided test of the null hypothesis $H_0 - \mu \leq 0$ – against the alternative $H_A - \mu > 0$. The estimates of the standard deviations of the means used in the test statistics are based on estimates of the variance–covariance matrices for events in the same year. The variance–covariance estimates are calculated from five years of monthly returns, where the monthly returns are calculated by cumulating the daily returns in the month. The sample sizes are given in the columns labeled "*n*." The column labeled "*p*-2" contains *p*-values for the one-sided two-sample test of the null hypothesis $H_0 - \mu_{more} \leq \mu_{less}$ – against the alternative $H_A - \mu_{more} > \mu_{less}$ – where μ_{less} and μ_{more} are the true means of the less advanced and more advanced firms, respectively.

221

Table 7.20. *Long-Term Performance of the Accounting Variables for TQM Firms with Positive and Negative Excess Percent Change in Employees – Manufacturing Firms Only*

Variable	Excess %ΔE	Full Sample			Less Advanced TQM Firms			More Advanced TQM Firms			
		Median (%)	p	n	Median (%)	p	n	Median (%)	p	n	p-wrs
NI/S	−	1.12	.17	28	0.32	.50	13	2.26	.15	15	.13
	+	0.62	.02	35	0.71	.02	18	0.55	.31	17	.60
			.55†			.81†			.34†		
NI/A	−	1.00	.29	28	−0.30	.71	13	2.76	.15	15	.03
	+	2.08	.01	35	1.23	.12	18	2.13	.02	17	.16
			.82†			.94†			.52†		
OI/S	−	1.19	.29	28	−2.39	.71	13	2.06	.15	15	.20
	+	0.08	.50	35	−0.17	.59	18	0.14	.50	17	.13
			.66†			.77†			.59†		
QI/A	−	2.37	.17	28	−3.14	.71	13	3.28	.06	15	.03
	+	2.86	.02	35	0.36	.41	18	6.33	.01	17	.04
			.91†			.94†			.80†		
S/A	−	1.74	.57	28	−26.74	.87	13	6.41	.30	15	.02
	+	1.40	.16	35	−2.65	.76	18	9.07	.02	17	.04
			.90†			.92†			.71†		

NI/E	−	-0.35	.71	28	-1.79	.87	13	0.41	.50	15	.16
	+	2.10	.25	35	2.16	.41	18	2.10	.31	17	.44
			.87†			.90†			.57†		
OI/E	−	1.51	.42	26	-5.73	.97	11	5.05	.06	15	.09
	+	2.35	.20	34	1.99	.41	18	2.35	.23	16	.12
			.82†			.81†			.60†		
S/E	−	-0.94	.57	28	-7.08	.87	13	0.25	.30	15	.24
	+	-1.78	.63	35	-14.16	.95	18	4.44	.17	17	.05
			.31†			.35†			.56†		

Note: Medians and *p*-values for the accounting performance variables for the manufacturing events only. For net income/sales (NI/S), net income/assets (NI/A), operating income/sales (OI/S), operating income/assets (OI/A), and sales/assets (S/A), the median excess unexpected performance for post-event years 3 to 5 is reported (expressed as percentages). For net income/employee (NI/E), operating income/employee (OI/E), and sales/employee (S/E), the median excess actual performance for post-event year 4 is reported expressed in units of $1,000s per employee. The rows labeled "−" and "+" correspond to events with negative and positive year 0 to 4 excess percent change in employees, respectively. Results are reported both for the entire sample of manufacturing events and for the subsamples of manufacturing firms with less advanced and more advanced TQM systems. The data were obtained as described in Tables 7.4 and 7.5 for the corresponding variables. Except as indicated by †, the columns labeled "*p*" contain *p*-values for the one-sided sign test of the null hypothesis H_0 – true median ≤ 0 – against the alternative H_A – true median >0. The sample sizes are given in the columns labeled "*n*." The *p*-values labeled "†" are for Wilcoxon rank-sum tests of the null hypothesis that the underlying distribution for the events with negative excess percent change in employees is not stochastically larger than that for the events with positive excess percent change in employees. The column labeled "*p*-wrs" contains *p*-values for the one-sided Wilcoxon rank-sum test of the null hypothesis that the underlying distribution of the more advanced firms is not stochastically larger than that of the less advanced firms.

223

Table 7.21. *Excess Cumulative Percent Daily Stock Returns for TQM Firms with Positive and Negative Excess Percent Change in Employee – Manufacturing Firms Only*

Year	Excess $\Delta\%E$	Less Advanced Full Sample			More Advanced TQM Firms			TQM Firms			
		Median (%)	p	n	Median (%)	p	n	Median (%)	p	n	p-wrs
1	–	−0.79	.39	28	−3.13	.70	13	2.70	.15	15	.17
	+	1.90	.14	34	1.07	.29	17	2.72	.17	17	.30
			.74†			.83†			.48†		
2	–	−7.24	.76	27	−15.64	.97	13	6.71	.17	14	.03
	+	5.20	.33	34	−5.44	.71	17	10.06	.12	17	.17
			.86†			.89†			.62†		
3	–	4.83	.48	27	−17.15	.98	13	17.44	.02	14	.00
	+	5.89	.05	34	−0.70	.34	17	18.75	.05	17	.08
			.85†			.99†			.41†		
4	–	6.50	.17	27	−13.45	.93	13	36.83	.01	14	.00
	+	10.66	.02	34	2.84	.22	17	18.14	.02	17	.12
			.72†			.96†			.31†		
5	–	23.59	.06	27	3.97	.54	13	41.07	.01	14	.09
	+	22.81	.00	34	24.54	.05	17	21.02	.02	17	.37
			.69†			.87†			.35†		

Note: Medians and p-values for the excess cumulative percent with-dividend continuously compounded daily stock returns for the manufacturing events only. The rows labeled "–" and "+" correspond to events with negative and positive year 0 to 4 excess percent change in employees, respectively. Results are reported both for the entire sample of manmufacturing events and for the subsamples of manufacturing firms with less advanced and more advanced TQM systems. The cumulative returns data were calculated from the daily returns data base compiled by the Center for Research in Securities Prices at the University of Chicago. Except as indicated by †, the columns labeled "p" contain p-values for the one-sided Wilcoxon signed-rank test of the null hypothesis H_0 – true median ≤ 0 – against the alternative H_A – true median >0. The sample sizes are given in the columns labeled "n." The p-values labeled † are for Wilcoxon rank-sum tests of the null hypothesis that the underlying distribution for the events with negative excess percent change in employees is not stochastically larger than that for the events with positive excess percent change in employees. The column labeled "p-wrs" contains p-values for the one-sided Wilcoxon rank-sum test of the null hypothesis that the underlying distribution of the more advanced firms is not stochastically larger than that of the less advanced firms.

Table 7.22. *Efficiencies of AR 1 Forecasts Relative to Value Line Analysts' Forecast for the Accounting Variables*

Variable	Year	Control Firms			Event Firms		
		Eff (%)	r-Eff (%)	n	Eff (%)	r-Eff (%)	n
NI/S	1	44.44	54.21	299	5.33	30.76	98
	2	25.01	36.25	288	1.65	30.96	96
	3–5	1.84	71.41	248	0.00	41.18	84
NI/A	1	47.63	50.35	299	20.72	55.06	98
	2	30.50	37.90	288	5.72	49.32	96
	3–5	4.11	92.48	248	0.09	82.70	84
OI/S	1	75.47	77.96	259	83.51	66.18	85
	2	34.94	37.70	249	37.03	82.96	84
	3–5	35.51	94.83	212	7.53	79.70	72
OI/A	1	72.61	82.46	259	96.25	68.19	85
	2	43.09	52.28	249	63.07	114.90	84
	3–5	61.11	188.40	212	13.58	110.44	72
S/A	1	50.57	66.11	299	79.37	75.39	98
	2	65.71	50.31	288	51.24	53.90	96
	3–5	83.12	95.02	248	40.07	75.41	84

Note: Efficiencies (Eff) and "robust" efficiencies (r-Eff) for AR 1 time series forecasts for net income/sales (NI/S), net income/assets (NI/A), operating income/sales (OI/S), operating income/assets (OI/A), and sales/assets (S/A) in post-event years 1 and 2 and the average of years 3 to 5. The efficiencies are expressed as percentages. The efficiency is calculated as the mean-squared error of the Value Line analysts' forecasts divided by the mean-squared error of the time series forecasts. The "robust" efficiencies are calculated in a similar fashion, except that the mean-squared errors are replaced by 5% trimmed mean-squared errors (the mean-squared error obtained after omitting the largest 5% of the squared errors). The performance measures and forecasts used to calculate the mean-squared errors for the analysts' forecasts were obtained from Value Line. The performance measures used to calculate the AR 1 forecasts were obtained from COMPUSTAT. The AR 1 model was estimated for each firm based on 11 years of data before and ending with event year 0 (i.e., t_{-10} to t_0).

analysts' forecasts. The efficiency is defined as the ratio of the MSE of the analysts' forecasts to the MSE of the AR 1 forecasts. Efficiencies of less than 100% show superior performance of the Value Line forecasts. The analysis was conducted separately for the control firms and for the event firms because the MSEs for the event firms contain a bias component due to their subsequent implementation of TQM. The results for the control firms do not include this bias component. Because the accounting data contain outliers and other deviations from normality and MSEs are very sensitive to these problems, a "robust efficiency" was also computed after trimming the largest 5% of the squared deviations.

Table 7.22 shows clear superiority of the analysts' forecasts. For the usual efficiency (based on the standard MSEs), there is no instance of superior performance of the AR 1 forecasts. For the robust efficiencies, there are only three instances (out of 30) in which the AR 1 forecasts had superior performance. Most of the robust efficiencies are well below 70%.

Firm Size and Calendar Year. Possible effects of firm size and year of TQM implementation were also examined. There were no clear differences in performance between event firms in the lower half of the size distribution and those in the upper half or between events that occurred in 1987 or earlier and those that occurred after 1987.

Quality Awards. To determine whether the results were biased by the selection of potential sample firms on the basis of quality-award-related search criteria, the analysis was also rerun after all firms that were identified as a result of quality awards had been deleted. The results are essentially unchanged, showing the same patterns of significance as for the full sample. In addition, a separate analysis was performed for the 39 events collected as a part of the first phase (Jarrell and Easton, 1997) of the study, which were not based on any searches relating to quality awards, and the 60 events collected in phase 2. The results of these analyses are also consistent. This stability lends further validity to the overall analysis and results.

Intra-sample Validation. The differences in performance between the more advanced and less advanced subsamples of TQM firms represent a very important intra-sample validation of the overall research design. Because, however, the development of the firms' TQM systems occurs over a multi-year period, it is possible that the subsequent development of a firm's TQM system could be influenced by financial performance early in the post-event period. This might create a kind of "TQM survivorship" bias whereby firms that had positive early financial results would be more likely to continue the kinds of efforts necessary to develop an advanced TQM system. There are a number of reasons this is not likely. This hypothesis assumes that managers expect early overall financial success from their TQM initiatives, that early success does not diminish the perceived need for major organizational change, and that early success drives the development of an advanced system as defined by the Baldrige Award criteria rather than just a continuation of initial efforts.

This issue was also examined empirically by conditioning on zero excess average year 1 and 2 stock returns and examining whether the difference in performance between the more advanced and less advanced firms persists in years 3 and 4. Two subsamples were constructed, one of the more advanced firms and the other of the less advanced firms, with zero median year 1 and 2 excess average stock returns. For these subsamples, the year 3 and 4 performance of the more advanced firms continues to be significantly better than that of the less advanced firms. This analysis provides evidence against the hypothesis that "feedback" due to early financial performance is the driver of the difference in the results for the more and less advanced firms.

Conclusion

This study provides clear evidence that the long-term performance of firms that implement TQM is improved. We believe the evidence of improvement is particularly strong when the overall analysis is considered. Specifically, both the results based on the excess unexpected performance of the accounting variables and excess cumulative stock returns are consistent. We also view the overall stronger performance of the more advanced TQM firms, which were identified independently by interviews, as both an important test of the research methodology and compelling evidence that the management methods comprising TQM are associated with improved performance. In addition, the results are even stronger when the analysis is limited to manufacturing firms. The study also examines whether downsizing, which might have occurred in conjunction with the implementation of TQM, could explain the positive performance we observed. This hypothesis is not supported by the data.

While no observational study can prove a causal relationship, this study is based on a carefully developed research methodology designed to provide evidence as compelling as possible on the impact of the adoption of TQM on corporate financial performance. Specifically, a carefully controlled event study approach was used rather than cross-sectional analysis, the sample of TQM firms was selected on the basis of in-depth interviews rather than on mail survey responses or public pronouncements, an established operational definition of a TQM system was the basis for selection (the Baldrige Award criteria), and the approach was further validated by comparison of the more and less advanced TQM firms. In addition, there is a plausible causal mechanism for the observed improvement performance – TQM, after all, focuses specifically on generating quality and operational improvements. Further, the management changes associated with the development of a TQM system are sufficient in scope that it is plausible that their effects are observable in overall corporate performance. Finally, even under the most unfavorable interpretation, the results of this study provide clear evidence against the proposition that the implementation of TQM actually hurts corporate performance.

It is important, however, to recognize the limitations on the generalizability of the results. This study examines whether TQM is associated with an improvement in the financial performance of companies that made serious efforts to implement TQM. This was done by comparing actual performance with a carefully constructed benchmark of what performance would have been without TQM. The finding that TQM improves the performance of the companies that implement it, however, cannot necessarily be generalized to a prescription that the companies that did not implement TQM would also have improved performance if they had. It is possible that there are enabling factors that would make TQM effective in some companies and ineffective in others. The decision to implement or not implement TQM may be based on managers' knowledge of these factors.

Appendix A

Sample of TQM Firms

TQM Firm	Year of Implementation
ADC Communications	1987
Advanced Micro Devices	1988
Air Products	1987
Albany International Corporation	1987
Alcoa	1990
Allied Signal	1991
Amdahl Corporation	1984
American Express[s]	1989
Analog Devices	1987
Applied Materials	1985
Arkansas Best Corporation[s]	1984
Armstrong World Industries	1983
Arvin Industries	1986
AT&T[s]	1988
Baldor Electric Co.	1987
Banc One Corporation[s]	1986
Bausch & Lomb	1989
Baxter International	1985
Black & Decker	1990
Boise Cascade	1990

Sample of TQM Firms (cont.)

TQM Firm	Year of Implementation
Cameron Iron Works Inc.	1984
Carolina Freight Corporation[s]	1984
Carpenter Technology Corporation	1987
Caterpillar	1983
Ceridian	1984
Chevron	1987
Chrysler	1985
Conner Peripherals	1989
Consolidated Freight[s]	1990
Corning Glass	1984
Cummins Engine	1983
Dana Corporation	1984
Diebold	1990
Digital Equipment	1989
Dun & Bradstreet[s]	1991
DuPont	1987
Eastman Kodak	1983
Ethyl Corporation	1986
Federal Express[s]	1986
Firestone Tire	1982
First Chicago[s]	1985
Fluke (John) Mfg. Co.	1990
Ford Motor	1984
FPL Group[s]	1986
Gaylord Container Corporation	1990
General Datacomm	1987
General Motors	1985
Goodyear Tire	1990
Goulds Pumps	1989
Grumman	1988
GTE Corporation[s]	1986
Hanna (M.A.) Co.	1990
Harris Corporation	1986
Hewlett Packard	1983
Hillenbrand Industries	1987
George A. Hormel & Co.	1986
IBM	1989
Integrated Device Technology	1989
Intel	1985
International Paper	1985
James River	1986
Johnson Controls	1986
Kulicke and Soffa	1988
Lubrizol Corporation	1988
Lyondell Petroleum	1989

Sample of TQM Firms (cont.)

TQM Firm	Year of Implementation
Micron Technology	1988
Millipore Corporation	1986
Minnesota Mining & Manufacturing (3M)	1984
Molex	1986
Moog	1989
Morton International	1991
Motorola	1983
Nashua Corporation	1981
National Semiconductor	1990
Pacific Telesis[s]	1989
Perkin Elmer Corporation	1984
PPG Industries	1986
Proctor & Gamble	1987
Raychem Corporation	1987
Roadway Services[s]	1989
Rockwell International Corporation	1986
Rogers Corporation	1983
Rohr Industries	1989
Scotsman Industries	1990
Sealed Air Corporation	1989
Snap-on Tools	1986
Square D	1987
Standard Register	1989
Sterling Chemical	1990
Storage Technology	1988
Sun Microsystems	1988
Tektronix	1989
Teradyne	1990
Texas Instruments Inc.	1982
Thomas & Betts	1987
Timken Company	1983
Union Camp Corporation	1987
Union Carbide	1988
Unisys	1988
United Technologies	1984
Varian Associates Inc.	1987
VLSI Technology	1989
Westinghouse Electric Corporation	1982
Weyerhaeuser	1989
Whirlpool Corporation	1990
WPL Holdings[s]	1987
Xerox Corporation	1983
Yellow Corporation[s]	1990

[s] A predominantly service company.

Appendix B

Interview Topics

General Category	Specific Approach
Training	Senior management training Awareness training Training of other management levels Workforce basic training Technical training Training for engineering
Teams	Workforce improvement teams Natural work-group teams Cross-functional teams Vertical teams Work cell teams Self-managed teams Project-oriented teams Management teams
Customers	Customer satisfaction surveys Customer complaint tracking Customer audits
Organizational structures	Senior management quality council Departmental quality councils Specific location quality councils Internal quality consultants
Planning/values	Written quality values and/or mission statement Hoshin planning/policy deployment Formal benchmarking Quality/customer satisfaction measures reported to senior management
Audits	Quality assurance audits ISO-9000 Baldrige self-assessments Other management systems audits
Team processes and tools	Problem-solving process Flow-charting Plan–do–check–act Seven basic quality control tools Seven management tools Root-cause analysis
Involvement and morale	Suggestion systems Employee quality recognition Employee morale survey

Interview Topics (cont.)

General Category	Specific Approach
Design and engineering	Design-for-manufacturability Concurrent/simultaneous engineering Design of experiments Taguchi methods Quality function deployment
Production	Statistical process control Just-in-time cycle time reduction/single minute exchange of die Activity-based costing Work cells
Suppliers	Supplier tracking Supplier certification Supplier quality audits Supplier training Joint supplier teams Ship-to-stock/production relationships Supplier integration into product development
Crosby[a]	Quality improvement teams Error cause removal system Corrective action teams Cost of quality/price of non-conformance Measure and display Quality education system training Zero defects days

[a] "Crosby" refers to the quality management system developed by Philip B. Crosby (1979) that was used by many companies as the basis of their initial quality management systems.

REFERENCES

Anderson, S. W., Daly, J., and Johnson, M. F. 1995. The value of management control systems: Evidence on the market reaction to ISO 9000 quality assurance certification. Working paper, University of Michigan Business School, Ann Arbor.

Barber, B. M., and Lyon, J. D. 1995. Detecting abnormal operating performance: The empirical power and specification of test-statistics. *Journal of Financial Economics* 41 (No. 3):359–399.

Brown, L. D. 1993. Earnings forecasting research: Its implications for capital markets research. *International Journal of Forecasting* 9:295–320.

Brown, L. D., Hagerman, R., Griffin, P., and Zmijewski, M. 1987. Security analyst superiority relative to univariate time-series models in forecasting quarterly earnings. *Journal of Accounting and Economics* 9:61–87.

Brown, L. D., and Rozeff, M. 1978. The superiority of analyst forecasts as measures of expectations: Evidence from earnings. *Journal of Finance* 6:1–16.

Crosby, P. B. 1979. *Quality Is Free*. New York: McGraw-Hill.

Easton, G. S. 1995. A Baldrige examiner's assessment of U.S. total quality management. In R. E. Cole (ed.), *The Death and Life of the American Quality Movement*. New York: Oxford University Press, 11–41.

Easton, G. S., and Jarrell, S. L. 1999. The emerging academic research on the link between total quality management and corporate financial performance: A critical review. In M. J. Stahl (ed.), *Perspectives in Total Quality*. Malden, MA: Blackwell, 27–70.

Fried, D., and Givoly, D. 1982. Financial analysts' forecasts of earnings: A better surrogate for market expectations. *Journal of Accounting and Economics* 4:85–108.

Healy, P., Palepu, K., and Ruback, R. 1992. Does corporate performance improve after mergers? *Journal of Financial Economics* 31:135–175.

Hendricks, K. B., and Singhal, V. R. 1996. Quality awards and the market value of the firm: An empirical investigation. *Management Science* 42 (No. 3):415–436.

Jarrell, S. L. 1991. Do takeovers generate value? Non-stock price evidence on the ability of the capital market to assess takeovers. Unpublished dissertation, University of Chicago, Graduate School of Business.

Jarrell, S. L., and Easton, G. S. 1997. An exploratory empirical investigation of the effects of total quality management on corporate performance. In P. Lederer and U. Karmarkar (eds.), *The Practice of Quality Management*. Norwell, MA: Kluwer, 9–53.

NIST. 1994. *Malcolm Baldrige National Quality Award 1995 Award Criteria*. U.S. Department of Commerce, National Institute of Standards and Technology.

Schipper, K. 1991. Commentary on analysts' forecasts. *Accounting Horizons* 5:105–121.

U.S. General Accounting Office. 1991. Management practices: U.S. companies improve performance through quality efforts (GAO/NSIAD-91-190).

CHAPTER 8

Implementing Effective Total Quality Management Programs and Financial Performance: A Synthesis of Evidence from Quality Award Winners

Kevin B. Hendricks and Vinod R. Singhal

Introduction

The past decade has witnessed a remarkable spread and awareness of total quality management (TQM) practices. Surveys indicate that TQM initiatives and adoption rates are increasing in the United States (Haim [1993]). However, studies by some management consultancy firms have raised concerns about whether investments in TQM programs have created economic value (see, e.g., the International Quality Study, a joint project by Ernst & Young and American Quality Foundation [1992] and Kelly [1992] that discusses the studies done by Arthur D. Little Inc., A. T. Kearney, and Rath and Strong). Although these studies report management perceptions as to whether TQM is beneficial or not, they rarely provide objective data and statistical evidence to support their claims. Nonetheless, these studies have received widespread publicity in the business press and seem to have left many firms confused about the value of TQM (see, e.g., Fuchsberg [1992a, 1992b], Mathews and Katel [1992], and Mathews [1993]). Ittner and Larcker's (1995a) survey results indicate that top management in many firms is concerned about the impact of TQM practices on financial performance, and is putting pressure on its quality departments to demonstrate whether investments in TQM have paid off.

Proponents of TQM have reacted to the negative publicity by reminding critics of the few well-publicized success stories of TQM, and have used these examples to make the case that TQM works. Others have revisited the theory of TQM to reiterate what TQM is, why there is nothing wrong with the theory of TQM, and what organizations must do to implement TQM successfully (King [1992] and Johnson [1993]).

234

Others have argued that the link between quality and financial performance is strong but hard to establish (Garvin [1991] and Stratton [1993]).

It is surprising and somewhat disturbing that claims and counterclaims about whether TQM programs have paid off financially are rarely supported by objective, rigorous empirical evidence. For example, the highly publicized International Quality Study did not provide any statistical data on the effectiveness of TQM programs, but reported that firms may waste millions of dollars on TQM strategies that do not improve performance and may even hurt it. Most studies on TQM report management perceptions as to whether TQM is beneficial, but make little effort to assess the basis for the perceptions. Similarly, studies which suggest that TQM improves operating performance rarely provide statistical evidence.

This chapter provides rigorous, objective evidence on whether implementing effective TQM programs affects the financial performance of firms. The evidence is based on our research that has been ongoing for five years. Our research uses the winning of quality awards as a proxy for effective implementation of TQM programs. Here, we describe key aspects of our research, and highlight and summarize our main findings. We discuss three sets of results.

First, we provide evidence on the financial performance of a sample of quality award winners by comparing their performance with that of a sample of control firms (Hendricks and Singhal [1995a, 1997a]). Publicly available accounting data are used to test for changes in various performance measures, such as operating income, sales, costs, total assets, and employment. Results are reported separately for two different periods. The first period, called the implementation period, begins six years before and ends one year before the date of winning the first quality award. The second period, called the post-implementation period, begins one year before and ends three years after the date of winning the first quality award.

Our results indicate that there is no difference in the financial performance of quality award winners and that of the control firms during the implementation period. We view this as good news, as it suggests that the costs of implementing TQM programs are not very high. Another interpretation is that the implementation costs are high, but firms get some quick and early benefits that balance these costs. Our results indicate that quality award winners significantly outperform the control firms during the post-implementation period. Over the post-implementation period, the mean change in the operating income of the award winners is 33% higher than that of the control firms. There is reasonably strong evidence that award winners do better on sales growth than do the control firms.

Over the same time period, the mean change in sales for the award winners is 15% higher than that for the control firms. We also find weak evidence that award winners are more successful in controlling costs than are the control firms.

Second, we provide evidence on the relation between the financial performance of quality award winners and such characteristics as firm size, the degree of capital intensity, the degree of firm diversification, the type of quality awards won, the timing of the first quality award, and the number of awards won (Hendricks and Singhal [1995a, 1995b]). We believe that central to TQM is a set of management and workforce practices that will affect different firms in different ways. However, there is little evidence on how the impact of TQM varies across firms. By studying the relation between firm characteristics and TQM, we provide evidence on the relative potential of TQM to affect the financial performance of firms with different characteristics and, therefore, provide a basis for setting expectations. It seems to us that expectations about how TQM can improve performance are based less on rigorous empirical evidence than on anecdotes, hype, and publicity. Furthermore, the expectations seem to be very high.

Our results indicate that less-capital-intensive award winners do better than more-capital-intensive award winners in both the implementation and post-implementation periods. Firms that have won awards from independent award givers (such as the Baldrige Awards and state awards) do worse than the firms that have won only supplier awards during the implementation period, but do better than supplier award winners during the post-implementation period. There is weak evidence that during the post-implementation period smaller firms do better than larger firms and that less diversified firms do better than more diversified firms. Finally, we do not observe any significant differences between the performance of single versus multiple award winners, and earlier versus later implementers.

Third, we provide evidence on the stock price performance of quality award winners. Using the event study methodology, we estimate the mean "abnormal" change in the stock prices of a sample of firms on the date when information about winning quality awards is publicly announced (Hendricks and Singhal [1996]). Our results show that the stock market reacts positively to quality award announcements. Statistically significant mean abnormal returns on the day of the announcements range from 0.59% to 0.67% depending on the model used to generate the abnormal returns.

We also compare the long-term stock price performance of the quality award winners with that of different samples of control firms (Hendricks and Singhal [1997b]). During the implementation period, we do not find any significant difference in the stock price performance of the quality award winners and that of the control firms. During the post-implementation period, the quality award winners significantly outperform the various control samples. Depending on the control sample used, the mean buy-and-hold abnormal returns range from 38% to 46%. This level of outperformance is economically significant, resulting in substantial wealth creation. For example, at the beginning of the post-implementation period, an investor would have to invest about 25% more money in the control firms than the award winners to achieve the same wealth at the end of the post-implementation period. We estimate that during the post-implementation period, the average award winner created $700 million worth of additional market value compared with the controls.

Since our results are based on samples of quality award winners, it is important to justify why it makes sense to use results based on award winners to infer the value of implementing effective TQM programs. We believe that there are at least two important reasons for using award winners. First, an important objective of quality award givers is to recognize firms that have done an outstanding job of implementing effective TQM programs. To maintain credibility and the value of awards, award givers have a strong incentive to give awards only to those firms that have significantly improved quality. Award givers typically decide on winners after conducting an independent evaluation and assessment of firms' quality practices and measuring firms' quality performance against some pre-established standards. For a firm to win such an award, it must undertake a strict and effective quality improvement program. Therefore, winning a quality award provides independent third-party certification that a firm has implemented an effective TQM program. By focusing on quality award winners, we avoid the biases associated with asking firms to judge for themselves the effectiveness of their TQM programs.

The second reason is that award givers exclude financial performance in the selection of winners because of technical, fairness, and confidentiality considerations. Thus, firms in our sample are not selected because of their financial performance (good or bad). By basing the results of our study on publicly traded firms that have won quality awards, we obtain information on financial performance independently of TQM practices. Thus, we avoid the biases associated with self-reports by firms on the impact of TQM on their financial performance.

Our results also provide evidence on the value of the quality award systems themselves. These systems have become an integral part of the TQM movement. This is shown by the fact that, besides the Malcolm

Baldrige National Quality Award, there are quality award systems in place in nearly 44 of the 50 states. Reimann (1995) indicates that about 40 new quality awards have been initiated outside of the United States, many of which are national quality awards. Furthermore, many firms have initiated quality award systems solely for their suppliers.

Quality award systems have also been a source of controversy. Critics have used the examples of financial setbacks experienced by some prestigious award winners to question the value of award systems because they do not guarantee that the winners will be financially successful. Some have criticized the framework and criteria used by various award systems for choosing the winners. Furthermore, the existence of different award systems has led to a debate about which system is better (Garvin [1991]). Others have questioned the motivational aspect of quality awards, claiming that firms are more interested in winning awards than in fundamentally changing their organizations to improve quality. While there is much debate about the value of quality award systems, it seems to us that both critics and supporters have passed judgment on the value of these systems on the basis of conceptual arguments and anecdotes rather than on rigorous empirical evidence. Evidence on the financial performance of quality award winners could help resolve the controversy about the value of these systems.

The second section of this chapter summarizes the empirical evidence on the effect of TQM on financial performance. The third section discusses our hypotheses on why effective implementation of TQM could improve financial performance and describes the various measures used. The fourth section describes the sample selection process and discusses various methodological issues. The fifth section discusses the empirical results for the full sample of quality award winners. The sixth section discusses the results on the relation between the characteristics of award winners and their financial performance. The seventh section describes the results that establish the link between the stock price performance of quality award winners. The final section summarizes our research, discusses the implications of our results, and outlines future research directions.

Review of Empirical Evidence on TQM and
Financial Performance

The extent of evidence on TQM is perhaps best discussed by Haim (1993). This study was commissioned by Conference Board Inc., New York, partly because the media reported mixed views during 1992 and 1993 concerning the effectiveness of TQM. Haim summarized the results of 20 empirical studies on TQM. Most of these studies were conducted by business organizations and consulting firms using surveys. Of the 20 studies reviewed, 15 provide evidence on the impact of TQM and related practices on internal, external, and bottom-line measures. Twelve of these studies rely solely on the perceptions of managers, 2 add external validity by combining perceptions of respondents with an analysis of company records, and 1 uses externally judged measures of both TQM and performance. Only 3 of the 20 studies report any kind of numerical measurement of the profitability impact of TQM. Other studies simply give opinions about whether or not TQM improved the bottom-line performance. Haim (1993) notes that in most studies the findings consist entirely of the opinions of managers who completed the surveys and are rarely based on objective data. Furthermore, there has been little independent measurement of TQM practices and their impact on financial or non-financial measures of performance.

The study by the U.S. General Accounting Office (1991) is one of three that Haim (1993) indicated made any kind of numerical measurement of the impact of TQM on profitability. This study's results are based on responses from 22 firms that were finalists or winners in the 1988 and 1989 Baldrige Award competition. The study measured performance using such measures as market share, sales per employee, return on sales, and return on assets. For the 15 firms that responded, 34 of the 40 reported changes increased and 6 declined. Responses were also favorable in the areas of customer satisfaction, quality, cost, and employee relations.

The second study is by Fitzerald and Erdmann (1992), who evaluate the impact of continuous improvement practices, a key element of TQM. Based on responses from 280 automotive suppliers, their survey shows that over a two- to three-year period, respondents reported an average 17% increase in profits from their continuous improvement efforts.

The third study is an internal study by International Business Machines (see Quality Management Update [1993]), which compared the performance of 57 business units that had scored 500 or more out of 1,000 on the Baldrige criteria with other business units that had not. These 57 units outperformed the other business units in areas of customer satisfaction, employee morale, market share, revenues, and profitability.

A common limitation of the studies just described is that they do not test for the statistical significance of the improvements in performance. Additional weaknesses include the survey nature of the data and the failure to control for industry and economy effects.

A more rigorous study is that by Easton and Jarrell (1998), who examine the impact of TQM practices on the financial performance of 108 firms by comparing the actual performance with a benchmark of how the firm may have performed had it not adopted TQM. They identified their sample firms by conducting interviews with the director or vice president of quality. On the basis of information gathered during the interviews, they included those firms that appeared to have made a serious effort to implement TQM approaches in the majority of their business. They measure performance over a five-year period starting at the approximate time their sample firms began to make a serious effort to implement TQM. Given that it can easily take three to five years to implement an effective TQM program, their results are more representative of what could be expected during a period of TQM implementation. They find evidence of significantly improved performance from year 3 onward. The results are uniformly stronger for the subsample of 44 firms that they identify as having more mature TQM programs. To our knowledge, the research described in this chapter and Easton and Jarrell's study are the first known attempts to use rigorous research methods with objective measures of performance to estimate the financial impact of TQM.

A number of empirical studies have examined the link between TQM and other measures of performance. Other studies have investigated different aspects of implementing TQM programs (Saraph, Benson, and Schroeder [1989] and Ittner and Larcker [1995b]). Still other studies have assessed the impact of TQM on non-financial measures of performance (Benson, Saraph, and Schroeder [1991], Flynn, Schroeder, and Sakakibara [1995], and Powell [1995]).

Concepts, Hypotheses, and Performance Variables

Concepts concerning how effective TQM programs improve financial performance can be broadly classified into three areas: (1) cost of quality, (2) total customer satisfaction, and (3) organizational innovation.

Cost of Quality

There are two competing theories on how improving the conformance quality level affects costs. Juran and Gryna (1980) trade off the appraisal and prevention costs with the internal and external failure costs to argue that the optimal conformance level implies a strictly positive proportion of defects. On the other hand, Deming (1982) and Crosby (1979) claim that the optimal conformance level is zero defects. This claim is based on the belief that making products of higher conformance quality is always less costly than making products of low conformance quality. Fine (1986) shows that when quality-based learning affects quality control costs, firms have an incentive to push toward zero defects. Garvin's (1983) study of the room air-conditioning industry and Abernathy, Clark, and Kantrow's (1981) study of the automobile industry show that manufacturers with higher conformance quality have lower costs.

Improving conformance quality can also affect revenues. If the performance level of similar products offered by different firms is stable and prices are similar across different firms, a product with a higher conformance level has a better chance of gaining market share than a product with a lower conformance level. If customers perceive improvements in conformance quality, they may be willing to pay higher prices. This could enable a firm to increase its revenues while maintaining its market share or vice versa. In summary, the cost-of-quality concept suggests that improving conformance levels should increase profits.

Total Customer Satisfaction

Totally satisfying customer needs and expectations is a key element of any effective TQM program. This point is reinforced by most award givers, as they assign a significant weight to how the award applicant has performed on customer satisfaction. Customer satisfaction is defined more broadly than simply providing a high-quality product. It includes developing systems to determine customer expectations, establishing communication links and long-term relationships with customers, responding to customer needs in a timely manner, being committed to customers, developing customer satisfaction indicators, and taking actions to improve these indicators. Higher customer satisfaction should generally lead to a higher customer retention rate, increased market share, and higher profitability.

Organizational Innovation

Many experts view TQM as a new organizational technology that enables an organization to utilize its human and other physical assets more productively. Key elements of this technology include training the workforce in non-traditional approaches to problem solving, involving employees in decision making, delegating decision making and responsibility farther down in the organization, teamwork, inter-functional problem-solving efforts, and changing the way employees are evaluated. Wruck and Jensen (1994) argue that TQM is an efficiency-improving organizational technology because (1) it encourages the use of the scientific method in everyday decision making at all levels of an organization; (2) it encourages the creation and utilization of specific knowledge, by transferring decision-making rights to those agents who have specific knowledge; and (3) it changes the performance measurement, reward, and punishment systems.

On the basis of these concepts, our first hypothesis is that implementing an effective TQM program will improve a firm's profitability. Our primary measure of profitability is operating income before depreciation, which equals net sales less cost of goods sold and selling and administrative expenses before depreciation, depletion, and amortization are deducted. This is a measure of the cash generated from operations before depreciation, interest, and taxes. It is therefore unaffected by the method of depreciating assets, the capital structure of the firm (debt–equity ratio), or the gains or losses from the sale of assets. Since the changes in operating income do not control for acquisitions and divestitures, this measure could mis-estimate the real change. To partially control for acquisitions and divestitures, other income-based measures considered in our analyses are annual operating income divided by year-end assets (return on assets), by annual sales (operating margin), and by year-end number of employees.

Our second hypothesis is that implementing an effective TQM program will increase revenues. A commonly cited benefit of TQM programs is that they can lead to higher customer satisfaction, which in turn could lead to higher sales (customers are willing to pay more or buy more). Net sales is our primary revenue measure. Other measures considered are asset turnover, which is annual sales divided by year-end assets, and sales per employee, which is annual sales divided by year-end number of employees.

Our third hypothesis is that implementing an effective TQM program will reduce costs. Reducing defects and rework, process improvements, and eliminating waste are key elements of an effective TQM program. Progress in these areas of TQM is expected to reduce costs. Our primary cost measure is the sum of annual cost of goods sold and the cost of selling and general administration divided by annual sales (cost per dollar of sales).

We also explore the effect of implementing an effective TQM program on capital expenditure, number of employees, and total assets. No specific hypotheses are offered for the direction of change on these variables, as arguments can be made for changes in either direction. For example, some believe that TQM programs require investment in people and capital, resulting in an increase in employment, capital expenditure, and total assets. Others believe that TQM programs increase the effective productive capacity of a firm because of process improvements and reductions in defects, rework, and waste, among other things. These improvements could result in a decrease in employment, capital expenditure, and total assets.

Sample Selection and Methodology

Sample Selection

Our sample of quality award winners is obtained from three sources: (1) announcements of quality awards in the *Wall Street Journal*, PR Newswires, Business Wires, and Dow Jones News Service Wire using "quality" and "award" as key search words; (2) lists of quality award winners published in monthly publications such as *Automotive Engineering, Business Electronics, Distribution*, and *Ward's Auto World*, and (3) lists from quality award givers of firms that have won their awards.

About 100 award givers are represented in our sample, some of which are listed in Table 8.1. Many of the award givers are customers who have developed quality award systems for their suppliers. Examples of such award givers include most major U.S. automobile manufacturing firms and many firms that have won the Baldrige Award in the large-manufacturing category. Award givers also include independent organizations such as the National Institute of Standards and Technology, National Association of Manufacturers, and various state award givers. A firm need not be a supplier to compete for awards given by independent organizations. Competing for independent awards is voluntary.

Our data base consists of nearly 2,800 quality award winners. To be included in the sample, an award winner must satisfy two criteria. First, it must be on the COMPUSTAT Annual Industrial File. Second, it must have continuous data for a minimum of six fiscal years, beginning from six years before through one year before the winning of the first quality award. The second criterion is imposed to reduce the noise in our analyses. There were 596 firms that met the first criterion, and 463 firms that met both criteria. For each of these 463 firms, we identified the year when the firm won its first quality award. Panel A of Table 8.2 gives the distribution of the year of winning the first quality award for the 463 firms. Nearly 25% of the sample firms won their first quality award in 1989. About 32% of the sample firms won their first quality award during 1983 to 1988, whereas 43% won their first award during 1990 to 1993.

Panel B of Table 8.2 gives summary statistics for the full sample of 463 firms based on the most recent fiscal year completed before the year of

Table 8.1. *Some Quality Award Givers Whose Award Recipients Are Included in the Sample*

Organizations That Give Awards to Their Suppliers	Independent Award Givers
Auto Alliance International Inc. (part of Mazda Motor Manufacturing)	Alabama Senate Productivity & Quality Award
Chrysler Corp.	Arizona's Pioneer and Governor's Award for Quality
Consolidated Rail	California Governor's Golden
Eastman Kodak Co.	State Quality Awards
Ford Motor Co.	Connecticut Quality
General Electric	Improvement Award
General Motors Corp.	Delaware Quality Award
Goodyear Tires	Florida Governor's Sterling Award
GTE Corp.	Maine State Quality Award
Honda of America Manufacturing Inc.	Maryland Senate Productivity Award
International Business Machines	Massachusetts Quality Award
Lockheed Corp.	Michigan Quality Award
Minnesota Mining and Manufacturing	Minnesota Quality Award
	Missouri Quality Award
National Aeronautical and Space Authority	National Association of Manufacturers (Shingo Prize)
New United Motor Manufacturing Inc.	National Institute of Standards and Technology (Baldrige Award)
Nissan Motor Manufacturing Corp., USA	Nebraska Edgerton Quality Award
Pacific Bell	New Mexico Quality Award
J. C. Penney & Co.	New York Governor's Excelsior Award
Sears Roebuck & Co.	North Carolina Quality Leadership Award
Texas Instrument Co.	Oklahoma Quality Award
Toyota Motor Manufacturing, USA Inc.	Oregon Quality Award
TRW Inc.	Pennsylvania Quality Award
Union Carbide	Rhode Island Award for Competitiveness and Excellence
Westinghouse	Tennessee Quality Award
Whirlpool	Texas Quality Award
Xerox Corp.	Virginia Senate Productivity & Quality Award
	Washington State Quality Award

Table 8.2. *Description of the 463 Quality Award Winners*

Panel A: Distribution of the Year When the Sample Firms Won Their First Quality Award

Year	Firms That Won Their First Quality Award in This Year (N)	Firms That Won Their First Quality Award in This Year (%)
1983	15	3.2
1984	5	1.1
1985	27	5.8
1986	53	11.4
1987	33	7.1
1988	23	5.0
1989	118	25.5
1990	52	11.2
1991	54	11.7
1992	61	13.2
1993	22	4.8
1983–1993	463	100.0

Panel B: Selected Descriptive Statistics for the Sample

Measure	Mean	Median	Standard Deviation	Maximum	Minimum
Total assets (million $)	4,879.9	924.5	14,043.1	207,666.0	3.5
Sales (millions $)					
Net income	4,571.2	1,078.1	11,664.8	127,337.0	7.7
(million $)	189.5	32.5	559.5	5,260.0	−1,669.0
Market value (million $)	2,688.0	580.9	6,718.0	72,710.8	2.9
Employed (thousands)	30.2	9.1	68.5	876.8	0.08
Debt ratio	.47	.45	.21	.98	.02

winning their first quality award. The information was collected from the COMPUSTAT Annual Industrial File. The average observation in the data set represents a firm with a net income of $189.5 million on sales of $4.57 billion with a market value of $2.69 billion. The smallest firm had sales of $7.7 million, while the largest firm had sales of more than $127 billion. The number of employees ranged from 82 to 877,000. And the debt–equity ratio (defined as the total debt divided by the sum of total debt and the market value of equity) similarly covered a wide range, from 2.1% to more than 98%. In all, the sample has firms from 180 distinct four-digit SIC codes and 42 distinct two-digit SIC Codes.

To pool observations across time, for each firm in our sample fiscal years are translated to event years using the following conventions. The fiscal year when the firm won its first quality award is denoted as year 0. The next fiscal year is denoted year +1, and the year after that as +2, and so on. The fiscal year before the year when the firm won its first quality award is denoted as year −1, and the year before this as year −2, and so on.

Choice of Time Period for Analyses

To estimate the net benefits of implementing an effective TQM program, financial performance must be examined both before and after the effective implementation of TQM. Ideally we would have liked to establish the time period of our analyses based on the date when the firms first started implementing the TQM program and the date when the program became reasonably effective. Unfortunately, precise determination of these dates is very difficult because it requires detailed information that firms typically do not reveal to the public. Hence, we used the following approach to identify the time period of analyses.

It is reasonable to expect that if a firm has an opportunity to apply for an award, it will apply soon after it has implemented an effective TQM program. It typically takes award-giving organizations about six to eight months to evaluate and certify the effectiveness of the program. Given this, we use year −1 as our best estimate of when the TQM programs of the award-winning firms started being effective. The literature suggests that it can take about three to five years to implement an effective TQM program (U.S. General Accounting Office [1991], Hockman [1992], and King [1992]). Given this, we made the choice to anchor the beginning of our estimation period six years before the year of winning the first quality award. The time period from years −6 to −1 is designated as the implementation period.

The time period after year −1 is considered the post-implementation period. For most firms in our sample, the 1993 fiscal year is the last year for which data are available on the version of the COMPUSTAT Annual Industrial File we used. The distribution of the year of winning the first quality award indicates that nearly 40% of the sample firms (firms that won their first quality award after 1989) would not have accounting information for year +4 (the fourth year after the year of winning the first quality award). Given this, we chose +3 as the end of the post-implementation period. The time period from years −1 to +3 is designated as the post-implementation period.

Creating Matched-Pair Samples of Comparison Firms

To provide a benchmark for the performance of our sample of quality award winners and to control for potential industry- and/or economy-wide influences, we created three control samples. We assumed that firms in the same industry and of similar size are subject to similar economic and competitive factors. In the first control sample, for each award winner we chose a control firm that (1) has the same country of incorporation, (2) has accounting data available over at least the same time period as the award-winning firms (i.e., over the years beginning six years before through three years following the year of winning the first quality award), (3) has its fiscal year ending in January to May (June to December) matched with firms whose fiscal year ends in January to May (June to December), (4) has at least the same two-digit SIC industry code, and (5) is closest in size to the award winner as measured by the book value of assets at the fiscal year end before the winning of the quality award, with the constraint that the ratio of the book value of assets of the control and award winner is always less than 3. The same control firm is not matched with more than one award winner in any one control sample.

We were able to find a control firm that met these conditions for 335 (72%) of the 463 award winners. The matching is good in terms of size. The percentages of matches with the same two-, three-, and four-digit SIC industry codes are 53%, 21%, and 26%, respectively. We feel that this control sample gives the closest matches, but we were unable to match 128 large firms.

To prevent any size bias from being introduced, a second control sample was generated by attempting to find matches for the 128 unmatched award-winning firms. This was done by relaxing the conditions on the fiscal year-end matching and allowing a single-digit industry matching. We were able to match an additional 59 firms, bringing the total matches to 394 firms (85%) of the 463 award winners. As expected, the matching is good in terms of size. The percentages of matches with the same one-, two-, three-, and four-digit SIC industry codes are 14%, 46%, 18%, and 22%, respectively. Of the 59 new matches, 54 are matched at the one-digit SIC code.

A third control sample was generated without any conditions on the fiscal year-end matching and without the requirement that the control be within a factor of 3 of the size of the award-winning firm. Specifically, when all the other conditions are met, we select as the control the one that is the closest in size to the award winner as measured by the book value of assets. We found a match for 431 (93%) of the 463 award winners. The only firms that are not matched are firms incorporated outside of the United States. The award-winning firms and controls are mismatched on size. The industry matching is similar to that in the first control sample.

We feel that the first control sample gives the best overall matches, but with potential biases since very large firms are not matched. The second control sample reduces these potential biases through the addition of another 59 firms by relaxing the industry matching while ensuring a good match on size. The third control sample matches all possible firms and does as well as the first control sample in terms of industry matching, but does poorly in terms of matching on size compared with the first and second samples. Each control sample had its own strengths and weaknesses; therefore, we ran our analyses using all three control samples. Since the results are similar across the three control samples, we report only the results obtained from the second control sample.

Empirical Results on the Financial Performance of Quality Award Winners

We report two sets of results. The first set includes the "abnormal" performance on an annual basis over 10 years. The abnormal performance is computed by subtracting from the percent change in performance of each award winner the percent change in performance of its control firm. These results identify time periods when operating performance significantly improves or worsens. We report results on an annual basis only for selected performance measures.

The second set of results includes the abnormal performance over longer time intervals with different starting and ending points. There are two reasons for focusing on longer time intervals. First, the pattern of changes in performance could vary across firms. For example, there could be a firm that had significant deterioration in performance in year −3 because of, say, a major investment in training as part of the TQM program, whereas another firm could have had a positive performance in year −3 because it had already started implementing its TQM program in year −5. In any particular year, such negative and positive changes in performance could cancel each other out, and the net outcome could be a statistically insignificant change in performance. Second, the philosophy of continuous improvement is a key element of TQM programs. The thrust of this philosophy is the making of small and incremental improvements on a regular basis, with these small improvements adding up to a significant improvement over longer time periods. If this is indeed the case, the changes measured on an annual basis may be small and, statistically speaking, insignificant, yet could be significant over longer intervals.

Specifically, we examine changes from years −6 to −1 (a 5-year period before evidence of an effective TQM program becomes apparent), −4 to −1 (a 3-year period before evidence of an effective TQM program becomes apparent), −1 to +1 (a 2-year period after evidence of an effective TQM program becomes apparent), −1 to +3 (a 4-year period after evidence of an effective TQM program becomes apparent), and −6 to +3 (the complete 10-year period). Recall that year −1 is our best estimate of when the TQM programs of the award-winning firms in our sample started being effective.

The mean and median results for the various performance variables are reported. To control for outliers, which can influence the mean values, all results are reported after symmetric trimming of the data at the 2.5% level in each tail. The results (not reported here) are similar using 5.0% trimming in each tail and winsorizing at the 2.5% or 5.0% level in each tail. Non-parametric results are basically the same with and without trimming and winsorizing. The student t (Wilcoxon signed-sign rank) statistic is used to test whether the mean (median) of the performance variable is significantly different from zero. All references to the significance levels of the results are based on one-tailed tests.

Differences in Performance between the Quality Award Winners and Control Firms

Operating-Income-Based Measures. Tables 8.3 through 8.7 report changes in various performance measures for the award winners after adjusting for the performance of the control firms. Table 8.3 reports the annual percent changes in operating-income-related measures. The mean and median changes in operating income of the award winners are higher than those of the control firms in 7 of the 10 years. The mean changes are positive and statistically significant in the following 3 years: −7 to −6 (15.87%, $p = .001$), −4 to −3 (14.38%, $p = .002$), and −1 to 0 (7.82%, $p = .012$). The median changes in these 3 years are also positive, with 1 year significant at the 1% level and the other 2 years significant at the 6% level or better. Note that not all of the statistically significant results are positive. The mean changes are negative and statistically significant in the following 2 years: −5 to −4 (−7.97%, $p = .014$) and +1 to +2 (−7.45%,

Table 8.3. *Annual Changes in Control-Adjusted Performance*

From Year	% Change in Operating Income			% Change in Operating Income/Assets			% Change in Operating Income/Sales			% Change in Operating Income/Emp.		
	Obs.	Mean	Median	Obs.	Mean	Median	Obs.	Mean	Median	Obs.	Mean	Median
−7 to −6	316	15.87	2.58	316	11.18	1.78	315	9.15	1.03	262	9.56	4.97
		(3.15)[a]	(1.63)		(3.21)[a]	(1.96)[c]		(2.84)[a]	(1.63)		(2.89)[a]	(2.63)[a]
−6 to −5	315	4.50	2.92	315	4.90	3.91	314	3.45	−0.35	262	−1.52	−1.44
		(1.19)	(0.72)		(1.53)	(1.47)		(1.16)	(0.66)		(−0.43)	(−0.80)
−5 to −4	313	−7.97	−2.57	313	−7.05	−3.36	312	−6.15	−3.28	263	−11.21	−4.22
		(−2.20)[b]	(−1.45)		(−2.16)[b]	(−1.56)		(−2.23)[b]	(−1.86)[c]		(−2.86)[a]	(−2.17)[b]
−4 to −3	317	14.38	8.31	319	13.49	−0.01	317	14.96	2.85	264	15.06	4.92
		(2.96)[a]	(3.00)[a]		(2.96)[a]	(1.64)		(3.44)[a]	(2.63)[a]		(2.78)[a]	(2.21)[b]
−3 to −2	319	5.30	1.05	315	8.26	1.02	318	4.26	1.45	264	5.85	1.28
		(1.24)	(0.81)		(2.10)[b]	(1.33)		(1.31)	(0.63)		(1.57)	(0.99)
−2 to −1	315	−1.14	0.71	314	0.80	0.50	315	0.22	1.23	261	0.13	−1.40
		(−0.32)	(0.48)		(0.27)	(0.67)		(0.08)	(0.84)		(0.04)	(0.03)
−1 to 0	314	7.82	2.48	299	4.89	0.30	314	6.91	3.41	259	9.16	6.04
		(2.26)[b]	(1.56)		(1.67)[c]	(0.65)		(2.66)[a]	(1.90)[c]		(2.76)[a]	(2.13)[b]
0 to +1	281	2.86	0.95	281	0.21	−0.75	281	0.81	−2.64	229	−0.61	−0.21
		(0.82)	(0.20)		(0.06)	(−0.35)		(0.26)	(−0.22)		(−0.15)	(−0.21)
+1 to +2	228	−7.45	−2.41	228	−6.91	−1.85	228	−5.80	−3.50	187	−9.34	−2.58
		(−1.85)[b]	(−1.19)		(−1.86)[c]	(−1.49)		(−1.63)	(−1.45)		(−2.08)[b]	(−1.22)
+2 to +3	195	5.95	−1.00	195	4.41	1.16	195	2.49	−1.80	165	8.89	0.94
		(1.27)	(0.80)		(0.90)	(0.46)		(0.56)	(−0.23)		(1.59)	(0.87)

Note: Mean and median changes are reported for operating income and for the ratios of operating income to assets, to sales, and to number of employees for firms that won quality awards. The student *t*-statistics for the mean and the Wilcoxon *z*-value for the median are in parentheses. Superscripts *a*, *b*, and *c* denote significantly different from zero at the 1%, 2.5%, and 5% level, respectively, for one-tailed tests.

$p = .032$). The median changes in these 2 years are also negative, with 1 year significant at the 10% level. Overall there are more years with statistically significant positive changes than negative changes. Furthermore, the magnitude of changes in the positive years are generally higher than the magnitude of changes in the negative years. Table 8.3 also gives the results for the percent changes in the ratio of operating income to assets, operating margin, and operating income per employee. The results for these measures are similar to those for the percent change in operating income.

Table 8.4 reports changes in operating-income-related measures over longer intervals. Over the 10-year period from −6 to +3, the mean (median) control-adjusted change in operating income is nearly 79% (30%). The mean and median changes in operating income are highly significant with a t-value of 3.47 and z-value of 3.00. The results are similar for the mean changes in the ratio of operating income to assets and in operating margins. The mean change in operating income per employee is positive but not statistically significant.

The results indicate that improvements in operating income start just before the winning of the quality award. For example, over the years from −6 to −1 and from −4 to −1 (the years before the winning of quality awards), the changes in operating income measures are positive but not significant. However, from year −1 onward, operating income starts to improve. The changes in operating income measures from years −1 to +1 and from −1 to +3 are positive and significant. In particular, the results from year −1 to +3 are highly significant. In general, the mean changes are stronger and more significant than the median changes, but the results are similar.

Overall, the results provide strong evidence that firms that have won quality awards outperform a control sample on operating-income-based measures. As we have argued earlier, firms are likely to win quality awards if they have an effective TQM program in place. The evidence supports our hypothesis that implementing an effective TQM program improves the operating income performance of the firm.

Sales-Based Measures. Table 8.5 reports the changes in sales-based measures over longer intervals. Over the 10-year period from years −6 to +3, the mean (median) change in sales of the award winners is nearly 43% (18%) higher than that of the control firms and is significant at the 2% level or better. The results suggest that award winners start outperforming the control firms just before the winning of the quality award. For example, over the years from −6 to −1 and from −4 to −1 (the years before the winning of quality awards), the changes in sales are positive but sta-

Table 8.4. *Changes in Control-Adjusted Performance over Various Time Periods Spanning More Than One Year*

From Year	% Change in Operating Income			% Change in Operating Income/Assets			% Change in Operating Income/Sales			% Change in Operating Income/Emp.		
	Obs.	Mean	Median	Obs.	Mean	Median	Obs.	Mean	Median	Obs.	Mean	Median
−6 to −1	325	7.90	−0.46	325	6.59	−1.79	324	1.57	−2.91	285	0.74	−3.22
		(0.61)	(−0.08)		(1.31)	(0.17)		(0.34)	(−0.69)		(0.08)	(−0.65)
−4 to −1	330	9.10	7.94	330	7.05	3.80	330	4.31	3.03	284	4.28	1.05
		(1.02)	(1.25)		(1.28)	(0.97)		(0.94)	(0.19)		(0.58)	(0.49)
−1 to +1	297	15.09	2.59	297	4.31	−4.84	297	7.84	0.22	253	12.40	−0.57
		$(2.75)^a$	(1.36)		(1.07)	(−0.52)		$(2.19)^b$	(0.95)		$(2.17)^b$	(0.67)
−1 to +3	210	33.61	21.29	210	18.26	10.16	210	18.51	2.43	182	24.92	7.56
		$(3.86)^a$	$(3.04)^a$		$(3.04)^a$	$(1.98)^b$		$(3.01)^a$	$(1.67)^c$		$(2.71)^a$	(1.53)
−6 to +3	205	79.01	30.02	205	14.41	3.87	204	15.20	−3.13	177	9.46	−6.04
		$(3.47)^a$	$(3.00)^a$		$(2.37)^a$	(1.56)		$(2.08)^b$	(0.41)		(0.67)	(0.14)

Note: Mean and median percent changes are reported for operating income and for the ratios of operating income to assets, to sales, and to number of employees for firms that won quality awards. The student *t*-statistics for the mean and the Wilcoxon *z*-value for the median are in parentheses. Superscripts *a*, *b*, and *c* denote significantly different from zero at the 1%, 2.5%, and 5% level, respectively, for one-tailed tests.

Table 8.5. *Mean and Median Percent Changes in Sales, in the Ratio of Sales to Assets, and in the Ratio of Sales to Number of Employees for Firms That Won Quality Awards*

From Year	% Change in Sales			% Change in Sales/Assets			% Change in Sales/Employee		
	Obs.	Mean	Median	Obs.	Mean	Median	Obs.	Mean	Median
-6 to -1	368	6.21 (0.66)	5.35 (0.43)	368	3.01 (1.51)	1.63 (1.64)[c]	315	-1.04 (-0.38)	-2.64 (0.73)
-4 to -1	368	2.80 (0.72)	2.92 (0.90)	368	2.47 (1.52)	3.72 (1.67)[c]	315	0.28 (0.15)	1.23 (0.27)
-1 to +1	324	5.16 (2.47)[a]	1.19 (1.63)	324	-2.59 (-2.18)[b]	-1.46 (-2.19)[b]	276	0.34 (0.24)	0.61 (0.35)
-1 to +3	225	14.67 (3.77)[a]	8.45 (3.06)[a]	225	0.83 (0.41)	0.18 (0.32)	194	2.49 (1.01)	4.28 (1.26)
-6 to +3	225	43.22 (2.34)[a]	18.16 (2.25)[b]	225	1.31 (0.46)	1.80 (0.58)	194	-4.78 (-0.94)	-1.07 (-0.67)

Note: Mean and median changes are reported for varying time periods after adjusting for the performance of the controls. The student *t*-statistics for the mean and the Wilcoxon *z*-value for the median are in parentheses. Superscripts *a*, *b*, and *c* denote significantly different from zero at the 1%, 2.5%, and 5% level, respectively, for one-tailed tests.

tistically insignificant. However, the changes in sales from years −1 to +1 and from −1 to +3 are positive and statistically significant. In particular, the mean change in sales from year −1 to +3 is 14.67% with a t-value of 3.77 (the median change is 8.45% with a z-value of 3.06).

The mean and median changes in the ratio of sales to assets from years −6 to +3 are positive but insignificantly different from zero. Over the years from −6 to −1 and from −4 to −1, the median change in the ratio of sales to assets is positive and significant at the 5% level (the means are also positive and weakly significant at the 7% level). The change in sales per employee is not different from zero for all the time periods shown in Table 8.5. Overall, the results provide reasonably strong evidence that award winners outperform the control firms on sales growth.

Cost-Based and Other Measures. Table 8.6 reports the annual percent changes in cost per dollar of sales. From years −6 to +3, the change in cost per dollar of sales of the award winners is −0.95% when compared with the control firms. The mean change from years −1 to +3 is about −0.90% and is weakly significant at the 7% level. None of the mean changes over other intervals and none of the median changes are significantly different from zero.

The weak evidence on costs is somewhat surprising given the conventional wisdom that improving quality reduces costs. It is plausible that although firms have been able to reduce costs by adopting TQM, much of the cost reductions have been passed on to customers in the form of lower prices. A better way to examine the relation between quality and cost would be to use cost per unit instead of cost per dollar of sales. Unfortunately, data on cost per unit are not available from publicly released financial statements.

Table 8.6 also shows that from years −6 to +3 the median change in the ratio of capital expenditure to assets is 8.04%, significant at the 5% level (the mean change is 2.44%). Most of this change can be attributed to the increased rate of capital expenditure from years −6 to −1 (the median change in the ratio of capital expenditure to assets is 6.07%, significant at the 7% level). This suggests that implementing TQM programs requires that firms increase their capital expenditure, perhaps on better process control systems or better equipment.

Table 8.6 also indicates that most of the changes in employment and assets occur from year −1 onward. The control-adjusted mean percent change in employment and assets is significantly positive from years −1 to +1 and from years −1 to +3. Similarly, the percent change in assets is significantly positive from years −1 to +1 and from years −1 to +3. Over

Table 8.6. *Mean and Median Percent Changes in the Ratio of Total Cost to Sales, the Ratio of Capital Expenditure to Assets, the Number of Employees, and Total Assets for Firms That Won Quality Awards*

From Year	% Change in Total Cost/Sales			% Change in Capital Expenditure/Assets			% Change in Number of Employees			% Change in Assets		
	Obs.	Mean	Median	Obs.	Mean	Median	Obs.	Mean	Median	Obs.	Mean	Median
−6 to −1	361	−0.27 (−0.47)	−0.16 (−0.09)	336	5.56 (1.03)	6.07 (1.49)	320	0.35 (0.05)	5.69 (0.72)	374	−1.93 (−0.21)	−4.98 (−0.41)
−4 to −1	361	−0.45 (−0.97)	−0.27 (−0.69)	336	−0.71 (−0.16)	3.94 (0.23)	320	2.33 (0.75)	0.64 (0.60)	374	1.80 (0.47)	−1.72 (0.33)
−1 to +1	323	−0.29 (−0.76)	0.22 (−0.59)	298	−7.76 (−1.73)^c	−3.94 (−1.40)	281	4.00 (2.07)^b	3.61 (1.59)	330	8.25 (3.71)^a	5.73 (3.45)^a
−1 to +3	224	−0.93 (−1.49)	−0.24 (−0.92)^a	205	−3.77 (−0.72)	−0.24 (−0.25)	197	9.70 (2.84)^a	3.49 (2.57)^a	229	14.03 (3.14)^a	6.89 (2.71)^a
−6 to +3	224	−0.95 (−1.02)	0.61 (−0.58)^a	205	2.44 (0.40)	8.04 (1.67)^c	197	9.47 (0.96)	8.83 (2.11)^b	229	33.11 (1.73)^c	18.26 (1.56)

Note: Mean and median changes are reported over varying time periods after adjusting for the performance of the controls. The student *t*-statistics for the mean and the Wilcoxon *z*-value for the median are in parentheses. Superscripts *a*, *b*, and *c* denote significantly different from zero at the 1%, 2.5%, and 5% level, respectively, for one-tailed tests.

the years –6 to +3, the mean (median) change in employment is 9.47% (8.83%). The mean (median) change in total assets over the same time period is 33.11% (18.26%).

Overall, the evidence weakly suggests that the award winners are more successful in controlling costs than are the control firms, and appear to increase their rate of capital expenditure. The award winners have higher growth in employment and assets than do the control firms.

Sensitivity Analyses

The control-adjusted results presented in the preceding analysis probably underestimate the true change in operating performance brought about by implementing effective TQM programs. There are two main reasons for this. First, the sample of award winners is based on information gathered from newswires and from award givers. It is conceivable that some of the firms in our control sample won quality awards about which we know nothing. Second, while winning a quality award indicates an effective TQM program, not having won a quality award does not necessarily indicate an ineffective TQM program. There is no easy way to know which firms in our control samples may have an effective TQM program in place. Therefore, it may be instructive to examine the performance of the award winners without adjusting for the performance of the control firms. This could give us an idea of an upper bound on the impact of implementing effective TQM programs. Tables 8.7 and 8.8 present these results for selected measures.

Table 8.7 shows that award winners experienced large and highly significant positive changes (unadjusted for control) in operating income and net sales for nearly all 10 years. Except from years +1 to +2, the mean annual percent change in operating income ranges from 6% to 26%, and for sales it ranges from 6% to 14%. Similar conclusions are reached when changes for operating income and sales are measured over longer time periods (Table 8.8). From years –6 to –3, mean increases in operating income and sales are a highly significant 148.40% and 155.07%, respectively (median increases are 92.86% and 84.78%, respectively). The mean increase in cost per dollar of sales is 1.11% (significant at the 1% level), whereas the median increase is 0.73% (significant at the 5% level).

We believe that the results presented in Tables 8.7 and 8.8 probably overstate the true change in operating performance brought about by implementing effective TQM programs. Our study uses data from 1977 to 1993, with most of the data from 1980 onward. For nearly 15 of these 17 years the U.S. economy was expanding. There were three recession-

Table 8.7. *Annual Changes in Performance*

From Year	% Change in Operating Income			% Change in Sales			% Change in Total Cost/Sales		
	Obs.	Mean	Median	Obs.	Mean	Median	Obs.	Mean	Median
−7 to −6	332	26.41 $(6.72)^a$	12.16 $(7.79)^a$	359	14.52 $(12.11)^a$	9.85 $(11.69)^a$	354	−0.38 $(-1.80)^c$	−0.23 (-1.34)
−6 to −5	335	18.22 $(6.07)^a$	12.57 $(7.07)^a$	359	14.44 $(13.57)^a$	11.24 $(11.97)^a$	354	0.21 (0.88)	−0.10 (0.39)
−5 to −4	333	5.98 $(2.62)^a$	5.99 $(2.92)^a$	359	9.82 $(9.82)^a$	6.80 $(9.03)^a$	354	0.44 $(2.15)^b$	0.25 $(2.11)^b$
−4 to −3	330	20.74 $(7.37)^a$	13.44 $(7.72)^a$	359	11.07 $(11.13)^a$	8.82 $(10.55)^a$	354	−0.27 (-1.52)	−0.37 $(-1.99)^b$
−3 to −2	338	17.02 $(7.24)^a$	11.94 $(7.77)^a$	359	11.43 $(14.59)^a$	9.70 $(12.56)^a$	354	−0.19 (-1.02)	−0.23 (-1.60)
−2 to −1	344	12.98 $(6.36)^a$	8.60 $(6.25)^a$	359	9.83 $(12.96)^a$	8.08 $(11.59)^a$	354	0.10 (0.68)	−0.06 (0.20)
−1 to 0	338	9.06 $(3.68)^a$	6.50 $(3.70)^a$	353	7.34 $(9.93)^a$	6.64 $(9.19)^a$	348	0.23 (1.41)	0.05 (0.95)
0 to +1	304	9.48 $(4.17)^a$	8.27 $(4.51)^a$	320	7.05 $(9.75)^a$	6.33 $(9.18)^a$	317	0.19 (1.08)	0.01 (0.96)
+1 to +2	250	0.28 (0.14)	2.84 (0.81)	262	3.41 $(4.77)^a$	2.80 $(4.47)^a$	260	0.46 $(2.42)^a$	0.23 $(1.82)^c$
+2 to +3	212	11.63 $(4.98)^a$	6.65 $(4.62)^a$	225	6.16 $(7.89)^a$	5.48 $(7.10)^a$	240	−0.01 (-0.07)	0.01 (0.01)

Note: Mean and median percent changes are reported for operating income and for the ratios of operating income to assets, to sales, and to number of employees for firms that won quality awards. The student *t*-statistics for the mean and the Wilcoxon *z*-value for the median are in parentheses. Superscripts *a*, *b*, and *c* denote significantly different from zero at the 1%, 2.5%, and 5% level, respectively, for one-tailed tests.

Table 8.8. *Changes in Performance over Various Time Periods Spanning More Than One Year*

From Year	% Change in Operating Income			% Change in Sales			% Change in Total Cost/Sales		
	Obs.	Mean	Median	Obs.	Mean	Median	Obs.	Mean	Median
−6 to −1	347	96.31 $(10.61)^a$	50.09 $(11.34)^a$	371	93.56 $(12.53)^a$	61.54 $(15.08)^a$	365	0.50 (1.39)	0.09 (0.59)
−4 to −1	343	59.24 $(9.93)^a$	33.97 $(10.51)^a$	371	41.85 $(15.19)^a$	29.71 $(14.62)^a$	365	−0.46 (-1.61)	−0.59 $(-1.91)^c$
−1 to +1	321	27.22 $(6.04)^a$	13.57 $(6.10)^a$	330	16.89 $(12.19)^a$	13.91 $(10.95)^a$	327	0.37 (1.57)	0.22 (1.59)
−1 to +3	224	41.29 $(6.28)^a$	22.97 $(6.28)^a$	230	30.69 $(11.16)^a$	23.02 $(9.59)^a$	229	0.69 $(1.91)^c$	0.51 (1.50)
−6 to +3	217	148.40 $(9.77)^a$	92.86 $(9.97)^a$	230	155.07 $(10.06)^a$	84.78 $(11.90)^a$	229	1.11 $(2.31)^a$	0.73 $(1.71)^c$

Note: Mean and median percent changes are reported for operating income and for the ratios of operating income to assets, to sales, and to number of employees for firms that won quality awards. The student t-statistics for the mean and the Wilcoxon z-value for the median are in parentheses. Superscripts a, b, and c denote significantly different from zero at the 1%, 2.5%, and 5% level, respectively, for one-tailed tests.

ary periods, which lasted for a total of 29 months. Furthermore, the inflation rate in the late seventies and early eighties was high. For example, the annual increases in the consumer price index ranged from 7% to 13% from 1977 to 1981. Since 1982 the annual increases have ranged from 3% to 4%. These observations suggest that economic growth and inflation could be partly driving the highly significant results reported in Tables 8.7 and 8.8. Clearly, these results must be interpreted with caution. It is also worth reiterating that most of the articles on TQM in the business press and many studies report evidence on the economic impact of implementing TQM without adjusting for potential industry-and/or economy-wide factors. In our view, this may have created overly optimistic expectations of what can be achieved with TQM.

Given the distribution of the years in which firms won their first quality awards and the availability of data from the COMPUSTAT Annual Industrial File, our results could be affected by two potential sources of bias. First, nearly 25% of the firms in our test sample won their first quality award in 1989. This clustering could influence the results. To test for this, we ran our analyses by excluding firms that won their first quality awards in 1989. Second, for the firms in our test sample, we have more data for the period before the winning of quality awards than for the period after the winning of quality awards. This is because many firms won their first quality award in the nineties. To ascertain whether our results are influenced by the loss of observations for firms in years +1 to +3, we ran our analyses with only those award winners that have complete data from years –6 through +3. In both cases, the results are similar to the results for the whole sample.

Relation between Firm Characteristics and Financial Performance

This section presents results on the relation between various characteristics of the quality award winners and their control-adjusted changes in financial performance. Our detailed arguments for developing the hypotheses and the detailed results are discussed in Hendricks and Singhal (1995b). Here we briefly summarize some of our main results. We examine the following characteristics:

Firm size: measured as a categorical variable (larger vs. smaller) based on the median of the sales in year –1 converted to constant 1990 dollars using the consumer price index.

Capital intensity of the firm: measured as a categorical variable (more vs. less) based on the median of the ratio of net property, plant, and equipment (converted to constant 1990 dollars) to the number of employees at the end of year −1.

Firm diversification: measured as a categorical variable (less diversified vs. more diversified) based on the median Herfindahl index of the firms in our sample. The Herfindahl index is the sum of the squared ratio of sales of each business segment to the firm's total sales (see Palepu [1985] for further discussion of the Herfindahl index).

Timing of effective implementation of TQM programs: measured as a categorical variable by classifying firms that won their first quality awards in 1986 or earlier as earlier implementers and those that won their first quality awards after 1986 as later implementers.

Type of award won (independent awards vs. supplier awards): measured as a categorical variable by classifying firms that won an independent award (such as the Malcolm Baldrige Award, state awards, and Philip Crosby and Associates award), anytime over the period covered as independent award winners and the remaining firms as supplier award winners.

Number of awards won: measured as a categorical variable by classifying firms that won awards from more than one award giver as multiple award winners and the remaining firms as single award winners.

Table 8.9 summarizes the main results on the relation between firm characteristics and control-adjusted performance during the implementation period. The table reports the mean change in operating income, operating margin, sales, and cost per dollar of sales. For each of the six characteristics, we report the means for each of the two subsamples and the *t*-value for the difference in means of the two subsamples.

The results in Table 8.9 indicate that the only statistically significant results are those for the degree of capital intensity and the type of award won. During the implementation period, less-capital-intensive firms' mean change in operating margin is 9.0%, whereas that of more-capital-intensive firms is −15.1%. Furthermore, the difference in means of the change in cost per dollar of sales is weakly significant at the 8.0% level: less-capital-intensive firms do better than more-capital-intensive firms in managing costs.

During the implementation period, independent award winners do poorly in terms of operating margin when compared with the supplier award winners. Independent award winners' mean change in operating margin is −24.2%, whereas that of supplier award winners is 2.5%. During the implementation period, independent award winners also do

Table 8.9. *Implementation Period's Results on the Mean Percent Change in Various Performance Measures when the Full Sample Is Segmented by Firm Characteristics*

Sample Characteristic	% Change in Operating Income, Mean	% Change in Operating Margin, Mean	% Change in Sales, Mean	% Change in Cost per Dollar of Sales, Mean
Smaller firms	-27.90	-8.00	-2.50	-0.20
Larger firms	1.30	2.00	-6.10	0.30
t-Value for the difference in mean	-0.91	-0.85	0.17	-0.32
Less-capital-intensive firms	2.80	9.00	2.40	-1.10
More-capital-intensive firms	-29.40	-15.10	-11.10	1.10
t-Value for the difference in mean	1.01	2.07[b]	0.61	-1.47
Less diversified firms	-20.40	-1.50	-2.60	-1.20
More diversified firms	-6.20	-4.60	-5.90	1.30
t-Value for the difference in mean	-0.45	0.26	0.14	-1.65[c]
Earlier implementers	-40.80	-1.10	-12.70	0.90
Later implementers	-0.50	-3.90	-0.50	-0.40
t-Value for the difference in mean	-1.17	0.22	-0.51	0.79
Independent award winners	-36.80	-24.20	-29.00	-0.10
Supplier award winners	-7.60	2.50	1.17	0.00
t-Value for the difference in mean	-0.72	-1.85[b]	-1.11	0
Multiple award winners	-20.20	-4.60	-3.70	1.30
Single award winners	-2.80	-0.70	-5.10	-1.70
t-Value for the difference in mean	-0.53	-0.33	0.01	1.91[c]

Note: Results are presented for the implementation period; t-values for the difference in means are also reported. Superscripts b and c denote significantly different from zero at the 1%, 2.5%, and 5% level, respectively, for one-tailed tests.

poorly relative to their controls as indicated by the mean change of −36.8% in operating income and the mean change of −24.2% in operating margin. Since winning independent awards is an indication that the firm has a more comprehensive TQM program, the higher cost of implementing such a comprehensive program could be the cause of poor financial performance during the implementation period for the independent award winners. It is also plausible that poor financial performance motivated these firms to adopt a comprehensive TQM program.

Table 8.10 summarizes the main results on the relation between firm characteristics and control-adjusted performance during the post-implementation period. First, smaller firms have a higher mean change in operating income than larger firms (49.1% vs. 24.4.%). The difference in means is significant at the 8.5% level. Somewhat stronger results are observed for operating margin, where smaller firms do significantly better than larger firms. Furthermore, smaller firms do better on cost reductions than larger firms.

Second, less-capital-intensive firms significantly outperform more-capital-intensive firms on operating-income-based measures. The mean change of 57.2% for less-capital-intensive firms is significantly higher than the mean change of 16.4% for more-capital-intensive firms. The results are similar for the mean change in operating margin. In terms of cost per dollar of sales, the mean change of −2.6% for less-capital-intensive firms is significantly lower than the mean change of 1% for more-capital-intensive firms.

Finally, independent award winners outperform supplier award winners. The mean change of 68.3% for independent award winners is significantly higher than that of 29.1% for supplier award winners. The results are similar for operating margin. Independent award winners have a higher mean change in sales than supplier award-winning firms (26.9% vs. 11.7%). Independent award winners also do better in terms of cost per dollar of sales than supplier award winners, but the difference is not significant at conventional levels.

To summarize, we observe some significant differences in financial performance of award winners across certain characteristics. Our results have implications for setting reasonable expectations regarding the potential payoffs from TQM.

The Relation between Quality Award and
Stock Price Performance

In one of our earliest attempts to examine the relation between quality awards and stock prices, we used the event study methodology to esti-

Table 8.10. Post-implementation Period's Results on the Mean Percent Change in Various Performance Measures When the Full Sample Is Segmented by Firm Characteristics

Sample Characteristics	% Change in Operating Income, Mean	% Change in Operating Margin, Mean	% Change in Sales, Mean	% Change in Cost per Dollar of Sales, Mean
Smaller firms	49.10	33.10	14.90	-2.00
Larger firms	24.40	7.30	14.50	0.30
t-Value for the difference in mean	1.38	2.04[b]	0.10	-1.78[c]
Less-capital-intensive firms	57.20	38.60	17.30	-2.60
More-capital-intensive firms	16.40	1.90	12.10	1.00
t-Value for the difference in mean	2.29[b]	2.95[a]	0.65	-2.8[a]
Less diversified firms	50.30	21.50	16.20	-1.10
More diversified firms	23.00	18.70	13.20	-0.60
t-Value for the difference in mean	1.52	0.22	0.36	-0.39
Earlier implementers	27.60	8.50	16.70	1.20
Later implementers	40.60	25.00	13.80	-1.60
t-Value for the difference in mean	0.66	-1.18	0.32	1.97[b]
Independent award winners	68.30	42.40	26.90	-1.70
Supplier award winners	29.10	14.60	11.70	-0.60
t-Value for the difference in mean	1.73[c]	1.75[c]	1.51	-0.68
Multiple award winners	33.50	16.30	15.10	-0.40
Single award winners	41.10	25.60	14.20	-1.40
t-Value for the difference in mean	0.42	-0.71	0.11	0.74

Note: Results are presented for the post-implementation period; t-values for the difference in means are also reported. Superscripts a, b, and c denote significantly different from zero at the 1%, 2.5%, and 5% level, respectively, for one-tailed tests.

mate the abnormal change on the day when information about winning quality awards is publicly announced (Hendricks and Singhal [1996]). Our event results are based on a sample of 91 announcements. Table 8.11 summarizes the main results for three models of estimating abnormal returns: the market model, the market-adjusted model, and the mean-adjusted model (see Brown and Warner [1985] for a detailed discussion of the event study methodology and these models).

The results in Table 8.11 show that the stock market reacts positively to quality award announcements. Statistically significant mean abnormal returns on the announcement day range from 0.59% to 0.67% depending on the model used to generate the abnormal returns. The reaction is particularly strong for smaller firms (mean abnormal returns range from 1.16% to 1.26%) and for firms that win awards from independent organizations such as Malcolm Baldrige and Philip Crosby (mean abnormal returns range from 1.31% to 1.65%). The reaction is strongest for smaller firms that win awards from independent organizations (mean abnormal returns range from 1.47% to 2.09%).

Although we argue that our event study results provide a lower bound on the value of implementing effective TQM programs, the lower bound is fairly low. Such a low value seems hardly likely given the efforts firms are making to implement these programs and the publicity surrounding the winning of awards. It is plausible that the market views the winning of quality awards somewhat cautiously, causing stock prices to adjust slowly over time as firms establish the benefits of their quality programs, and/or that the market has already reflected the value of TQM programs before firms announce their quality awards.

The small magnitude of abnormal returns observed in our event study motivated us to examine the long-term stock price performance of award winners. In Hendricks and Singhal (1997b) we examine the long-term stock price performance by comparing the performance of a sample of nearly 600 quality award winners against various control samples. Specifically, we create three control samples by matching award winners to control firms on such factors as industry, size as measured by the market value of the equity, and the ratio of book value of equity to market value of equity. We examine stock price performance by computing the abnormal buy-and-hold returns separately for the implementation period (which begins six years before and ends one year before the date of winning the first quality award) and post-implementation period (which begins one year before and ends four years after the date of winning the first quality award). Abnormal return is the difference between the return of the award winner and that of its control firm.

Our results indicate that during the implementation period there is no

Table 8.11. *Mean Abnormal Returns for 91 Announcements of Quality Award Winners and Subsamples of These Winners*

Sample Description	Sample Size	Market Model	Market-Adjusted Model	Mean-Adjusted Model
All firms	91	0.59 (0.03)	0.66 (0.02)	0.67 (0.03)
Small firms	45	1.16 (0.02)	1.26 (0.02)	1.20 (0.03)
Large firms	46	0.03 (0.46)	0.06 (0.42)	0.15 (0.34)
Independent award winners	26	1.31 (0.00)	1.50 (0.00)	1.65 (0.00)
Supplier award winners	65	0.30 (0.22)	0.31 (0.21)	0.27 (0.27)
Small firms and independent award winners	14	1.47 (0.02)	1.83 (0.01)	2.09 (0.01)
Large firms and independent award winners	12	1.11 (0.01)	1.13 (0.01)	1.14 (0.02)
Small firms and supplier award winners	31	1.02 (0.08)	1.00 (0.09)	0.79 (0.16)
Large firms and supplier award winners	34	−0.35 (0.19)	−0.31 (0.22)	−0.20 (0.33)

Note: Returns are expressed as percentages. Abnormal returns are computed using the market model, market-adjusted model, and mean-adjusted model. One-tailed *p*-values are in parentheses.

difference between the stock price performance of the quality award winners and that of the various samples. The mean abnormal returns are −2.8%, −0.05%, and 6.75%, depending on the control sample used. These means are insignificantly different from zero.

The results are very different for the post-implementation period. Award winners significantly outperform the control samples. The mean abnormal returns are 37.84%, 44.70%, and 46.32%, depending on the control sample used. These means are significantly different from zero at the 2.5% level or better in two-tailed tests. This level of outperformance is economically significant. For example, an investor would have to invest anywhere from 21% to 26% more money in the control firms (depending on the control sample used) than in the award winners to achieve the same wealth. Rough estimates of the abnormal market value created by the average award winner are $548 million, $774 million, and $923 million, depending on the control sample used.

A few other studies have examined the relation between the TQM and stock price performance. Adams, McQueen, and Seawright (1996) find marginally positive stock price responses on the day of announcement for the 12 publicly traded Baldrige Award winners during 1988 to 1994. Anderson, Daly, and Johnson (1995) examine the stock market's reaction for a sample of 221 ISO 9000 certified firms. They find that the mean abnormal return is not significantly different from zero. In their study of 108 firms, Easton and Jarrell (1998) find that median cumulative abnormal return is a statistically significant 16.05% at the end of year 5, with most of the gains occurring during years 4 and 5. Heller (1994) reports that a portfolio of 150 TQM firms had a statistically significant abnormal change of 4.95% in stock prices over the years 1989 to 1992. Heller (1994) identifies the TQM firms by applying criteria developed from the Baldrige Award and other popular sources of information on TQM. Finally, the U.S. Department of Commerce News (1995) reports the results of a buy-and-hold strategy of investing on the first trading day in April of the year a publicly traded firm won the Baldrige Award (or the date the winner went public) to October 3, 1994. Under this strategy, the 12 publicly traded Baldrige winners beat the Standard & Poor's 500 index by almost 3 to 1.

Summary and Future Directions in Research

This chapter has described and summarized our research on whether implementing effective TQM programs improves the financial performance of firms. The winning of a quality award is used as a proxy for the effective implementation of TQM programs. Table 8.12 summarizes

Table 8.12. *Key Control-Adjusted Results for the Implementation and Post-implementation Periods*

Performance Measure	Implementation Period	Post-implementation Period
Change in operating income (%)	7.90	33.61[a]
Change in operating return of assets (%)	6.59	18.26[a]
Change in operating margins (%)	1.57	18.51[a]
Change in operating income per employee (%)	0.74	24.62[a]
Abnormal stock price performance using:		
Industry-matched control firms (%)	6.75	37.84[c]
Industry-size-matched control firms (%)	-2.80	46.32[b]
Industry-size-book-to-market-matched control firms (%)	-0.05	44.70[b]
Change in sales (%)	6.21	14.67[a]
Change in total cost/sales (%)	-0.27	-0.93
Change in number of employees (%)	0.35	9.70[a]
Change in total assets (%)	-1.93	14.03[a]

Note: Superscript *a* denotes significantly different from zero at the 1% level for one-tailed tests; *b* and *c* denote significantly different from zero at the 1% and 2.5% level, respectively, for two-tailed tests.

some of our key results for the implementation and post-implementation periods.

The evidence indicates that during the implementation period there is no difference in the performance of the quality award winners and that of the control firms. This suggests that implementing an effective TQM program may not necessarily result in poor performance during the implementation period. This is important, because managers often worry about the direct and indirect costs of implementing TQM programs. While these costs may be real and high, perhaps TQM programs provide at least some early benefits that outweigh the costs of implementation.

The evidence clearly indicates that during the post-implementation period, award winners significantly outperform the control firms. During this period the mean change in the operating income of the award winners is 34% higher than that of the control firms. Over the same period the mean changes in the ratios of operating income to assets and to sales are also higher relative to the controls by about 18%. Award winners experience mean abnormal stock returns of about 40%. Consistent with the results on operating income and stock prices, we find strong evidence that award winners do better in terms of growth in sales. We find weak evidence that award winners are more successful in controlling costs than are the control firms. The growth in employment and in total assets of award winners is higher than that of the control firms.

The post-implementation period results are consistent with the notion that once an effective TQM program is in place, firms should experience improvement in performance. It could also be that firms use quality awards to send a credible and verifiable signal about quality to the marketplace. Thus, the improvement in performance is due to the favorable reaction of customers.

Overall the evidence clearly indicates that implementing effective TQM programs leads to improved financial performance. Given the recent controversy about the financial benefits of TQM, our evidence should be reassuring to firms that have made significant investments in TQM. For those firms that have chosen not to invest in TQM, our results provide a compelling reason to consider investing in TQM.

Quality award systems have been an object of criticism. Our results suggest that such criticism is unwarranted and misplaced. Organizations that give quality awards seem to give them to firms that subsequently show better financial performance. We believe that quality award systems play a critical role in promoting awareness of TQM practices, motivating and challenging firms to improve quality, providing a benchmark against which a firm can evaluate the progress of its TQM programs, and providing feedback to firms that have applied for an award. Since quality award winners show improved financial performance, it is important that government and businesses continue to provide incentives and resources for developing and administering quality award programs. It seems to us that such programs have a substantial payback.

We also provide evidence on the relation between the financial performance associated with effective implementation of TQM programs to such characteristics as firm size, the degree of capital intensity, the degree of firm diversification, the type of quality awards won, the timing of the first quality award, and the number of awards won. We find that less-capital-intensive firms do significantly better than more-capital-intensive firms in both the implementation and post-implementation periods. Firms that have won awards from independent award givers (such as the Baldrige Award) do worse than the supplier award-winning firms during the implementation period, but do better than the supplier award winners during the post-implementation period. There is weak evidence that during the post-implementation period smaller firms do better than larger firms, and that less diversified firms do better than more diversified firms. We do not observe any significant differences between the performance of single and multiple award winners. This suggests that the incremental benefits of winning additional awards may be low, and chasing too many awards may not have a significant impact on financial performance. The evidence also indicates that differences between the performance of earlier and later implementers are insignificant. This suggests that firms that are late in implementing TQM still benefit from TQM.

The key implication of the results on the relation between firm characteristics and financial performance is that the impact of TQM can vary quite significantly across firms. Firms should be realistic in forming expectations about the potential of TQM. It seems to us that expectations about how TQM can improve performance are based less on rigorous empirical evidence than on anecdotes, hype, and publicity. Furthermore, the expectations seem to be very high. High and unrealistic expectations could be a main reason for some firms' dissatisfaction with their TQM programs.

There are a number of avenues for future research. First, there is considerable interest among managers and academicians in identifying "best or effective" quality management practices. Practices can be labeled best or effective if they improve performance. Given the results of our study, it might be fruitful to focus on quality award winners in order to identify best practices. Second, our results indicate that during the implementation period some subsamples of award-winning firms do significantly worse than the controls. It would be interesting to examine whether this is because of the cost of implementing TQM programs or simply because firms adopt TQM after experiencing poor financial performance. Finally, recent research has documented that financial and organizational mechanisms such as management buyouts, leveraged buyouts, and recapitalizations have created value through significant improvements in operating performance (see Jensen [1993] for a review of this literature). However, these studies do not provide much information on what operating actions led to the improvements in performance. It would be interesting to determine whether managers in these firms adopted elements of TQM and, if so, what is unique about their implementation approach. This could also clarify the role of incentives and organization structure in the adoption of TQM.

REFERENCES

Abernathy, W. J., K. B. Clark, and A. M. Kantrow, "The New Industrial Competition," *Harvard Business Review*, 59, 4 (1981), 68–81.

Adams, G., G. McQueen, and K. Seawright, "Quality Awards and Stock Prices: A microanalysis," Working paper, Brigham Young University, Marriott School of Management, 1996.

Anderson, S. A., J. D. Daly, and M. F. Johnson, "The Value of Management Control Systems: Evidence on the Market Reaction to ISO 9000 Quality Assurance Certification," Working paper, University of Michigan Business School, 1995.

Benson, P. G., J. V. Saraph, and R. G. Schroeder, "The Effects of Organizational Context on Quality Management: An Empirical Investigation," *Management Science,* 37, 9 (1991), 1107–1124.

Brown, S. J., and J. B. Warner, "Using Daily Stock Returns: The Case of Event Studies," *Journal of Financial Economics*, 14 (1985), 3–31.

Crosby, P. B., *Quality Is Free*, McGraw-Hill, New York, 1979.

Deming, E. W., *Quality, Productivity and Competitive Position*, MIT Center for Advanced Engineering, 1982.

Easton, G. S., and Jarrell, "The Effects of Total Quality Management on Corporate Performance: An Empirical Investigation," *Journal of Business*, 71, 2 (1998), 253–307.

Ernst & Young and American Quality Foundation, *International Quality Study: The Definitive Study of the Best International Quality Management Practices – Top-Line Findings*, Ernst & Young, Cleveland, OH, 1992.

Fine, C. H., "Quality Improvements and Learning in Productive Systems," *Management Science,* 32, 10 (1986), 1301–1315.

Fitzerald, C., and T. Erdmann, American Automotive Industry Action Group, *Actionline*, October (1992).

Flynn, B. B., R. G. Schroeder, and S. Sakakibara, "The Impact of Quality Management Practices on Performance and Competitive Advantage," *Decision Sciences*, 26, 5 (1995), 659–691.

Fuchsberg, G., "Total Quality Is Termed Only Partial Success," *Wall Street Journal*, October 1 (1992a), B1.

—"Quality Programs Show Shoddy Results," *Wall Street Journal*, May 14 (1992b), B1.

Garvin, D. A., "Quality on the Line," *Harvard Business Review*, 61, 4 (1983), 65–75.

—"How the Baldrige Award Really Works," *Harvard Business Review*, 69, 6 (1991), 80–94.

Haim, A., "Does Quality Work? A Review of Relevant Studies," Conference Board, Report Number 1043, New York, 1993.

Heller, T., "The Superior Stock Market Performance of a TQM Portfolio," *Center for Quality Management Journal*, 3, 1 (Winter 1994), 23–32.

Hendricks, K. B., and V. R. Singhal, "Implementing Effective Total Quality Management (TQM) Programs and the Financial Performance of Firms: An Empirical Investigation," Report prepared for the U.S. Department of Labor, September 1995a.

—"Firm Characteristics, Total Quality Management, and Financial Performance: An Empirical Investigation," Working paper, College of William and Mary and Georgia Institute of Technology, 1995b.

—"Quality Awards and the Market Value of the Firm: An Empirical Investigation," *Management Science*, 42, 3 (1996), 415–436.

—"Does Implementing an Effective TQM Program Actually Improve Operating Performance? Empirical Evidence from Firms That Have Won Quality Awards," *Management Science*, 43, 9 (1997a), 1258–1274.

—"The Long-Run Stock Price Performance of Quality Award Winners," Working paper, College of William and Mary and Georgia Institute of Technology, 1997b.

Hockman, K. K., "Does the Baldrige Award Really Work?" *Harvard Business Review*, 70, 1 (1992), 137.

Ittner, C. D., and D. F. Larcker, "Measuring the Impact of Quality Initiatives on Firm Financial Performance," Working paper, University of Pennsylvania, Wharton School, 1995a.

—"Total Quality Management and the Choice of Information and Reward Systems," *Journal of Accounting Research*, 33, Supplement (1995b), 1–34.

Jensen, M. C., "The Modern Industrial Revolution, Exit, and the Failure of Internal Control Systems," *Journal of Finance*, 48 (1993), 831–880.

Johnson, T. H., "To Achieve Quality, You Must Think Quality," *Financial Executive*, May–June (1993), 9–11.

Juran, J. M., and F. M. Gryna, *Quality Planning and Analysis*, McGraw-Hill, New York, 1980.

Kelly, K., "Quality: Small and Midsize Companies Seize the Challenge – Not a Moment Too Soon," *Business Week*, November 30 (1992), 66–69.

272   **Kevin B. Hendricks and Vinod R. Singhal**

King, R., "Using Total Quality Management to Improve Bottom-Line Results," GOAL/QPC 9th Annual Conference, Boston, October 26, 1992.

Mathews, J., "Totaled Quality Management," *Washington Post*, June 6 (1993), H1.

Mathews, J., and P. Katel, "The Cost of Quality: Faced with Hard Times, Business Sours on Total Quality Management," *Newsweek*, September 7 (1992), 48–49.

Palepu, K., "Diversification Strategy, Profit Performance and Entropy Measure," *Strategic Management Journal*, 6 (1985), 239–255.

Powell, T. C., "Total Quality Management as Competitive Advantage: A Review and Empirical Study," *Strategic Management Journal*, 16 (1995), 15–37.

Quality Management Update, "IBM's Good News," January–February (1993).

Reimann, C. W., "The Evolution and Impact of Quality," Talk given at the Minnesota Quality Award Conference, November 2, 1995.

Saraph, J. V., P. G. Benson, and R. G. Schroeder, "An Instrument for Measuring the Critical Factors of Quality Management," *Decision Sciences*, 20, 4 (1989), 810–829.

Stratton, B., "Why You Can't Link Quality Improvement to Financial Performance," *Quality Progress*, February (1993), 5.

U.S. Department of Commerce News, "Quality Management Proves to Be a Sound Investment, Says NIST," NIST 95-05, February 3, 1995, Washington, DC.

U.S. General Accounting Office, "Management Practices, U.S. Companies Improve Performance Through Quality Efforts," GAO/NSIAD-91-190, Washington, DC, 1991.

Wruck, K. H., and M. C. Jensen, "Science, Specific Knowledge and Total Quality Management," *Journal of Accounting and Economics*, 18, 3 (1994), 247–287.

CHAPTER 9

Public Policy Implications

David I. Levine

The research presented in this volume suggests several implications for public policy. First, policy should support research on what makes workplaces effective. A goal of this research should be to create and validate measures of whether front-line employees solve problems for customers. Such measures would be valuable for investors, top managers, and regulators as well as customers. Second, employers need measures of which employees have skills in problem-solving. Finally, the government should remove legal barriers to new work practices.

The introduction to this volume drew three conclusions from the research literature on effective workplace practices. The first is that innovative human resource management practices can have large, economically important effects on productivity, profitability, and (long-term) stock market value. These positive results do not rely on any single innovation. Instead, they come from a system of related work practices designed to enhance worker participation, decentralization of decision-making, and flexibility in the design of work.

The magnitude of the effects suggests that in a well-functioning marketplace, new workplace practices should diffuse rapidly. In fact, the second conclusion is that while most contemporary U.S. businesses have adopted some forms of innovative work practices aimed at enhancing employee participation, only a small percentage have adopted a comprehensive system of innovative work practices.

The contrast between these two conclusions suggests the third: a number of obstacles impede the move to a system of innovative practices. These obstacles include the abandonment of organizational change initiatives when limited policy changes do not improve performance, the

The author thanks the Sloan Foundation for financial support. These recommendations draw from Levine (1995, 1998) and Ichniowski et al. (1996).

costs of other organizational practices needed to make new work practices effective, long histories of labor–management conflict and mistrust, resistance of supervisors and other employees who might not fare as well under the newer practices, and the lack of a supportive institutional and public policy environment.

This list of obstacles suggests three paths for public policy. First, the government should provide the public good of identifying good practices in workplaces. Second, the government should create metrics that make it easier for employers, regulators, top executives, customers, and investors to see which employees and suppliers are constantly solving problems. Finally, the government should remove legal barriers to new work practices.

These recommendations lend coherence to the dozens of disjointed government policies that affect the workplace, including accounting rules that fail to measure training as an investment, skills standards that define problem-solving differently in different states or industries, and procurement policies that emphasize low bids over quality. The win–win approach of measuring who solves problems can foster the goals of government, business, and employees.

In the past decade, many governmental policies have taken important strides toward making the nation's implicit workplace policy more friendly to high-skill workplaces. These efforts range from the highly successful Malcolm Baldrige National Quality Award to creating a framework of voluntary skills standards for employees. Nevertheless, more can be done, and what we are doing can be done more effectively.

Research on What Works

This volume summarizes what we know about what works at work. In a rare consensus, careful case studies, industry studies, and cross-industry studies all point to the research conclusions summarized in the preceding section. In spite of the progress achieved so far, the government has a responsibility to provide the public good of additional research.

For example, a number of important gaps remain in our understanding of what works at work. Nearly all of the research to date has focused on manufacturing businesses, so research in the service sector is needed. New research is also needed to address the effects of new workplace arrangements on outcomes of particular concern to workers, such as safety, job security, and the level, inequality, and volatility of earnings. Further research is needed to investigate more thoroughly whether new work systems work best in certain environments. Are new work systems less effective in declining product markets? How can such factors as technology and organization size modify the basic research conclusions?

The research presented in this volume is quantitative. Coupled with past studies and overviews, the balance of the evidence supports the hypothesis that innovative workplace practices work, at least sometimes. These studies reveal enormous variation, although their above-average attention to providing rigorous controls helps reduce many sources of error. While additional measures can help, there will always be omitted variables, and quantitative studies will never explain all the variation we observe.

To complement these quantitative studies, we will always need detailed qualitative studies that shed light on crucial details of how to implement innovative practices successfully. Ultimately, results will be convincing only if they show up in both qualitative and quantitative studies.

Finally, research to date has identified a number of barriers to the diffusion of successful workplace innovations. Future research must lead to a better understanding of these barriers. Such an understanding will help us to explain the limited adoption of new work systems in many sectors of the U.S. economy. It will also help us to identify possible market failures and to design appropriate policies.

Certifying Organizations Where Employees Solve Problems

A key goal of this research on workplaces should be to identify what combinations of work practices lead to successful organizational performance. As several chapters in this volume have noted, success on the Baldrige Quality Award criteria, for example, predicts future financial success (Easton and Jarrell, Chapter 7; Hendricks and Singhal, Chapter 8). More generally, we need to create and validate reliable measures of which organizations are building up the capabilities of their employees to work together to solve problems. Although the interests of stakeholders such as managers, employees, customers, and regulators sometimes differ, all of these groups have an interest in measuring this set of competencies.

Organizations as varied as the American Institute of Certified Public Accountants, the Association for Investment Management and Research (which charters financial analysts), the Financial Executives Institute, and the Organization for Economic Cooperation and Development have issued reports emphasizing the need for better measures of nonfinancial aspects of investment. International organizations, governments, industry, and the accounting profession must work together to create standard measures of workplace investments that are comparable across time, across nations, and across companies.

Customers want to know which organizations have employees trained, empowered, and motivated to solve their problems. Thus, it is not surprising that large customers as varied as Ford, AT&T, and Motorola use certifications related to the Baldrige criteria in order to measure the capacity of their suppliers to continuously improve their products and processes.

Companies face an important problem when trying to certify the quality of their goods, services, or production process – a profusion of awards and certifications. A supplier that hires workers who solve problems and that collects data from its customers to improve its products and services is a good supplier. Suppliers currently need to pass separate certifications to sell to a car company, an airplane company, and to different parts of the U.S. government.

The government must work with large private-sector customers to create certifications that measure which companies produce high-quality goods and services and are organized to improve their quality. Suppliers of high-quality goods and services usually rely on their workers for help in improving quality. Thus, these efforts to purchase from high-quality suppliers should not only save the government money but also increase the quality of jobs.

Top managers want to know how efficiently and productively a corporation is using and building up its valuable human resources. Such a performance measurement system is commonly called a "balanced scorecard" (Kaplan and Norton, 1996). A balanced scorecard including both financial and nonfinancial measures can be used by investors, boards of directors, and top executives for the several purposes served by narrower financial measures: valuing the enterprise, evaluating managerial success, and monitoring performance to look for opportunities to improve. A well-validated measure of workplace investments would be highly useful for creating a balanced scorecard.

The balanced scorecard should supplement traditional financial measures with nonfinancial measures, including measures of workplace outcomes (such as employee satisfaction and defect or rework rates), measures of workplace investments and practices (for instance, the proportion of employees enrolled in training programs or the proportion of employees who have submitted suggestions), measures of innovation (such as R&D spending or sales from products developed in the past five years), and measures of effectiveness in building a good reputation with customers (such as customer satisfaction or warranty return rates).

Managers should compare these performance measures across divisions and over time and should compare performance on these measures with that of the best-performing companies in the industry (and sometimes the globe).

At AT&T, for example, top management requires each division to complete the Baldrige Award application and report its score. This application points out weaknesses in investing in the organization's capabilities. In addition, managers are rewarded on the basis not only of their financial performance, but also of their success in building up two important assets – employee satisfaction and customer satisfaction.

A balanced scorecard can predict future financial performance more accurately than past financial measures alone. Financial results are lagging indicators of performance: they show the results of investments that have already paid off, but do not predict whether the company will maintain or improve its performance. In addition, they provide little guidance about what actions might be appropriate in improving future performance. By contrast, evaluating a balanced scorecard can help stakeholders distinguish between companies that are investing in the long term and those that are simply pumping up current earnings at their employees' or customers' expense.

Measuring performance is only the first step, however. Once organizations have established a balanced performance measurement system, top managers can use it to improve incentives within the organization. Few divisional managers are rewarded for long-term improvements in the performance of their operations. Once top managers have established divisional targets for nonfinancial performance measures, they should link divisional managers' pay to these indicators.

Investors want to know if the company is investing in building a high-quality reputation or if it is cutting costs at the expense of its customers' and employees' goodwill. As noted in the Introduction, under current accounting rules the investments that managers make in building a high-quality workforce and in producing high-quality goods show up in the short run only as lower earnings.

The government should restructure its accounting rules to put investment in people and in quality on a more even footing with investment in plant, equipment, or research. The government can work with industry and the accounting profession to create standard measures of product quality and of workplace investments that are comparable across time and across companies. Only then can investors determine which companies are investing for the long term. It is desirable to use dollar metrics (e.g., investment in training) when possible, but nonfinancial metrics can also be useful. The key is that they are comparable across time and across companies. Measures as varied as Baldrige scores or hours of training are candidates for this standardization.

Even before these changes are made in the accounting rules, a balanced scorecard can improve management's relations with investors and other stakeholders – that is, improve corporate governance. Good corporate governance is needed to lengthen both managers' and investors' time horizons and to reward managers for investing in assets that will lead to sustained improvements in performance.

Few corporations report their trends in quality, customer satisfaction, or human resource development to investors. Yet if financial stakeholders are well informed about a company's efforts to invest for the long term, they will be more likely to forgive the temporarily lower earnings that accompany these investments.

To build a trusting relationship with investors, managers can benefit from the creation of a strong, independent board. Only a strong board will have the credibility to certify to shareholders that management is pursuing a carefully planned strategy to build shareholder value.

The board should focus on two areas: improving the company's methods of measuring performance and ensuring that compensation systems reward top managers accordingly. As the elected representatives of the company's investors, it is the board members' responsibility to monitor and support the kinds of management practices that will generate and sustain improvements in productivity and quality over the long run. CEOs and other executives should not face pressure from the board to destroy employee or customer loyalty in the long run for the sake of short-term returns.

Regulators want to know which workplaces have high levels of employee involvement in problem-solving. For example, all recommendations for effective safety and health programs stress the key role of employee involvement. If the certification for workplaces includes measures of employee involvement in solving safety problems, the Occupational Safety and Health Administration should take that competency into account when regulating (Kochan and Osterman, 1995; Levine, 1997).

Measuring employee involvement can also improve the long-lived tax subsidies for employee stock ownership plans (ESOPs). When the U.S. Congress created the ESOP program, an important motive was to increase worker commitment and productivity. Unfortunately, "there is no evidence whatsoever that employee ownership itself automatically causes improved productivity or profitability except when combined with employee involvement" (Blasi and Kruse, 1991). The ESOP subsidy could be restricted to workplaces with empowered employees; it is in these workplaces where stock ownership is most likely to enhance value creation (Blasi and Kruse, 1991: 253; Freeman, 1991).

Certifying Employees Who Solve Problems

There is a saying in the computer industry: "Standards are wonderful – there are always so many to choose from." The standards that certify what our students and workforce have learned are becoming as complicated as the standards in the computer industry.[1]

Currently, a number of industries and almost all of the states are creating separate standards that measure skills in problem-solving and working in groups – the key skills employers say they need. Thus, someone who has good skills at solving problems in one industry might receive no credit for these skills when he or she moves to another industry.

Our skills standards should be created from a common set of building blocks that measure these key skills. Employers will bother learning the meaning of skill certifications only if the certifications apply to all applicants regardless of the state in which the applicants went to high school or the industry of the applicants' previous employer.

Standards for measuring how well students work together in groups and solve problems have the additional benefit of helping schools understand what they need to do in their move away from "chalk and talk" toward making education both more interesting and more relevant. Such standards can also increase the motivation of students, as they understand that employers will recognize and use these measures of their competencies.

Eliminating Legal Barriers

Labor law in the United States poses barriers to new work systems. The National Labor Relations Act makes it illegal for employers to discuss "conditions of employment" with company-sponsored committees of employees. Such a committee is an illegal "company union." Thus, committees of workers that make recommendations about safety, training, or even work schedules are typically illegal.

One possible solution is legalizing all forms of employee involvement. Unfortunately, this approach ignores cases where company unions are a threat to workers' right to form their own unions. A majority of Americans support the right of employees to form their own organizations free

---

[1] The points in this section are elaborated in Levine (1998).

280 **David I. Levine**

of management domination in order to bargain with management and to protect employees' rights (Freeman and Rogers, 1993: 30–32). Moreover, the strong opposition of the U.S. labor movement to this type of reform makes it likely that it will do little to increase cooperation and involvement at work.

Just as important, the current legislative vehicle that attempts to legalize more forms of employee involvement, the TEAM Act, does not appear to be politically viable – it was vetoed by President Clinton in 1996. Even if it passed, it remains unclear whether the TEAM Act would achieve its objectives. The Labor–Management Reporting and Disclosure Act of 1959 established rules concerning the election of representatives and the reporting requirements for labor organizations. Under the definition of "labor organization" in this act, these rules apply to many company-established forms of employee involvement. Because the TEAM Act leaves this definition unchanged, many forms of representative employee involvement would be subject to these strictures. Hence, many nonunion forms of employee representation might remain illegal even if the TEAM Act passed (Estreicher, 1997).

An alternative to legalizing all employee involvement groups including company unions is keeping the current law, unless the employees of an organization have approved an employment relations committee (Levine, 1997). This committee, in turn, would be able to approve other employee involvement mechanisms that would otherwise run afoul of the law. In organized worksites, the union would serve as this employment relations committee. In other workplaces, either a democratically chosen employee council or a direct vote would have to approve each exemption.

To ensure lack of employer domination, the employment relations committee would have to meet minimum standards. A typical set might include the following. Participants would be guaranteed against loss of pay or benefits and against any retribution for their participation (or for choosing not to participate) in any element of the employee oversight system. The members would be chosen in a free and fair manner, not by management. In addition, any mechanism would have to ensure proportional representation of hourly employees. Mechanisms ranging from random choice among volunteers to elections with secret ballots would be permissible. The initial establishment of an employment relations committee would have to be approved by a majority of the workforce.

Oversight by an employment relations committee would make it unlikely that employers would propose sham involvement mechanisms or that they would implement employee involvement primarily to weaken a union organizing campaign. If the employees ever felt other involvement groups were a sham, they could rescind their approval and the plans would no longer be legal.

At the same time, this oversight would increase employees' confidence that the proposed involvement program was in their best interest. There is some evidence that employee involvement programs are more successful in unionized establishments; presumably, part of the advantage is due to the union's role in discouraging employers from implementing exploitative programs for short-term gain.

Conclusion

Workplaces with high levels of worker skills and involvement appear capable of improving workplace effectiveness, yet remain relatively rare. This pair of results suggests that important barriers slow the adoption of new systems of work practices.

Public policy has a role in removing barriers that slow adoption and in providing public goods that may speed adoption. Typical public goods include research and creating a system for measuring which companies are investing in their workers' capabilities for continuous improvement. Improving the capacity of investors, employees, regulators, and managers to measure investments in individuals' and organizations' capabilities and removing legal barriers to employee involvement are relatively minor changes. Nevertheless, together they promote workplaces that provide higher performance for both employees and employers.

REFERENCES

Blasi, Joseph, and Douglas Kruse, *The New Owners*, HarperBusiness, New York, 1991.

Estreicher, Samuel, "Nonunion Employee Representation: A Legal/Policy Perspective," Paper presented at the "Nonunion Forms of Employee Representation" conference, Banff, 1997.

Freeman, Richard, "Employee Councils, Worker Participation, and Other Squishy Stuff," *Proceedings of the Industrial Relations Research Association*, Madison, WI, 1991, pp. 328–337.

Freeman, Richard B., and Joel Rogers, "Who Speaks for Us? Employee Representation in a Nonunion Labor Market," in Bruce E. Kaufman and Morris M. Kleiner, eds., *Employee Representation: Alternatives and Future Directions*, Industrial Relations Research Association, Madison, WI, 1993.

Ichniowski, Casey, Thomas Kochan, David I. Levine, Craig Olson, and George Strauss, "What Works at Work: A Critical Review," *Industrial Relations*, 35, no. 3 (Summer 1996), pp. 299–333.

282   **David I. Levine**

Kaplan, Robert S., and David P. Norton, *The Balanced Scorecard*, Harvard University Press, Cambridge, MA, 1996.

Kochan, Thomas, and Paul Osterman, *The Mutual Gains Enterprise*, Harvard University Press, Cambridge, MA, 1995.

Levine, David I., *Reinventing the Workplace: How Business and Employees Can Both Win*, Brookings Institution, Washington, DC, 1995.

—"Reinventing Workplace Regulation," *California Management Review*, 39(4) (1997), pp. 98–117.

—*Working in the 21st Century: Government Policies to Promote Opportunity, Learning and Productivity*, Sharpe, Armonk, NY, 1998.

Index

accounting variables: event study of TQM effects, 189–90; results of TQM event study, 194–204, 210–25

analysts' forecasts: alternatives when unavailable, 190–1; in analysis of TQM effects on performance, 177–80; compared with AR 1 model forecasts, 209, 225–6

apparel industry: assembly using modular system, 40, 42–4; assembly using progressive bundle system, 40–2, 62, 64–5; characteristics of, 63–4; labor-intensive nature of manufacture, 40; modeling performance effects in, 53–8; performance effects of modular assembly, 51–8; sweatshop operations, 59. *See also* modular production system; progressive bundle system; unit production system

automation: complement to high-involvement work practices of flexible, 143–4, 160–4; programmable, 96

bundle system. *See* progressive bundle system

business firms: adopters and non-adopters of modular systems, 45–52; development and performance of modules in, 68–74; distribution of TQM firms by industry, 192–3; effect of downsizing on financial performance, 206, 208–9; MDG sector industrial plants, 86; offering rapid replenishment, 48–9; performance of module adopters, 53–8; reasons for

adopting modular systems, 46–8; sample of TQM firms, 228–30

case studies: learning from, 15–19; meta-analysis of individual, 19–20; within single industry, 20–3; spanning many industries, 23–7

certification of organizations where employees participate, 275–9

change, organizational: evolutionary, 139; revolutionary and competence-destroying, 139–40

CNC. *See* computer numerical control (CNC) technology

Commission on the Future of Worker–Management Relations, 33

compensation system: apparel industry bundle system, 65; apparel industry modular system, 66; group-based, 85, 87, 89

competency traps, 141

computer numerical control (CNC) technology, 89, 95; programming for machine tools, 95

Conference Board, evidence on TQM effectiveness, 238–9

control firms: characteristics related to financial performance, 259–63; portfolio for event study of TQM effects, 187–8

Cronbach's α, 129–31

data: for analysis of modular production system, 38–40; for analysis of TQM effectiveness, 243, 245–6; comparison of